Dangerous Schools

Irwin A. Hyman, EdD
Pamela A. Snook, RN, MSN

Dangerous Schools

What We Can Do About the Physical and Emotional Abuse of Our Children

Jossey-Bass Publishers • San Francisco

Jossey-Bass books and products are available through most bookstores. To contact Jossey-Bass directly, call (888) 378-2537, fax to (800) 605-2665, or visit our website at www.josseybass.com.

Substantial discounts on bulk quantities of Jossey-Bass books are available to corporations, professional associations, and other organizations. For details and discount information, contact the special sales department at Jossey-Bass.

 Manufactured in the United States of America on Lyons Falls Turin Book. This paper is acid-free and 100 percent totally chlorine-free.

Library of Congress Cataloging-in-Publication Data

Hyman, Irwin A.
    Dangerous schools : what we can do about the physical and emotional abuse of our children / Irwin A. Hyman, Pamela A. Snook.
— 1st ed.
        p. cm.
    Includes bibliographical references and index.
    ISBN 0-7879-4363-0 (acid-free paper)
    1. School violence—United States.   2. School discipline—United States.   3. Students—Assaults against—United States.   4. Child abuse—United States.   5. Teacher-student relationships—United States.   6. Discrimination in education—United States.   7. Schools—United States—Safety measures.   I. Snook, Pamela A.   II. Title.
    LB3013 .H897 1999
    371.7'8—dc21

                                                            98-58074

FIRST EDITION
HB Printing   10 9 8 7 6 5 4 3 2

Contents

To Alan Reitman.
You made this book possible.

Acknowledgments

Many people have contributed to the development and writing of this book. We are deeply grateful for the legal expertise of Dr. Jacqueline Stefkovitch, who read the entire first draft, corrected legal points, and made many valuable suggestions. Special thanks are due to Alan Reitman and Loren Siegal of the ACLU, who provided significant input to Chapter Nine under immense time pressure. Also, we are grateful to Mike Winkler of The Pennington School for his review of Chapter Nine. Dr. Catherine Fiorello reviewed the entire manuscript and was very helpful in providing research, suggestions, and articles that enhanced the book. Kenneth Cassie provided invaluable editing and conceptual contributions to the introduction. We also acknowledge the contributions of graduate students Stanley Savage, Susan Levy, Joyce Spangler, and Tamara Southerling for their research on specific topics. Thanks to Stuart Hart and Cynthia Price Cohen for their contributions about international law, Rabbi Elliot Strom who reviewed the discussion of God and spanking, Principal Mark Collins for his suggestions on performance pressures, psychologist Robert Griffin for his direct contribution to the book and his ongoing advocacy against school abuses, and Dr. Lee Kern who offered valuable insights about several sections of the book. Thanks to Leslie A. Williamson, Esq., Chris Gronning, Esq., James Garbarino, Ph.D., and Marshall Croddy for their varied and unique contributions. We deeply appreciate the courage and persistence of Caryn Kunz, Sandy O'Brien Warner, their families, and other survivors who have contributed directly and indirectly to this book. Special thanks go to Richard Chan who saved us in our hour of need when the computer crashed in the middle of writing this book. Finally we thank Susan and Rachael Hyman and Don, Judy, and Jim Snook for their support and encouragement.

Dangerous Schools

Introduction

Most people worry about danger in schools because of disruption and violence by students. However there is another, less obvious but much more pervasive and insidious danger in schools. That danger comes not from students but from school staff, who physically and psychologically assault students in the name of discipline.

Through the media, we are constantly warned about dangerous schools. The public perceives schools as plagued and sometimes controlled by disruptive, disrespectful students who are too often violent. Schools are frequently portrayed as places in which children and teachers are likely to be victimized. We are alarmed about the increase in the intensity and horrific nature of deadly assaults in and around schools, especially by and against younger students. Despite our fears, this book will demonstrate that the problem of student violence is vastly overreported and exaggerated, resulting in severe, punitive disciplinary policies and procedures that are dangerous and both psychologically and physically toxic.

You may worry about your child being robbed, assaulted, or even shot by fellow students in school. But how often do you think about the much more frequent and dangerous occurrences when students are physically and verbally assaulted by school staff? How often do you consider the damage done when students' constitutional rights are undermined in the name of discipline? This is the other side of the school violence coin, which is almost never reported.

Every day, when you send your children to school, you trust that they will be nurtured, protected, and taught what they need to know. You reflect a belief in an unwritten social contract. This contract, which is based partly on the legal doctrine of "in loco parentis," gives the power of parenthood to schools. You trust that as surrogate parents the schools will discipline your children in a just and equitable manner. You believe that your children will be protected from the predations of peers and school staff alike.

Contemporary parents, forced to balance the demands of dual employment and child rearing, must increasingly rely on this social contract with schools. Schools are increasingly expected to assume expanded roles as the economic and social pressures of modern life overburden parents. Yet, in the name of discipline and "law and order," schools are breaking this crucial contract.

The incidence of educator-induced violence far exceeds that of offenses committed by students. Yet it is little studied, mostly ignored, and in some settings greatly encouraged. We are going to tell you about the nature, extent, and implications of these assaults and why they make schools dangerous and toxic to students. Whether or not your child is a target of these attacks, there are things you can and should do about this problem. Consider a few examples.

How would you feel if your thirteen-year-old daughter came home crying bitterly that she had been strip-searched for a missing $10 bill? Consider your reaction if your six-year-old had been tied to a chair and had his mouth taped shut by his first-grade teacher. Think about the consequences to your seventeen-year-old of sitting through periodic schoolwide lockdowns in which children and staff are required to remain in their classrooms while police and drug-sniffing dogs roam the halls and paw through the lockers.

You would feel as impotent, angry, and resentful as the many parents we have helped whose children have been maltreated by educators. Throughout this book, we will tell you their stories. But first, we want to tell you why we wrote this book about a problem that seems minimal or nonexistent to most Americans. (*Note:* Before going further, it seems useful to clarify the use of the pronouns *I* and *we* throughout this book. Except for occasional first-person quotes, *I* refers to the senior author, Irwin Hyman, whose thirty years of experience are the basis for much of this book. *We* refers to both authors, since Pamela Snook contributed mightily to research, editing, and writing.)

Why We Wrote This Book

For over thirty years as a school psychologist I have worked with parents, students, and schools to improve discipline. In all these years I have seen numerous examples of the abuse of students in the name of discipline. There are too many cases where students are victims of dangerous and toxic but legally sanctioned, routinely used, and pedagogically promoted disciplinary practices. These include emotionally and physically damaging disciplinary procedures such as paddling, punching, kicking, verbally assaulting, strip-searching, and confining students for long periods.

I addressed the issues of corporal punishment and emotional abuse in my 1990 book, *Reading, Writing, and the Hickory Stick: The Appalling Story of Physical and Psychological Abuse in American Schools*, a summary of numerous research studies begun in 1976 with the founding of the National Center for the Study of Corporal Punishment and Alternatives (NCSCPA) at Temple University. There we have demonstrated the ineffectiveness of corporal punishment and the advantages of positive techniques of prevention and remediation. The Center and the book have helped advocates eliminate school corporal punishment in twenty-five states, bringing the total from two, which had already banned it, to twenty-seven in the course of two decades.

I have testified in many horrific cases of school paddlings. As I will describe later in this book, I have evaluated children whose bruises and other injuries would clearly qualify as child abuse if the damage were inflicted by anyone but an educator. You will even read about two cases in which educators have publicly defended paddlings of teenage girls that resulted in extensive vaginal hemorrhaging and psychological trauma. Public acceptance of these practices has slowly eroded, so that now only twenty-three states allow educators to apply a wooden paddle to the behind of a student.

I hoped that my 1990 book, along with the research of my graduate students and of other scholars and the efforts of advocates, would have eliminated the last vestiges of support for corporal punishment in American education. Unfortunately, those efforts have hit the wall of the solid South and mostly rural legislatures. Conservative citizens, especially those in the Bible Belt, have asserted their God-given right to delegate the power of the paddle to educators. Even my own state of Pennsylvania, powered by a rurally dominated legislature, still maintains that swatting students is a good idea.

Until recently, I thought I had no reason to write another book about student victimization. But as my reputation as an expert on physical abuse of schoolchildren grew, I discovered a need to understand other types of maltreatment of schoolchildren. Despite the many gains in eliminating school paddlings, other punitive and antidemocratic procedures have infiltrated the schools.

Beyond Corporal Punishment: Constitutional and Psychological Issues

In recent years, we have witnessed a more subtle erosion of already fragile faith in the few constitutional protections afforded students since the 1960s. These protections should safeguard them from arbitrary and overly intrusive disciplinary procedures and police tactics. As the standard for invading students' privacy continues to be lowered, the toxicity spreads from individuals to our society. Students who doubt our founders' concept of justice and equity lose faith in the rule of law. They can become cynical adults. This cynicism may explain why Americans vote in smaller proportions than do citizens in all other democracies.

The desire for safe and drug-free schools has generated frightening excesses of enforcement. It seems that lately there are relatively large numbers of police patrolling our schools, arresting children, and conducting massive locker searches. Now do not get us wrong. We know that in certain cases, police are a blessing. But police, in general, are trained to interdict, interrogate, and incarcerate. Excessive police invasiveness too easily becomes an instrument of oppressive power in the hands of authorities.

Police tactics can poison a democratic, nurturing learning atmosphere. They include search and seizure, undercover agents, and strip searches. Strategies such as the use of undercover agents have great potential for harm and are largely ineffectual. You will read about one such agent, who seduced a fifteen-year-old girl. After he was dismissed, another school welcomed him, enabling him to find a similar victim. You will be outraged by cases of strip searches that never resulted in the discovery of any contraband but that psychologically devastated young boys and girls.

Until relatively recently, before our nation's exaggerated beliefs about the extent of school crime, schools wisely protected children of tender years and foolish intentions from heavy-handed police procedures. Police are not trained in understanding the culture of schools and schooling. Nor are they trained to understand and deal with the complex developmental issues of children and adolescents who are struggling to achieve, to be accepted, and to be respected.

Let us give you a specific example of why we are so concerned. Like it or not, boys in our society will get into fights in and around schools. In the best of all possible worlds, we would teach all children conflict resolution techniques that reduce the need to resolve problems with violence. Unfortunately the urge to violence is deeply embedded in our society. Over 90 percent of our children learn at an early age that it is OK for a bigger, stronger person (parent) to solve problems by hitting, slapping, and spanking.

Spanking is the cradle of violence in a country of devoted spankers. In addition, our populace loves to watch real-life violence in sporting events. We are devoted to disaster movies, heroes who win by use of lethal force, and live court coverage of the trials of alleged perpetrators of violence, such as O. J. Simpson. We are a nation of "violence junkies."

So why should it surprise us that young people fight? The shock to us is how we now handle this problem. Instead of devoting massive resources to halt fighting in schools by programs of prevention, education, and treatment, we now arrest kids. Until recently, we expected trained educators, psychologists, counselors, and administrators to deal with routine school fights. This was especially clear in special schools designed for aggressive, alienated, and disturbed students. Yet all of a sudden we are finding in clinical practice, in consultations with schools, and in the experience of colleagues in the field that police are now routinely called in when children fight in any type of school setting.

Again, do not get us wrong. We do not approve of fighting and we even impress upon the kids with whom we work that it is illegal to hit someone else. However, most schools have survived for centuries without the use of police force to deal with these routine issues. History and social science tell us that punishment-based policies are doomed to failure, especially in climates of social inequity. In America there are large gaps between the rich and the poor, people of color and those who are not, and a legal system that most citizens believe favors the rich. Despite these quandaries, the actual rates of school violence by students suggest that the public does not truly comprehend the scope of the problem.

Murder and Mayhem in the Schools: How Bad Is It?

On October 1, 1997, Luke Woodham, a sixteen-year-old student in Pearl, Mississippi, fatally shot his mother. He then went to school where he killed his ex-girlfriend and another girl, and wounded other students. The media eagerly fed this event to a public, seemingly ravenous for gore and violence. Two months later, fourteen-year-old Michael Carneal opened fire on a high school student prayer group in Paducah, Kentucky. Within months other widely publicized school slayings were repeated in Edinboro, Pennsylvania, Springfield, Oregon, and Fayatteville, Tennessee.

These school murders triggered frenzied activity by policymakers and citizens throughout the country. Many of them were already alarmed by what they perceived as dangerous increases in school crime during the past decade. Violence in the schools had finally gotten out of hand. The public was convinced that youth violence had increased to such a level that police, schools, and the courts needed to really get tough. School boards desperately turned to corrections and security experts for help. As a result, school safety began to rival prison management as a major growth industry in America. If this trend continues, school safety could become a dominant and potentially destructive force in educational planning.

School Violence: A Brief History

School violence by and to students has been a part of European, English, and American schools for centuries. For example, students in seventeenth-century France were often armed and feared by schoolmates and ordinary citizens. They commonly engaged in duels, brawls, mutinies, and beatings of teachers.

English students frequently caused mutinies, strikes, and violence between 1775 and 1836. Some of the mutinies were violent enough to require military intervention. By comparison, American schools were tame. However, problems related to sex, drugs, gambling, and violence have been common throughout the centuries. At the turn of the century, gang warfare between different ethnic groups in the big cities was not uncommon. Gang rumbles in the 1950s were immortalized in the musical *West Side Story*. We do not even really know the extent of school violence during all these years—there were no reliable reporting procedures. It is possible that, based on historical accounts, periodic school violence was much worse than it is now.

It is difficult for the public to sort reality from media hype and political rhetoric. Unfortunately, recent and continuing public tirades about increases in school violence are based on misinformation. Since the 1970s we have collected reasonable data about school violence and can demonstrate that it has not increased. In fact, in recent years it has decreased, as has the overall crime rate. For instance, school shootings, for which there are no reliable statistics prior to the mid–1990s, have dropped from fifty-five in the 1992–93 school year to around forty in 1997–98. Of course, this number is still unacceptable, but it is hardly epidemic with a school population of over fifty million students.

The sheer number of media accounts makes many think that the problem of school crime is much worse than it is. For instance, we studied reports of school crime from 1960 to 1975 and 1990 to 1995 in the *New York Times*. For most years the actual number of incidents were vastly outnumbered by the volume of articles about each incident. Increasing the volume were editorials and quotes from politicians calling for tougher school discipline, more police in the schools, and tougher court sentences for juveniles.

Unfortunately, what has increased is the use of guns, the tendency of younger children to commit more horrific crimes, and the national media coverage of local school murders in white, middle-class communities. Murders committed by white children receive more extensive national media coverage than do similar offenses committed by minority students. This contributes to the stereotype that poor minority youth in the cities routinely commit crimes both in and out of schools. Most poor minority children do not commit crimes and inner-city schools are generally as safe as schools in predominantly rural areas that serve poor white students. Because of stereotyping, the public is aghast when school crimes are committed by middle-class, rosy-cheeked white students in rural America.

National trends reveal modest fluctuations in school violence over the last several decades. What sometimes appear to be large increases in school crime, especially as reported in the media, may be artifacts of reporting procedures. For instance, when Philadelphia schools reported their crime statistics for 1990–91, beeper possession was not an offense. However, officials decided that beepers might, among other things, be used for drug deals and banned them. By 1992–93, during the second year beeper possession was considered an offense, there was a 428 percent increase in this so-called crime. This change accounted for a 5 percent total increase in school crime in 1992–93, contributing to the belief that schools had become more dangerous.

In 1996, the *Philadelphia Daily News* printed a widely quoted series on school violence. One of the major flaws in the reporting was that violent incidents (never clearly distinguished from nonviolent offenses) that occurred inside schools were lumped with those that occurred on school grounds and among students traveling to and from school. These data were interpreted to portray schools as being much more violent than they actually were. Further, there were no data reporting what percentage of the crimes were committed by students.

My colleagues and I used government surveys to track rates of violence in different settings over a number of years. The result? Schools are actually one of the safest places for children. For instance, in 1992, 12 percent of rapes, robberies, and assaults occurred in the home and 6 percent in school buildings.

Even in some of the most violent cities, children are safer in schools than anywhere else. For example, in 1991, the aggravated assault rate in Chicago was 1,502 per 100,000 citizens, while the public school rate was 325 per 100,000. The Los Angeles homicide rate for 1991 was 29.30 per 100,000 persons while the public schools in Los Angeles reported 3 homicides, one of which was accidental. These data all indicate that schools, with little or no significant police presence, are one of the safest places for children. While police may be needed in some situations, we must consider their effects on the learning climate.

The Toxic Impact of Police Tactics in the Schools

Responding to misperceptions of the real extent of school violence, schools have increasingly adopted law enforcement rather than educational models for violence reduction. For instance, there is little or no evidence for the efficacy of many popular contemporary youth violence prevention approaches based on police or correctional procedures. These include the use of metal detectors, increased police presence in schools (as opposed to trained school staff), searches of lockers and students, student and staff I.D. cards, a ban on the use of beepers on school grounds, school uniforms, boot camps, mandatory sentencing, and adjudicating delinquent adolescents as if they were adults. Further, many of these approaches may only put youth more at risk of abuse by punitive corrections workers, police, judiciary personnel, and punishment-oriented educators.

Our observations and anecdotal reports suggest that schools are relying more on police intervention for what previously had been considered routine disciplinary matters such as fighting and minor property destruction. In exceptional cases where police involvement remains necessary, an overdependence on police intervention can decrease the willingness of school authorities to develop alternative procedures to deal with school disruption. A possible unintended consequence might be the undermining of school authority. That is, students may perceive school authorities as impotent and may feel more free to act out in the absence of police. All these approaches focus on violence committed by students and do not address the conditions of schools and acts of educators that may increase school disruptions.

This book examines school violence from the other side of the coin. Educator violence against students, including verbal and physical assaults and the undermining of students' constitutional rights, erodes rather enhances school safety. In this book, we explain how unnecessarily harsh and punitive disciplinary practices against students create a climate that contributes to school violence. This issue is little recognized and hardly researched.

So why is this information important for you to know? The increased climate of punitiveness toward children makes it more difficult to convince school boards, legislators, judges, and juries that harsh discipline is really toxic. If citizens believe that youth are dangerous and that schools are out of control, they will conclude that youthful offenders deserve draconian punishments. We have become a country of punishment promoters whose policies make us the most punitive of all the Western democracies. In this book we tell you why we believe this to be true, what you should understand about our society in order to develop strategies for litigating a case of student victimization, and how to bring about political change.

America the Punitive

The United States, based on data from 1998, incarcerates 668 citizens for every 100,000 residents. This is higher by a wide margin than any other country for which data exist. Russia and South Africa are our closest competitors. We are also the only Western democracy that uses capital punishment in the flawed belief that it deters crime. This emphasis on punishment by jailing would be great if it worked, especially with juveniles.

Most crimes are committed by males between the ages of around fifteen to twenty-five. Fifty-three percent of all identified murderers in 1993 were under the age of twenty-five. Since there will be a 20 percent increase in the juvenile population by 2005, experts predict a doubling of juvenile arrests for violent crime by 2010. Of course experts could be wrong, because violent crime in the United States fell 12 percent in 1995 and has continued to drop.

Compared to most Western democracies, America is returning to an eighteenth-century model of punishment and retribution in dealing with misbehavior, deviancy, and delinquency. However, every study conducted that compared punishment with prevention in juvenile detention centers demonstrates that education, rehabilitation, and therapy are much more successful than punishment in decreasing the rearrest rates. But many Americans reject reliable scientific data because they are subject to a pattern of thought we call the Singapore Syndrome.

The Singapore Syndrome

The Singapore Syndrome is a set of irrational, antidemocratic beliefs that emerged as a result of reactions in 1994 to the proposed public flogging of eighteen-year-old Michael Fay, an American student living in Singapore.

The disease is reflected in the American public from an April 8, 1994, *Newsweek* poll in which respondents were told, "A young American in Singapore is to receive a severe caning under the law there for punishing vandalism. Do you approve or disapprove?" Thirty-eight percent approved and 52 percent disapproved of a practice that has long been banned in America. It is practiced in an authoritarian country certified by our State Department as having an unacceptable human rights record.

Soon after the Fay story broke, right-wing California Assemblyman Mickey Conroy, obviously suffering from the Singapore Syndrome, tried unsuccessfully to reinstate paddling in schools and institute public floggings of juveniles convicted for graffiti offenses. He was joined by conservative politicians throughout the country in attempts to reintroduce flogging into our penal codes.

One of Conroy's fellow travelers was Florida Representative Berly Burke, whom I debated on *Oprah*. She was quoted as saying, "Bruises, welts, and broken bones do not constitute child abuse," and, "We need to get tougher to reduce crime." She helped write a get-tough bill that was passed in the Florida legislature but vetoed by Governor Childs. The bill guaranteed parents that they could beat away on their kids without worrying about those pesky child abuse investigators.

Burke's thinking was reinforced by Supreme Court Justice Antonin Scalia, who claimed that caning is probably constitutional and an improvement over the more horrible things that were done in 1791, when our forefathers defined cruel and unusual punishment. He derides our twentieth-century understandings of the relation between cruelty, torture, and justice. We wonder if he approves of the constitutions or laws of Afghanistan, Iran, Iraq, Libya, and Saudi Arabia?

Trying Children as Adults: A Return to the Nineteenth Century

In 1899, courts began to recognize that childhood is different from adulthood. Juvenile courts were established to intervene on behalf of children when their parents were unable to raise them properly. Since then, vast amounts of psychological, social, developmental, and medical research has demonstrated that children and youth are different from adults. However, America the punitive has begun to reject this notion. In part, this is due to the media's eagerness to sensationalize individual cases of youth violence. Particular groups, such as inner-city African American and Hispanic youth, have been demonized in cinematic portrayals of violent lifestyles. Since the well-publicized spate of school shootings, and despite an anticipated counter campaign by the National Rifle Association (NRA), white country boys brandishing hunting rifles may soon be demonized in the media.

This demonization of youth contributes further to the lynch mentality of many Americans. Rather than understanding why a boy like eleven-year-old Andrew Golden (of Jonesboro, Arkansas) would shoot his classmates, the first reaction of many citizens and officials was to find a way to try him as an adult. This reflects a growing belief in retribution and revenge for criminal activity, which contributes further to the toxicity of schools.

The political right's push toward punishment has extended beyond schools and the jails. But, in a strange alliance, moderate to liberal jurists and conservative politicians are willing to eliminate juvenile courts as they exist along with current laws for trying children and youth. Liberals feel that the closed proceedings of the courts and the indeterminate sentences, which were originally developed to protect children, tend to deny them their constitutional rights. While acknowledging children and youth should not be treated as adults, these critics seek better guarantees of due process rights. Moderates and conservatives tend to believe that the system is too lenient. They feel that it protects predatory youth who deserve adult sentences for committing violent crimes.

How Others View Us

On November 20, 1989 the General Assembly of the United Nations adopted a major international covenant, the Convention on the Rights of the Child. As of 1998, 191 countries had ratified this comprehensive document that spells out the nature of childhood and the rights of children. These include freedom from both psychological and physical maltreatment in all settings including school, home, and the criminal justice system.

Even though President Clinton signed the Convention on the Rights of the Child on February 16, 1995, it was never sent to the Senate for "advice and consent" in order for the president to ratify it on behalf of our country. Perhaps the major reason that this humanistic treaty has not been ratified is that it may be interpreted as prohibiting parents and schools from spanking, paddling, or psychologically maltreating children. In fact, Senator Jesse Helms let it be known that there is no way he would let a bunch of foreigners tell us how to discipline our children.

Conservatives' refusal to adhere to contemporary, democratic views about punishment is further illustrated by the Senate's failure to review the American Convention on Human Rights. This treaty, already signed by President Jimmy Carter, is still languishing in some dusty bin of the Senate, awaiting their "advice and consent." Since it was signed by the president, it is theoretically binding on the United States due to our membership in the Organization of American States. It specifically forbids the execution of youth whose crimes were committed below the age of eighteen.

Technically, American judges could cite either of the above treaties in their opinions about corporal or capital punishment of juveniles since these treaties are widely accepted among democratic nations. Obviously, American jurisprudence tends to ignore these treaties. For instance, a study by Amnesty International found that among the Western democracies the United States had the highest rate of execution of juveniles from 1980 to 1986.

Given these data, it is interesting to see how we are viewed by other Western democracies in terms of our punitiveness. Several recent court cases illustrate that to many Europeans, the American justice system is nothing short of barbaric in its harsh treatment of the accused.

In a case over the extradition of an American convicted in absentia of murder, the defendant's French attorneys referred to the American judicial system as "regressive [and] inhumane." They berated America, a purported model of democracy and civil liberties, for sentencing children and the mentally handicapped to death. Media reports from Italy and England reinforced the view that many citizens of those countries agree with these sentiments.

We do not know how the citizens of other Western democracies would view the slow erosion of schoolchildren's rights in America. By many measures it appears that our children have more opportunities than any in history. As one of the first countries ever devoted to universal mandatory education, surely we value education. Our democracy is built on the assumption of an educated populace.

If children were highly valued as torchbearers of democracy, education would be our nation's highest priority. Schools would be modern and air-conditioned, teachers would be well paid and have the highest academic credentials. Administrators would match their successful counterparts in corporations in terms of intelligence, creativity, flexibility, and leadership.

However, how we claim to value education is contradicted by how we support it financially. Almost every poll reveals that if asked the questions in an objective and straightforward manner, most Americans support education. They are willing to pay higher taxes to improve education. Unfortunately, this is negatively affected by the constant cacophony against raising taxes, the general distrust of politicians and government, and the persistent portrayal of schools overrun by violent youth.

The demonization of youth, especially by an aging population, may contribute to some collective unconscious belief that children are the "imps of darkness" described in earlier times. In a country that ranks in the top three among Western democracies in the belief in Satan, it is not hard to understand that many Americans still subscribe to admonitions to beat the devil out of children in both home and school. Why else would America be among the four Western democracies that still allow children to be paddled in school?

We are increasingly relying on punishment and a spirit of meanness to solve social and school problems. As a result, we now have more people and a higher proportion of our citizenry in jail than any other Western democracy. Yet imprisonment or the fear of incarceration do not end crime. In other words, punishment is not very effective in changing behavior.

The Failure of Punishment

History and social science research demonstrate that when punishment doesn't work immediately, it has to increase in frequency, duration, and intensity. Since the concept of punishment is so central to the theme of this book, we would like to start by giving you a scientific definition of the term. Simply stated, *punishment is any act by the punisher that decreases the chances that the punishee will repeat a particular behavior or misbehavior.*

Now, don't get us wrong. We are not fuzzy-thinking, ivory-tower liberal intellectuals who think that punishment should never be used. Of course we sometimes need to use punishment, especially when it works. From our work with parents, educators, law enforcement officials, and a variety of agencies, we know that we need rules, structure, and consequences for bad behavior. But we also know that punishment is generally the least effective way to change or stop bad behavior, teach good behavior, and change negative attitudes to positive ones. Let us give you a simple example of the problem of dependence on punishment.

Think of the analogy of a rat in a cage. We want to stop certain rat behaviors. We know from years of research that punishment can make a rat in a cage avoid normally preferred acts such as mating or eating a particular rat treat. The usual punishment is a mild electrical shock. But rats can learn to accommodate and become increasingly insensitive to punishments, just like people. Therefore, for the punishment to retain its effectiveness, we have to shock a rat more frequently, for longer periods, and with higher levels of voltage. Through increasing the punishment we can continue to stop mating and eating behavior. But as punishment levels increase, eventually we wind up with either a very disturbed or very dead rat. As we will demonstrate in this book, when it comes to punishment, people are not much different from rats.

You might object to this analogy because people are not rats, or at least most people are not. But almost a hundred years of research on learning demonstrates that the basic principles of reward and punishment apply equally to all creatures. Let us give you an example of how punishment is minimally effective in people because authorities are limited in their power to increase the frequency, intensity, and duration of most punishments.

Most people we know have exceeded the speed limit at one time or another. Some have received frequent tickets, have had their insurance rates increased, and have even had their driver's license revoked. While none of our friends have ever admitted to going to jail for speeding, we know that incarceration is sometimes a penalty, especially in cases of drunk driving. However, even drunk drivers generally have to commit repeated and heinous offenses to go to jail.

What is our point? Simply put, if punishment (speeding tickets, fines, and so on) worked, why do people who get ticketed continue to speed? In other words, if tickets were really a punishment, based on the scientific definition, people would not continue to speed after the initial ticket. Our national policy of punishing speeders has not worked that well. If we really wanted to eliminate speeding, we could do at least two things. We could educate everyone to really believe that speeding can kill them and others and is therefore morally reprehensible. Alternatively—or in addition—we could give large rewards each year to those who do not speed. This is technologically feasible. There are already devices that prevent inebriated drivers from starting their cars and therefore it would be simple to add a speeding monitor. Manufacturers could install monitors, but their use could be decided by each driver. To avoid a Big Brother horror, people could voluntary submit the data from their monitors for rewards each year.

Now we are sure you think the voluntary-monitor idea is silly. But just think about it. If insurance companies were willing to forego some initial profits by offering huge reductions each year for drivers who do not speed, there would be fewer costly accidents and the insurance companies and society would benefit. But just as you realize how improbable this scenario is in America, we see a reward-oriented scenario to deal with misbehavior and delinquency just as improbable in most contemporary schools.

Schools appear to be increasingly driven by policies and politics of punishment. Many believe that safe and orderly schools require automatic punishments based on zero tolerance policies. The routine and unquestioning acceptance of these policies is not only undermining and distorting students' understanding and belief in constitutional rights, it is absolutely bound to the simple fact that such policies just do not work. The main point of this book is that the intensifying and automatic use of punishment, as opposed to prevention of misbehavior and violence in schools, makes the schoolhouse toxic for too many children.

This Book Is Not About Teacher Bashing

Despite our observations on the rise of toxic discipline, this book is not a wholesale condemnation of all schools and educators. Pam and I grew up in families that highly regarded educators. Most of our close relatives have been or are teachers. I started my professional career as a teacher and my children have had many exemplary teachers. As a professor I have taught many excellent future teachers and have consulted with numerous exceptional educators for over thirty years.

Teaching is a terribly difficult and demanding profession. Good teachers should be paid as much as other professionals. But even good, decent, and enthusiastic teachers can be defeated if they work in toxic schools. Fledgling teachers are quickly shaped by veterans in their building. If the school climate is positive, new teachers are likely to become positive. Despite college training, formal supervision, and school district guidelines, new teachers' outlooks are strongly influenced by what they hear from their colleagues.

Much of the seminal training of novice teachers occurs informally in the faculty lounge. This is where teachers generally collect in the morning before school, at breaks, and at the end of the school day. This is where new teachers are acculturated to the climate of the school. The way teachers talk about students, parents, colleagues, and the community offers a good measure of the health of the school. A toxic climate is typified by teachers' constantly complaining, demeaning, and denigrating students and the school. A positive climate is typified by happy, relaxed, and friendly discussions about a variety of topics and objective problem solving related to student issues.

The climate is ultimately determined by the leadership of the school. If the principal is liked and respected, teachers will tend to treat each other and the students decently. If the principal is considered ineffectual, self-serving, or authoritarian, this will take its toll on faculty—who will vent their frustrations on students and parents.

Whatever teachers become, we believe that most begin their careers as idealistic professionals who want to help students. People become educators for a variety of reasons. Most like kids and aspire to teach. If they are really mismatched with a career in education, they will usually find out in their practice teaching and during their first few years on the job. During their careers, the majority of teachers do not intentionally or maliciously maltreat children. An unknown proportion of those who are abusive do not even realize how damaging their behaviors can be. This group is remedial and can be helped by adequate supervision, continuing education, and consultation with other staff such as school psychologists.

Even where the climate is poisoned, there are teachers who struggle against all odds to be respectful and considerate, and to maintain high expectations for all their students. Even in the midst of urban blight and rural poverty, there are principals and teachers who create climates of hope and encouragement for their students. They create schools that promote democratic ideals through both the content of the curriculum and the processes of democratic teaching that they model. This book addresses the other side of the educational coin. We are concerned about educators who are inherently punitive and autocratic. We are alarmed about educators who believe exaggerated and distorted accounts of school crime and youth violence. They become agents of dangerously punitive policies that victimize students.

. . .

In conclusion, we believe that school disciplinary practices, driven by the politics of punitiveness, make schools dangerous for too many children. They are dangerous because they are toxic to children's emotional and physical well-being. Throughout this book we will refer to toxic or dangerous practices we believe poison the climate of schools and undermine democracy.

We believe that this book will really make you think about where we are going as a nation. You may think that our portrayal is of doom and gloom. But we obviously have hope. Otherwise, why write this book? Why continue to work with schools and parents? We believe that when the majority of Americans are given the facts, rather than hysterics or propaganda, they will opt for just and equitable reforms in schools. At the end of this book you will find a plan of action to change American schools from authoritarian enclaves to exemplars of democracy.

In schools that encourage participatory democracy, students and staff understand the need to respect each other's rights. Democratic schools provide students with a sense of shared responsibility with school staff for assuring the safety of all. Further, these schools will encourage students to participate in democracy when they become adults. But before considering these broad issues, let us first turn to a toxic and dangerous practice that is still allowed in the schools in twenty-three states.

Chapter 1

Physical Maltreatment in the Classroom

Whack! Smack! The long arcing swing of the paddle ended abruptly against her behind. She leaned over with both hands tightly gripping the edge of the counter. Her pants offered little protection from the earnest efforts of the man with broad shoulders and powerful arms. Her eyes were filled with tears as she cried in anger and outrage.

In her seventeen years she had never experienced such excruciating pain. Unbeknownst to her and in reaction to the trauma, her uterus began to contract with increasing force as the blows struck her buttocks. The paddling occurred during normal menstruation and she would later need medication to stem the heavy menstrual hemorrhaging.

The short break since the last two swats offered little relief from the mounting pain. The cries of the other girls who were present and the stone-faced demeanor of the powerful disciplinarian increased her feelings of outrage. The situation was hardly relieved by what seemed like gallows humor from the other man who entered the scene. Through her tears she heard him giggle and say, "Save one for me." He later denied this, but then, it is easier to believe the master than the victim whose perceptions are distorted by pain. He certainly did not object to what was happening.

Although she was a physically and emotionally mature seventeen-year-old, Shelly Gaspersohn could only think, "I want my mother." She ruefully remembered that her parents had warned her not to allow herself to be degraded. Her later descriptions of the incident were similar to those of rape victims. In describing this experience, which occurred on December 1, 1982, Shelly said, "I felt humiliated and violated. That and the pain caused me to start to cry. I never thought anything could hurt so much." And her educational experience was not unique. Since then, I have heard unceasing litanies about tears and humiliation caused by the "board of education."

Let us fast-forward to a recent and quite similar situation. On January 31, 1997, seventeen-year-old Bria Rose was bent over as the powerful, large man administered one smashing blow with a paddle to her behind. The meeting of the wooden paddle and her unprotected flesh resulted in a smack so loud that it was heard through a closed door. The force of the blow caused Bria to lose her grip on the desk and fall against it. An adult woman stood by to witness this act of what many would consider sadistic, sexual savagery.

The smack caused Bria to become overwhelmed by pain, tears, shame, and humiliation. The resulting bruises were still visible at the end of two weeks. Following the paddling, Bria developed unscheduled menstrual bleeding that lasted for twenty days. Her gynecologist told her that she might have internal damage to her reproductive system. The single powerful swing of a paddle, she tearfully recounted, was "no doubt in my mind whatsoever, about the worst experience in my life."

Now before we go any further, we want to say that we are not writing this book for aficionados of sadomasochistic sexual practices. While some might get their jollies from reading about the experiences of Shelly and Bria, we can assure you that those experiences were not jolly for the two young women. Neither girl's life experiences had prepared her to be beaten by a trusted and respected male caregiver. Both the paddlers were admired coaches. Shelly's was coach Glenn Varney, former disciplinarian at Dunn High School in Harnett County, North Carolina. The witness was Vice-Principal Roger Lee McKoy.

What was Shelly's horrendous offense? Before I answer that question, let me give you a little background. Shelly was an honor student in her senior year. She had no record of disciplinary infractions. Rather, she was a considerate, well-behaved, deeply religious young woman. She was an accomplished flutist and a member of the all-state band who enjoyed school. She was hardly someone who would require the infamous "last resort" that many educators claim is necessary to maintain law and order in the schools. Now, what horrible act did Shelly perpetrate?

Shelly's indiscretion, common to seniors, was playing hooky and constituted the only recorded rebellious act of her school career. How was it that Shelly, a girl who never broke school rules, committed this sin worthy of a flogging? At the urging of her close friend, Renee Byum, the two skipped classes and spent the day driving around looking for Renee's boyfriend. Not being accomplished truants, both were caught.

The girls were offered the choice of corporal punishment or a five-day in-school suspension (ISS). In-school suspension at Dunn High School meant sitting with other punishees all day in a monitored room. Theoretically, teachers from all classes provide assignments for each day. Like many similar programs, teacher cooperation in providing schoolwork is inconsistent. Often students are left with long periods of idle time because of no work assignments.

Shelly and Renee accepted the ISS, partly because the cruel reputation of the disciplinarian, Glenn Varney, the strapping, paddle-swinging assistant principal and football coach, preceded him. After several days of in-school suspension, Shelly became worried about keeping up with her pre-calculus class as she was not being supplied with assignments. According to school policy, a student could volunteer for three licks with the paddle for each day of parole from ISS. Shelly, Renee, and some other ISS students volunteered to take their licks from Varney in order to return to regular class. The result was the incident already described.

But surely, Shelly's minor offense (committed in the rural South), the aberrant punishment, and the subsequent events could not possibly be mirrored fifteen years later in a Northern state. Wrong!

As you will read a little later, Shelly's litigation and appeals are a matter of documented history. Bria's complaint was only filed three months before this book was begun. Therefore, I must be careful not to violate the rights of the various litigants as I describe her case.

Bria alleges that preceding the paddling, a former best friend had been verbally harassing her for about one month, possibly over issues of jealousy and competitiveness. Bria had been taught to "turn the other cheek" so she tried to ignore the insults and negative statements. On January 31, 1997, she was hit by the backpack of her ex-friend, who was walking past her. Bria, who believed that this act was done purposefully, exclaimed, "Excuse me!" They exchanged words and her former friend left for the parking lot.

As soon as Bria left the building she was again confronted and was allegedly called a "bitch." Bria, who reports that she had never before struck anyone or been in a fight, pushed her ex-friend.

The altercation between the two girls was interdicted by Mr. Hale, assistant principal and Bria's former soccer coach at South Webster High School. Similar to Shelly's case, Bria was offered the choice of a paddling or a three-day suspension. She was given the weekend to make a decision. In her mind there was no choice. She felt that, because of academic blocking schedules and her participation on the school basketball team, she would miss too much work and let the team down if she accepted the suspension. She also reasoned that since Mr. Hale was a trusted caregiver, and considering that this was a "first offense," he certainly would not hit her enough to cause any real damage.

Unlike Shelly's, Bria's pain was witnessed by a female, Mrs. Hickman, rather than a male teacher. It is somewhat surprising that a professional woman would countenance discipline directed at the behind of a sexually mature female. Like Shelly, Bria had no life experiences that prepared her to be beaten by a male caregiver—a formerly admired and respected coach—while being forced to bend over in a passive position and offer her buttocks as a target for the infliction of pain. Bria, a model student, a child who strove to please adults and authority figures and to make her parents proud, a child who had never been in any school trouble, suddenly felt transformed into one of the "bad kids." Associated with this, she experienced a considerable amount of physical pain.

One would wonder what we have learned about child abuse in the fifteen years since Shelly Gaspersohn was legally and brutally battered by a school official. Obviously Mr. Hale and Mrs. Hickman had not learned much. Nor had Mr. Paul White, the superintendent, and the school board of Bloom-Vernon School District.

As the tale unfolds, it is clear that the majority of legislators in those twenty-three states where student paddling is still legal have learned nothing. For students in these states, any reasonable definition of child abuse stops at the schoolhouse door. Yet advocacy groups have worked hard in almost every state to inform legislators about the problem of allowing educators to smack students. We hope that the story of Shelly (which received national attention in the 1980s), coupled with the contemporary story of Bria, will convince enough parents, educators, and policymakers to stop the continuing abuse.

These two cases tell a story that we have heard too many times. The ages of students, the resources of parents, and the locations may be different. But the scenarios are remarkably similar and attest to the stupidity, arrogance, and outright malice that school and public officials can demonstrate when confronted by parents who want justice for their own children and protection for others. Let us continue to consider the similarity between the two cases.

Bruised Behinds and Battered Minds

Both the Gaspersohns and the Roses were quickly taught about the ability of school officials to trivialize a family disaster. In over twenty years of experience with these types of cases, I am still amazed by reports of many school officials' reactions. They are adroit at trivializing, denying, lying, evading, and stonewalling when parents have legitimate complaints about physical and emotional damage done to their children in the name of discipline.

When Shelly arrived home after the beating, her mother was shocked and horrified by the large welts on Shelly's buttocks. An examining physician became so enraged that he filed child abuse charges against Coach Varney. In the vast majority of states at that time, teachers were immune to child abuse charges. Of course, if Shelly's parents had administered the beating they could have been arrested.

Complaints by the Gaspersohns to the principal, superintendent, and school board fell on deaf and hostile ears. Despite the fact that the beating left bruises for three weeks and caused menstrual hemorrhaging and long-lasting emotional trauma, the school officials trivialized the whole event.

Unlike the majority of brutalized students, who are almost always from poor or working-class families, Shelly Gaspersohn had parents with the resources to hire an attorney. Research and personal experience indicate that parents without financial resources are further victimized and bullied into submission by the power of school authorities. The Gaspersohns hired Renny Deese, an experienced lawyer devoted to civil rights issues, and filed suit against the school and Glenn Varney.

A similar scene ensued when Bria arrived home. Seeing Bria's injuries, her mother was also horrified. Mrs. Rose took her bruised daughter to the local urgent care center. Like Shelly, Bria was prescribed a painkiller to help her to deal with the bruises, which lasted about two weeks. Unfortunately, Motrin did not stop the unscheduled menstrual bleeding, which lasted for twenty days following the paddling. Bria went to a gynecologist who, she reports, indicated that she might have some internal damage. The examining physician followed standard protocols when abuse is suspected. He advised Bria's parents to report the incident to an attorney.

Like the Gaspersohns' complaint, the Roses' complaint to various authorities was not taken seriously. Mrs. Rose expressed incredulity that school officials could get away with what would be a criminal act if perpetrated by a parent or other caregiver. She was further disturbed when she was not "allowed" to file criminal charges with law enforcement officials.

But the Roses found, as others in rural, conservative communities have discovered, that the very law enforcement and child abuse authorities who should protect children's rights are reluctant to override the judgments of school authorities. Mrs. Rose alleged that the investigator from Scioto County Children's Services found her complaints "unsubstantiated." She was allegedly told by the investigator that he supported paddling in schools and if "they did more of it the kids would be better."

Like Mrs. Gaspersohn, Mrs. Rose began to research the issue of corporal punishment in her state schools. She discovered that her district reported the most paddlings in the state and that an alleged survey revealed that it is supported by the community and at least 81 percent of the students. She was allegedly told by the superintendent, "No judge or jury in America would convict the teacher for this paddling."

In neither of the two cases did the school officials realize the extent to which their behavior brought out and rallied protective parental instincts. In both cases the mothers were extraordinarily courageous and persistent in their struggles for justice for their children and others who might be similarly victimized.

The Roses were fortunate, as were the Gaspersohns, to find an attorney more devoted to civil liberties and children's rights than to big bucks. Most lawyers know that, even in the best of situations, they are not going to profit much in these types of cases. Attorney Phyllis Schiff was outraged by the physical and emotional abuses Bria suffered.

Justice—North Carolina Style

The Gaspersohns had their day in court, they had their appeals, and they learned some lessons about children's rights and justice for schoolchildren that have helped future generations. Marlene Gaspersohn became a vociferous advocate against paddling. Her message has spread through her activities in the Lutheran Church, letters to politicians, television appearances, and testimony in Congress. The saga of her persistent but failed litigation is described in detail in *Reading, Writing, and the Hickory Stick* and will be reviewed here briefly.

There were two claims. The first was that "Glenn Varney's violent and forceful striking of the plaintiff . . . required [her] . . . to undergo medical treatment, limit her activities and general enjoyment of life." Compensatory damages of $5,000 were requested. In retrospect, that was a small sum, considering the effect of the paddling on Shelly's life.

The second was that Glenn Varney willfully and maliciously struck Shelly, with the approval of the Harnett County School Board. Therefore, $50,000 in punitive damages was claimed.

The trial took place on December 12, 1983, before Judge James Pou Bailey. I was there because I had conducted an extensive psychological evaluation of Shelly and was to serve as an expert witness. The setting and Judge Bailey fulfilled every stereotype that one might associate with rural justice. I had a sense of foreboding when I learned that the examining physician was not allowed to testify that he had filed child abuse charges and that other testimony was restricted and distorted by the judge when he charged the jury.

After three days of testimony, in just fifteen minutes, twelve men and women of Harnett County, North Carolina, rendered a verdict of "not guilty." They decided that Coach Varney had not used unreasonable force. Their decision supports the justification that educators can beat and bruise students' behinds as long as it is done in the name of discipline.

The jury, mirroring a popular belief, most likely were expressing the conviction, "I was spanked and paddled as a kid and I turned out OK." If you can't take a little humiliation, how can you deal with the real world?

How many times have I heard the same old rationalizations? Some members of the jury may have been shocked by Shelly's beating. They may have thought about what they would have done if their physically mature young daughter suffered the same fate. Yet they may have felt constrained by North Carolina law in determining what is reasonable when a grown man hits a young woman with a wooden paddle and by Judge Bailey's charge. After all, the judiciary in this case appeared stuck in nineteenth-century thinking. Here are the two cases they used as precedents.

In the 1837 decision in *State* v. *Pendergast,* the North Carolina Supreme Court ruled that the whipping of a six- or seven-year-old girl can leave bruises and can be severe up to the point of causing "long lasting mischief." A stipulation was that the beating must be inflicted "honestly in the performance of duty."

To show that they were more forward thinking than the judges in 1837, the contemporary Supreme Court of North Carolina took a big leap into the twentieth century. However, in their misguided and unaccustomed efforts at progressive thinking regarding children's rights, they were only able to reach forward to 1904 and the decision in *Drum* v. *Miller.*

In *Drum* v. *Miller,* a child received serious injury as a result of his teacher throwing a pencil that struck the child's eye. In that case the court exonerated the teacher since the act was "not prompted by malice."

In contemporary education, most professionals recognize that students are harmed by discipline that inflicts severe physical or emotional pain. Even if one is not aware of the research and literature on school discipline, common sense and usual practice should dictate the stupidity of forcefully hitting an adolescent girl with a wooden paddle. Either the paddler is too dumb to know better or is prompted by maliciousness. Guilty in either case!

It may have been too much to expect citizens and the judiciary to challenge a legal interpretation of "reasonable force" based on knowledge and beliefs about children and education that were over a century old. Those were times when child, wife, and racial abuses were common and accepted. When I faced that jury in Harnett County, I assumed that they knew at least something about what we have learned in this second part of the twentieth century about developmental psychology, pediatric medicine, education, and children's rights. I was wrong!

Take one example of their distorted thinking. The school board, the judge, and the North Carolina Supreme Court made a big issue of the fact the Shelly "asked" for the beating. It is clear that she had no way of knowing how severely she would be hit for this very first disciplinary offense in her school career. The school's own rules indicated that a variety of punishments were available. It was not difficult to surmise that Shelly was not a hard-core delinquent. After all, she asked to be paddled so that she could quickly get back to her schoolwork, not to return to a life of crime.

Well, the Gaspersohns had their day in court and went as far as they could in appeals. It wasn't until I did the research for *Reading, Writing, and the Hickory Stick* that I realized what they were up against. Basically, they tried to take on a typical rural oligarchy. Lined up against them were the beliefs and traditions of a tightly knit right-wing political establishment rooted in fundamentalist, Southern Baptist doctrines.

Judge Bailey belonged to a group of far-right political operatives. His buddies from his "good old boy" network included Hoover Adams, publisher of the avowedly right-wing *Dunn Daily Record,* Thomas Ellis, a wealthy right-wing scion, and Senator Jesse Helms. In fact, Helms, in his first column as a writer for the *Tar Heel Banker,* house organ of the North Carolina Banker's Association, touted his friend Pou Bailey. I was familiar with the social agenda of such staunch supporters of far-right political and religious operatives. I had little faith that they would stray far from the often repeated misquote from the Bible, "spare the rod and spoil the child."

Following the trial, one of Shelly's married sisters, in an un-related event, complained about long-standing religious classes taught in the Dunn public schools. While the school's own attor-ney ruled that the classes were unconstitutional, Hoover Adams's paper led a campaign against canceling the religion classes. Media hostility against the Gaspersohns and threats against their per-sonal safety caused them to give up their manufacturing business and leave Dunn.

Shelly gave up any thought of teaching and studied electrical engineering. She later started a business and became a mother. However, her love of children eventually emerged as a dominant force in her life. She now teaches mathematics in public school. According to her mother, Shelly continues to experience stress whenever she thinks about that beating by Coach Varney sixteen years ago.

Is Paddling of Adolescents' Buttocks Sexual Harassment?

Since the predation of Coach Varney in rural North Carolina, there have been some changes in the way Americans think about females' bodies. Congress has passed laws forbidding sexual ha-rassment. The infamous Anita Hill hearings sensitized Americans to the issue. The American Association of University Women pub-lished a landmark study in 1993. This study, which will be described in Chapter Five, alerted the public to the negative emotional im-pact of all types of unwanted sexual behaviors. Most people con-sider buttocks to be in the domain of sexuality, though this probably does not include the somewhat questionable penchant of many male athletes to publicly pat their buddies' behinds. How-ever, sexual harassment does encompass unwanted touching, grab-bing, and groping students' derrieres.

When the Rose family called me and detailed the events, I could not help but think about Shelly's case and the change in the law regarding sexual harassment since 1982. Bria's trauma, like Shelly's, was similar to that of a rape victim. The major difference is that Bria was assaulted after the passage of Title IX. When I talked to Phyllis Schiff, Bria's attorney, it was difficult to contain my excitement. Could this be the case that would end all paddling of female students? Then, if that occurred, would it not be sexual discrimination to paddle only males? Ideally, this case would go to trial and Bria would win.

Bria's claim, unlike Shelly's, was filed in federal court. This is very important because it removed jurisdiction from the local oligarchy. Among the twelve charges is that a paddle in the hands of Coach Hale was a "deadly weapon" as defined by Ohio law. Under Title IX, Bria charges that Mr. Hale and the Bloom-Vernon Local (BVL) School District permitted and tolerated "illegal and/or inappropriate relationships between male BVL employees and female BVL students [thereby creating] . . . an offensive, sexist, hostile atmosphere."

The school board asked the United States District Court for the Southern District of Ohio to throw out the case. On March 9, 1999, Judge Susan Dlott agreed with the school board that a paddling that caused bruising and menstrual hemorrhaging was not brutal, inhumane, or sadistic and, therefore, was not at a level sufficient to be considered a breach of Bria's constitutional rights. The judge ignored the evidence of emotional injury and supported the decision by citing cases of brutal beatings that did not "shock the conscience" of federal judges in other districts. Judge Dlott saw no connection between the paddling of an adolescent female by a male educator and sexual harassment as defined in federal statutes. She based her decision in part on the flawed *Ingraham* v. *Wright* Supreme Court decision which we will discuss later.

The Roses are infuriated but still committed to protecting other students. Without people like the Roses, students throughout the country would not have a chance. Their efforts have resulted directly or indirectly in the banning of corporal punishment in two local school districts. The publicity surrounding the case and the family's support of other victims resulted in Mrs. Rose receiving the Child Advocate of the Year Award from the Ohio Center for Effective Discipline.

Exactly What Is Corporal Punishment?

Most dictionaries tell us that corporal punishment is the purposeful infliction of pain or confinement as a penalty for an offense. At home, most corporal punishment is done by spanking buttocks with an open hand. Other popular pain-infliction techniques used by parents include, in descending order of frequency, slapping, hair and ear pulling, punching, pinching, whipping, arm twisting, shaking, and kicking. Since educators were once children, they tend to model their spanking experiences at home when they enter the school. Educators are assumed by training to be more learned than the average parent. Years ago educators concluded that it made no sense to hurt their hands when forcefully striking the behinds of their errant students. Contemporary educators almost always use wooden paddles.

For the last twenty-two years I have tracked cases from all over the country and never cease to be amazed by the variety of ways in which schoolchildren can be hurt. For instance, some educators prefer the flexibility and ease of swatting behinds with leather. Rather than swatting with wooden paddles, some Oklahoma teachers have used a leather weapon shaped like the sole of a size 12 or 13 cowboy boot.

Other weapons documented at the NCSCPA include rubber hoses, leather straps and belts, switches, sticks, rods, ropes, straight pins, plastic baseball bats, and arrows. Punching, slapping, kicking, and shaking are popular forms of "getting children's attention." A favorite of coaches seems to be ramming students up against lockers. If lockers aren't available, any convenient wall will do.

Ramming students against a wall was once institutionalized by the Madison Valley Schools in Montana. Apparently some school staff believed that they could not educate their students without "racking" them. One particular teacher, Arthur Hartman, had developed racking to a fine art. It was not until a colleague and I evaluated the posttraumatic symptoms of six of Hartman's victims that we discovered that racking consists of picking students up by their necks and shaking them. In some cases racking was enhanced and extended by holding the student up against the wall to enhance the effects of mild strangulation. Eileen and Michael White, both veterinarians, had no children of their own in the school, but they were so enraged by this discipline-by-throttling philosophy that they organized the parents of the victims. Because of their empathy for the children and their fear for their children not yet in school in Ennis, Montana, they expended their own time and resources to organize litigation against the school district. In addition, they lobbied the state legislature and helped ban any type of corporal punishment in Montana schools.

Some teachers have gone well beyond the buttocks to creatively inflict pain. Not to be outdone by the stars of cable television's Food Channel, some educators in the Midwest injected hot Tabasco sauce in the mouths of errant students. Some of the children suffered the additional pain caused by having it smeared on their faces. Children with disabilities appear to be particularly vulnerable to abuse. For instance, a twelve-year-old in a special education class claimed that his teacher and her aide banged students' heads into their desks, twisted their arms, and even tried a little strangulation as punishment.

The dictionary definition at the beginning of this section does not tell the whole story. For instance, if one sticks by the provision that corporal punishment involves the *purposeful* infliction of pain, this could offer an escape from prosecution when a child is seriously damaged or even killed. I was involved in a case in which a student had been blowing spit bubbles in the air. The teacher claimed that this "disgusting, unsanitary act" caused her to "instinctively" smack him on mouth. The bleeding, pain, and emotional trauma so outraged the parents that they sued the school.

The teacher's defense was based, in part, on school board regulations that defined corporal punishment as an "intentional" act. She stated that she hadn't intended to hit the child, and therefore her instinctive act had not violated the school board sanctions. Rather than face the plaintiffs in court, the school board settled the case and removed the term *intentional* from the definition. However, in other cases, parents have lost in litigation when educators have successfully pleaded that they did not intend to cause serious harm.

We believe that corporal punishment in the schools includes any disciplinary procedure intended to cause physical pain. This can include forcing ingestion of noxious foods as mentioned earlier, preventing children from going to the bathroom, forcing children to assume uncomfortable postures for extended periods or to spend long durations in a time-out chair or confined space, and imposing painful physical drills. We believe it is important to broadly define corporal punishment to make the public and policymakers aware of the variety and seriousness of legalized pain-inflicting disciplinary procedures. Any infliction of pain, especially when carried to extremes or when the student has problematic medical conditions, can cause serious injury or even death.

For instance, teacher Craig Gordon claimed that his discipline of Michael Waechter, an orthopedically handicapped thirteen-year-old student, was not intended to cause the child's death. School authorities had been notified of Michael's heart problem, and Michael's parents claim that his teacher was also informed. According to a report in the *Detroit News,* as the students were lining up on the playground, Michael and another boy were lagging behind. "The two of them were tussling—not fighting" reported the school superintendent. For this horrendous offense, Gordon ordered the two boys to do a "gut run," which was a 320-yard disciplinary sprint. After twenty feet, Michael dropped dead.

There is a phenomenon that I call the "activity punishment continuum." At the active end are various drills, such as the "gut run" and push-ups. At the fixed end of the continuum are activities that force students to stay in one place for long periods. An angry parent from Wisconsin called me to complain about her child's teacher, who drew a circle on the blackboard which was a few inches above the tip the student's nose. She then made the child stand on tippy-toe and place his nose in the middle of the circle. While some of the teacher's victims might have been runners who relished long stretching exercises, it is doubtful that any trainer would agree with the motivation of the teacher, the duration of the exercise, or the painful consequences, which include painful muscle spasms. Not quite as exotic as this exercise is the much used and abused behavioral technique of time out.

Terrible Time Out: A Special Case of Corporal Punishment

Time out, which we call deprivation punishment, is different from a straightforward punishment. Instead of direct retribution, time out works by removing the child from a positive situation. If students enjoy being in the classroom, time out increases the probability that they will want to act appropriately when returned to that setting. We do not know of any research about the frequency of use of time outs by teachers, but this popular disciplinary technique has certainly had an impact on parents.

A 1992 poll showed that 38 percent of parents responded that they used time out and preferred it to spanking. This is an 18 percent increase over a similar poll in 1962. Unfortunately, like any punishment, this procedure is often overused.

Returning to the scientific definition—the one under which punishment can be justified as a constructive act—a punishment is a procedure that decreases the chance that a misbehavior will recur. So if a teacher repeatedly uses time out with the same child and the misbehavior does not stop, then—by definition—the procedure was not punishing. Further, there is little indication that increasing the duration of time out beyond very narrow limits increases its effectiveness—it just gets the child out of the way and increases the satisfaction of the person inflicting the penalty. Most of the abuses that I have dealt with have occurred when teachers have placed students for many hours in storerooms, closets, and specially designed boxes. In some cases, children have been tied to time-out chairs for long periods.

Experts generally agree that time out should not be more minutes than the child's age. Also, it should be used in conjunction with positive reinforcement programs. While the research on effectiveness shows that the correct duration is best determined by what works, duration should be dictated by common sense. If time out does not work after repeated use, it is clear that it is not an effective punishment and should be stopped.

Here is a somewhat bizarre case of in which paddling and time out were served up as a punishment cocktail. It illustrates how the lure of punishment can distort reason for professionals who should know better. Shirley, a high-achieving, happy, outgoing first grader, became aware of some disturbing marital conflicts between her parents. Because of her ruminations about fear of divorce, Shirley started to sob uncontrollably one day in class.

Shirley's teacher took her to the principal, who came up with a brilliant solution. "Bend over and touch your toes," said the principal, "I have a perfect way to stop your crying." When Shirley responded as requested, she found that a paddle on the behind was the proposed solution. Of course, this remedy only resulted in an increased flow of tears.

The next solution was even more brilliant. Shirley was escorted to a clothes closet across from the nurse's office. The collective wisdom of the principal and the nurse resulted in sitting Shirley on a stool in the closet. Shirley was still crying as the nurse turned off the light and closed the closet door. When this didn't stop the crying, the nurse decided on a more direct approach—she stuck a sock in Shirley's mouth to muffle the crying!

Shirley's mother was incredulous that this could happen in school. She was outraged that Shirley was so traumatized by the experience and that her daughter developed many stress symptoms, including fear of returning to school.

Going to the Bathroom: Right or Privilege?

Did you know that teachers are not supposed to leave their classrooms without a legally designated adult in charge? Now we are not saying that they always follow the rules, especially if they have painful urgency to go to the bathroom. But we know of teachers with urinary infections, spastic colons, and other conditions who have had to take work leaves because they could not remain in the classroom for sufficient periods. Despite our sympathy for teachers, we find it difficult to understand why so many of them are not empathetic to similar physical needs of students.

We believe a type of corporal punishment occurs when teachers forbid bathroom privileges to students who are in acute pain because of the need to go. The problem is often compounded when the student feels it necessary to publicly beg the teacher to go, is forced to run out of the class without permission, or has an accident. We know that some students request to go to the bathroom to escape from the class, to meet a friend, or to have a smoke. We also know that unsupervised bathrooms can be vandalized by angry students. However, as most principals know, there are relatively simple solutions to these problems, including keeping track of who goes to the bathroom and how much time they spend there.

Many people can recall at least one incident in their school careers when they or a close friend was punished by denial of an urgent request to go to the bathroom. Many of the cases we have heard were of students who did not have records of misbehavior. Refusals are often based on a teacher's reflexive need to refuse bathroom privileges except at assigned times. Here are just a few examples of the problem culled from our research on worst school experiences. Interestingly, only females reported worst school experiences in this category.

> My first bad experience in school was in kindergarten. The bathroom was located inside the classroom but you still had to raise your hand to use it. I sat with my hand raised for a long period of time and wet my pants.

I ended up sitting on a radiator for my underclothes to dry. This experience was a personal embarrassment for many years.

My worst school experience was when I was in fourth grade and I had to go to the bathroom. Prior to this, other students who were allowed to go to the bathroom were not returning to class. When I needed to go to have a bowel movement, the teacher would not let me go because she thought I would not come back. The pain got so unbearable that I could not hold it in any longer and went in my pants.

When I was in third grade, someone had a bowel movement in their pants. The teacher asked who did it and no one answered. She made us line up, bend over and she stuck her nose right up to our buttocks to smell who did it. I felt so humiliated. This incident damaged my sense of privacy, my respect for the teacher, and instilled in me a fear that sooner or later another teacher would do this to me or my class.

We have documented cases where children took notes from their physicians to school requesting that they be permitted to go to the bathroom when required. In one case, despite the child's urinary infection, her third-grade teacher insisted that she could only go to the bathroom at the assigned times. The child was kept home from school until the infection disappeared.

We continually hear examples of this particular type of painful punishment. We believe that the problem is in part caused by administrative rigidity resulting from the need for the orderly and predictable use of bathrooms so that no students appear unescorted in the hallways. However, this is a poor reason to cause children pain and embarrassment. While students and parents frequently complain to school authorities, at least one student took his case to the Supreme Court.

Jerry Boyett, a senior in Luverne High School in Crenshaw County, Alabama, was refused permission to go to the bathroom. He was suffering from diarrhea, but the teacher, Lalar Tomberlin, indicated that she saw no signs of distress. Boyett claimed that students have a constitutional right to use the bathroom when needed. His attorney claimed that this right is based on liberty interest and bodily integrity. Boyett's claim was denied by three Alabama courts. In 1997, the Supreme Court refused to hear the case, thereby denying students the legal right to go to the bathroom, even when in dire pain.

The Pedagogy of Pain

As part of ongoing research at the NCSCPA we have documented the pedagogy of pain. In one particularly interesting study we asked adults to describe their worst school experiences when they were students. Here are some selected anecdotes to demonstrate how heads were as often targets as were behinds.

> My teacher used to physically punish the boys by holding and slamming their heads against walls. He also seemed to like making the whole class exercise in the winter with no jackets for entire recess as punishment, etc. He was very sarcastic, always putting us down, yelling, demeaning.

> I was waiting in line at lavatory to go in a stall when two girls came out at the same time. I was second in line and went into second stall. When I came out, the nun was waiting for me. Apparently the girl behind me claimed I had cut in front of her. The nun proceeded to yell and to take my head and bang it into the tiled wall. Despite what I had to say, she made me feel as if I was wrong and consequently felt embarrassed.

> In second grade my teacher accused me of screaming out in the class. When I told her it wasn't me and the girl who had screamed admitted it was her, she still insisted that it was me and banged the side of my head into the chalkboard.

> If a student did not know an answer or rustled a paper at the wrong time, he would be set upon by teacher. Ridicule and physical abuse were most often used by this teacher. Most distressing of all was when the teacher would rip a student out of his seat (for what appeared to be innocuous behavior) and smash his head against the blackboard. As a witness to this event, I would cover my eyes for fear of seeing blood and brains all over the blackboard.

> In parochial school in the second grade I was bad in math. After receiving a "zero" on a test, the nun called me outside the classroom and proceeded to smack my head into the wall until I passed out.

> In seventh grade, I had sprained my foot and was unable to participate in gym class. For some reason the gym teacher and I didn't click. When I had to

sit on the outer wall of the gym and watch others, my sprained foot was lying across a boundary marker. The teacher kicked it to the other side of the line and made my foot worse.

A teacher took a book and slammed it on my sprained wrist just because I didn't know the answer to his questions.

In eleventh grade I stepped over a row of seats in the auditorium and was caught by the teacher. I was paddled on the stage in front of a hundred students. It hurt me more emotionally than physically.

When I was seventeen years old I was in class when I felt a very heavy menstrual flow. I asked several times to go to the bathroom until the teacher finally agreed to let me go. He seemed angry when I returned. He said I had been in the bathroom too long and he took me into the hallway. He pinned me up against the wall so that my feet did not touch the floor and screamed at me for what seemed to me like hours.

My parents were immigrants who had learned only enough English to enable them to become citizens. Because they spoke only Italian at home, I had trouble with English. My teacher slapped me in the face every day whenever I responded to her in Italian.

The nun in my third grade class was determined to improve my penmanship. Every time I wrote something messy, she slammed my knuckles with a five-foot metal ruler. It hurt bad. She also put grapefruit pits in anyone's shoes who wasn't standing up straight and used duct tape on their mouths for a whole day if they spoke out of turn.

These anecdotes were selected from hundreds that we have collected in our studies of peoples' worst school experiences. When the worst experience involved corporal punishment, adults often report vivid memories of the event and sometimes reexperience some of the emotional trauma. While most school guidelines for the use of corporal punishment suggest that it should be done in private, this is not always the case. In many cases, public smacking adds to the humiliation and embarrassment felt by the students. As is illustrated by the students with the sprained foot and sprained wrist, educators can target injured body parts for abuse. Sometimes the justification for smacking kids is bizarre, as is shown in the case of the student from the Italian-speaking home.

These cases demonstrate the insidious potential toxicity of any institution that empowers officials to inflict pain. That power is invariably abused. In the schools, the victims are children who have no right to due process or to parental oversight. Educators can, in the name of discipline and often for minor indiscretions, inflict punishments that have potential to cause lifelong trauma. This practice undermines the basic tenets of fairness and justice that are the underpinnings of our democracy. It gives the lie to the premise that the punishment should be justified by the nature of the crime.

Crime and Punishment in the Schoolhouse

One of the major defenses of corporal punishment is that it is a last resort. Now that term certainly has heavy-duty implications about the nature of student crime. To our minds, this argument is nothing more than an excuse to abuse students.

Get this picture. A poor, martyred teacher, struggling in the trenches, must each day face hordes of students, some who would be feared by Ghengis himself. In this power struggle, teachers can't allow chaos to reign. Supposedly, after teachers have used up their extensive armamentarium of tried-and-true disciplinary techniques and students still don't respond, swatting is the only solution. After all, a good whack is the only thing some kids understand. Right!

After hearing this argument over and over until I was sick of it, I decided to study the types of school crimes that call for the last resort—rather than relying on the myths perpetrated by its supporters. None of the reports give credence to any of the arguments used by pro-paddlers. For instance, some of these studies—conducted over a twenty-year period—examined press clippings of smacked and whacked students who claimed that they were injured by educators. Among other things, we wanted to see if these cases of injured children really reflected the last resort explanation.

Most cases involved teachers or principals, but others such as bus drivers, janitors, and even a school board member have gotten in their whacks. Now remember, these cases represent a tiny fraction of the potential pool of injured children, since the parents had to raise a big enough stink to interest the media. Most parents of injured children are emotionally unwilling or economically unable to take on the school board.

While the damages caused to the children ranged from severe bruises to internal injuries to death (three cases), over 80 percent of the offenses were nonviolent. Nonviolent misbehavior included talking out of turn, cursing, truancy, cigarette-related offenses, inadequate academic behavior (a kindergartner was injured for incorrectly pronouncing words during a phonics lesson), and staying in the bathroom too long. Violent infractions, by our definition, included fighting, throwing lethal objects, or engaging in potentially harmful pranks. Note that no case involved real violence. School discipline manuals do not recommend taking a paddle to the behinds of students who attack staff or peers with guns or knives. Whatever happened to the "make the punishment fit the crime" adage? So much for the last resort argument!

Is Corporal Punishment Abuse?

In recent years there has been a raging battle regarding the relationship between spanking and abuse. I present this fully in my book *The Case Against Spanking* (Jossey-Bass, 1997). Let me summarize the issue, since it is quite relevant to school paddling. Prospankers, fueled by vociferous support from the religious and political right, maintain that spanking is a God-given right and the responsibility of all parents. Since it is justified in the Bible and it is practiced by most American parents, it can't be considered abuse. Do-good liberals, "so-called" experts in parenting, and government officials have no business violating the sanctity of the home.

Most child abuse workers, professors, researchers, and child advocates claim that spanking, even when it consists of a few swats on the behind, is an act of violence and therefore abuse. When done with "weapons" such as belts, clothes hangers, and switches, swatting invariably leaves bruises and welts and therefore rises to the legal definition of abuse. Even when it does not do physical damage, it is considered subabusive because it is invariably done in anger, causes some pain, and often results in tears.

We propose a middle ground. Even though common spanking may not cause physical damage, it is abusive by intent. The purpose is to cause pain. We don't buy the argument that it is just a way to get children's attention. There are lots of other ways to get someone's attention.

Academics, pediatricians, and parenting experts who support spanking claim that it should be limited to two- to six-year-olds, never be done in anger, and should consist of two or three non-damaging swats by hand to the behind. All experts whom we know of with reasonable credentials consider the use of a wooden paddle or other weapon to be abusive. Except for self-proclaimed experts such as preachers, politicians, and parents from the far religious right, no experts who are pro-spankers (that we know of) support school paddling.

The real irony is that twenty-three states support the right of educators to legally abuse students. The bruises caused by paddlings would result in child abuse charges if caused by anyone other than a teacher! This has been supported in Georgia, for example, in a case against Berrien County School District. The Court of Appeals, considering pictures of the bruised and battered behind of Chris Mathis, decided that even though the bright red bruises revealed the outline of the paddle, it was not abuse.

Florida is a state not necessarily known for its abhorrence for corporal punishment. However, the Court of Appeals of Florida, First District, rendered an opinion that serves as an effective measure against pro-spanking educators. Several administrators were sued by the parents of paddled children who sustained bruises lasting more than a week. The administrators were shocked to discover that their actions qualified them for the Department of Health and Rehabilitative Services Registry of Child Abusers. The court agreed with state officials that when bruises last six or seven days, abuse has occurred. While the court should be commended for protecting children's flesh, we would be happier if the time of healing were not used as a yardstick for determining abuse.

The Demographics of Abuse

When I started serving as an expert witness in corporal punishment cases, it quickly became clear that swatted students, especially those who were abused, were almost never from upper-middle-class or wealthy families. Both abusive and so-called subabusive paddlings are rarely used on the children of the rich, the powerful, or the influential. Guess who is getting the brunt of it. Who else but poor children! Most of the victims reside in rural areas of predominantly rural states that comprise the majority of the twenty-three states on the "hit" parade. So the casualties in the war against children's behinds become victims of where they live, which is predictably the rural South and Southwest.

Not only are victims subject to regionalism and classism, there are also elements of ageism, sexism, and racism thrown in for good measure. The paddlees are mostly young boys in elementary school. Since minority children are more likely to be poor than are others, they get more than their share of beatings. In regard to African Americans, I used to think that this was pure racism, but as I began to really study this sensitive aspect of the issue, I uncovered some disturbing information.

When white-dominated schools allowed white teachers to batter African American students, there appeared to be clear evidence of racism. The most recent federal data on swatting comes from the 1994 Office of Civil Rights Bi-Annual Surveys of School Civil Rights Compliance. Of that year's public school children, 2.5 percent of the black students reported being paddled, as did 1.4 percent of the American Indians, 1 percent of the whites, and .60 percent of the Hispanics. Put another way, of the 470,683 reported paddlings out of a total population of roughly 42.5 million students, 38.75 percent were black, even though they make up only 16.9 percent of the total population. This often prompted charges of civil rights violations by child advocates of both races. And in fact, in some of the cases we were able to establish civil rights violations. However, as African Americans have gained more control over the schools attended primarily by black children, they have increasingly voiced support for paddling.

In recent years, black teachers, administrators, politicians, and even some professionals have attacked me and other anti–corporal punishment child advocates as being insensitive to diversity and black culture. A few researchers even claim that while there is definitely a relationship between parental spanking and aggression in Caucasian children, this does not hold up for black children. These views are countered by leading African American professionals such as Harvard child psychiatrist Dr. Alvin Poussaint and former associate director of Children's Hospital National Medical Center and past president of the National Committee for the Prevention of Child Abuse, Dr. Frederick Green. So why would any black professional support a practice widely used by slave owners to oppress and control their people?

The best explanation was given to me many years ago by Dr. Green. He said, "What makes you think they [African Americans] listen to me any more than many whites listen to you? They turn to their preachers for parenting advice." Many African American preachers are associated with the Southern Baptist Church or small, basically conservative Protestant denominations. They reflect the same "spare the rod" mentality as the majority of their white counterparts.

We are especially disturbed by the argument that black children need corporal punishment because it is part of their culture. Don't these African American pro-paddlers realize that this kind of rhetoric enhances the arguments of racists? Let's look at the slippery slope this kind of distorted thinking causes. If African American kids respond well to hitting by black adults, why shouldn't they do just as well if they are hit by others? If hitting is useful, necessary, and even required for raising and educating black children, they must be genetically different from all others. If they are different from other races, we should modify the curriculum to include hitting, or at least the threat of hitting, in all schools for black children, regardless of socioeconomic status.

If there is no relation between hitting and aggression in African Americans, the more black adolescents misbehave, the more we should hit them. Finally, since black culture depends on the infliction of pain on children, why not reinstitute flogging for African Americans in the military, in courts, and in prisons. But we must be culturally sensitive. We will only allow black military officers and cops to hit offenders. You can see the flaws in this type of thinking.

You might just as well argue for a return slavery. That is where Africans in America learned about the benefits of whips, paddles, and leather straps. But from what we have observed, African American children are getting more than their share of swats, according to Office of Civil Rights surveys.

Because of many methodological limitations, the data reported in the Office of Civil Rights surveys underestimate actual school paddlings. However, in recent years they reflect a vastly improved picture. When I first started analyzing data in 1977, I estimated that at least two million swats occurred each year in schools. At that time only New Jersey and Massachusetts forbade paddling. Despite tremendous progress, however, anti-paddling advocates have hit the wall delineating the demographics of pain. When someone labeled the band of rural conservative states as the Bible Belt, they might not have thought of the metaphor of the belt on the behinds of schoolchildren.

Here are the 1994 figures for the "hit" parade in order of total proportion of students hit in each state that still allows paddling. The estimate for the absolute number is given in parentheses. Arkansas, 13.4 percent (56,262); Mississippi, 10.9 percent (55,012); Alabama, 7.3 percent (30,541); Tennessee, 5.3 percent (44,842); Georgia, 3.39 percent (42,398); Texas, 3.36 percent (114,213); Louisiana, 3.3 percent (26,323); Oklahoma, 3.0 percent (15,765); South Carolina, 1.6 percent (9,995); Missouri, 1.4 percent (13,178). The rest report less than 1 percent and include Arizona (165), Colorado (31), Delaware (292), Florida (16,434), Idaho (6), Indiana (4,806), Kansas (196), Kentucky (1,263), New Mexico (1,988), North Carolina (8,788), Ohio (2,965), Pennsylvania (771), and Wyoming (2).

These are underestimates because they don't include children in private and church-related schools and those who are home schooled. The data also don't include cases in which paddlers do not report swats to the school administration or figures from schools that keep no records, poor records, or lie on the federal survey forms.

The bottom line—it is absolutely amazing that while virtually every other Western democracy is able to educate its children without paddles, America cannot. The few exceptions are all English-speaking, and they—Canada, New Zealand, and Australia—all have some limitations and regional restrictions on hitting. From a distant perspective, one might be led to believe that perhaps the children from states like Mississippi, Georgia, and Texas are just a lot meaner and less controllable than those from the rest of the world or much of America. They therefore need more lickings than their less mean peers in other climes. But if they need what they get and get what they need to beat the meanness out of them, why is it that as adults they tend to become some of the meanest, furthest out-of-control cops, judges, and politicians in the world?

One of our early studies looked at the relation between regional support for corporal punishment (as determined by analysis of newspaper editorials) and other factors in the region. The results showed that the regions most favorable to corporal punishment also had the lowest educational expenditures per capita, the highest dropout rates, and the highest illiteracy rates, and were among the lowest in terms of the amount of money spent on psychological staff as a percentage of school budgets.

A final demographic fact is of interest. Those who support a return to more punishment as a solution to school violence problems just haven't thought this out. Few educators hit big, tough, potentially violent students. Picture this. Ms. Jones is confronted by John, a burly sixteen-year-old student, alienated and angry, who has a knife in his hand. Ms. Jones states, "Now you put that knife down, John. I will teach you to bring a knife to school. Bend over, I'm going to paddle your behind." Sure! Corporal punishment is not the answer to real school violence—and it tends to increase rather than decrease the attraction of violence for students. Children subjected to violence when they're small and can't defend themselves can often hardly wait until they're big enough to get back at the system and the people in it.

Who Does Most of the Hitting?

Research has consistently shown that the best predictor of hitting is personal history. In general, the more you have been swatted as a kid, the more likely you are to swear by it and use it. As the old saying goes, "I was hit as a kid and look at me now." So, to start with, the educators who hit most were generally those who were paddled or spanked most frequently at home. But what does this type of experience do to them as adults?

One study in Tennessee found that teachers who paddled students the most were more rigid in their views, had more emotional problems, and tended to be less experienced and more impulsive than their colleagues. Other studies indicate that strong support for paddling is associated with less knowledge about the literature on discipline and the wide range of alternatives available. Pro-paddling educators also tend to score high on measures of punitiveness and authoritarianism.

An old but interesting study done in 1975 in Pennsylvania showed that support for school spanking ranged from school board presidents (81 percent), principals (78 percent), administrators (68 percent), teachers (74 percent), and parents (71 percent). Only 25 percent of the students surveyed favored corporal punishment. If this study were repeated in many conservative states, the results would probably be similar. This seems to suggest that the further adults are removed from students the more likely they are to have fond memories of paddling. Besides, it did not do them any harm, right? After all, the more you support paddling, the more likely you are to be a powerful school board member than you are to be a plain old teacher or parent. The filter of memory is certainly a selective and often distorting shaper of attitudes and behavior.

There are many explanations for the match between position in the school hierarchy and support for paddling. It is not hard to understand that students, the targets of paddling and the least powerful people in the hierarchy, are less likely to endorse it.

In states and communities that are basically conservative, higher-level positions may be most likely to be awarded to officials who reflect the most conservative values. School boards are often stepping stones for people with higher political aspirations. In conservative states, presidents of boards probably need to present "get tough" personas in order to assure their political futures.

When deciding on school policy and practice, administrators may be the least intellectually oriented and least likely of school personnel to depend on social science data. This is suggested by the fact that on the Graduate Record Examination, used for admission into graduate school programs in education, administrators tend to have the lowest scores. Once admitted to graduate programs, their training tends to focus on the politics of administering schools rather than the science of pedagogy. All widely used texts on the science of teaching that mention corporal punishment argue against its use. Assuming administrators have some exposure to this literature, it appears that they may be more strongly governed by political determinants than by what they learn in graduate school about the science of pedagogy. Another possible factor is that in rural areas, coaches—too often philosophically wedded to punitive measures to motivate athletes—are frequent recipients of administrative positions.

Favorably, our recent research in Pennsylvania indicates that over two-thirds of the school districts have either abolished corporal punishment or claim it is not used. Nonetheless, statewide approval of a ban seems remote. Some claim that the state has a dual legislature comprising Philadelphia and Pittsburgh on one hand and "Mississippi" on the other.

Does God Approve of School Paddling?

How often have spankers defended their practice by quoting the Bible? The famous passage "Spare the rod and spoil the child" is from a biblical proverb credited to Solomon. Let's get something straight from the beginning—this is a misquote.

In the closest contemporary translation of the original Hebrew, Solomon urges, "He who spares the rod hates his son, but he who loves him disciplines him early" (Proverbs 13:24). Now, we do not deny that Solomon recommended spanking. For instance, he says in Proverbs 22:15, "If folly settles in the heart of a lad, the rod of discipline will remove it." While we do not agree with Solomon's recommendations, we have to give him credit for being progressive. He says in Proverbs 23:13–14, "Withhold not correction from the child: for if thou beatest him with the rod, he shall not die." We believe that Solomon was really recommending an end to the stoning of recalcitrant youngsters. A rod was less likely to kill a kid than stoning, a common punishment in his day and one that would invariably be fatal.

Throughout Proverbs, Solomon stresses the need for wisdom and learning. As a progressive, if Solomon were alive today, we believe that he would heed his own advice by considering the overwhelming research and expert opinion that spanking is a bad idea. He would also understand how transgenerational modeling of violence affected the children of his seven hundred wives and three hundred concubines. He certainly modeled violence for two of his sons, Rehoboam and Jeroboam.

After Solomon's death, when his exiled son Rehoboam returned to become king, he told his advisers to communicate to the citizens, "My father flogged you with whips, but I will flog you with scorpions" (1 Kings 12:11). As a ruler, Rehoboam ignored his father's teachings about wisdom and modeled his penchant toward beating as a punishment. His advocacy for beatings backfired when his chief of forced labor was pelted to death by rebellious Israelites. His cruelty finally ended in his downfall when Jeroboam went to war against him.

It is clear that Solomon never talked about "spoiling" children. So how did Solomon's suggestions for parenting get distorted? The riddle is solved by Ian Gibson in his book *The English Vice,* where he explains that the phrase "Spare the rod and spoil the child" was first used in 1664 by the English author Samuel Butler. Butler's satirical poem "Hudibras" describes an amorous lady's request that her lover, Sir Hudibras, submit to a whipping as proof of his love. This is also interpreted as Butler's mockery of the practices of fanatics who accept flagellation in the name of religion. In the poem the lady says:

> But since our sex's modesty
> Will not allow I should be by,
> Bring me, on oath, a fair account, And honour too, when
>   you have done it;
> And I'll admit you to the place
> You claim as due in my good grace.
> If matrimony and hanging go
> By dest'ny, why not whipping too?
> What medicine else can cure the fits
> Of lovers, when they lose their wits?
> Love is a boy, by poets styled,
> They spare the rod and spoil the child.

In this poem, the lady tells her knight that he needs to be whipped in order to be an adequate lover. No one is absolutely sure how this last quoted line came to be invoked as the words of Solomon and God to justify spanking. So the next time someone talks for God, set them straight.

I am always fascinated by fundamentalists' reliance on Solomon for parenting advice rather than Jesus. Nowhere in the New Testament does Jesus recommend the use of violence against children or adults. Whenever I do a workshop in the Bible Belt I ask all the teachers who think that Jesus would recommend paddling students to raise their hand. Invariably, one or two literalists comply and then I let them and the rest of the group argue about the messages of Jesus about punishment, forgiveness, and how to treat children.

Why Is Paddling So Bad?

To summarize the effects of hitting children to change their behavior, we draw on all the research from parental spanking and school paddlings. There is clear, consistent evidence that increases in spanking are associated with higher instances of depression, delinquency, and low self-esteem. Critics contend that spanking only contributes a small amount to these problems. It is true that for most people, low levels of spanking make a small contribution to a variety of emotional problems. However, this contribution is consistent across almost all studies. It is almost like saying that since a small amount of poison will only make you a little sick, it is OK to continue to be poisoned.

Studies consistently show that as spanking becomes more frequent and severe, the effects are increasingly negative. While many people may survive severe spankings, almost all violent, angry, and aggressive juveniles have histories of frequent hittings by caregivers. There is very convincing evidence that witnessing and experiencing corporal punishment results in modeling of aggression. The old saw that "violence breeds violence" is supported by this finding. For instance, how can anyone justify paddling emotionally disturbed, abused, and aggressive schoolchildren who have become that way because of the infliction of pain by caregivers? Legislators can.

After extensive hearings, in which I have testified on behalf of the American Psychological Association, we couldn't even get Congress to pass a law forbidding the spanking of children classified as emotionally disturbed, blind, deaf, retarded, or learning disabled. Guess who sabotaged our efforts. Legislators from Texas, North Carolina, and other pro-spanking states who just did not want to hear our data and logic. As a result, federal and state monies intended to help children with disabilities can also be used, often against the advice of experts, to make their disabilities worse.

Schools with high rates of corporal punishment also have high rates of suspension and are generally more punitive than schools with low rates of corporal punishment. They also tend to have lower achievement. Further, punitive climates actually exacerbate the problem of school violence.

Safe schools are often characterized by students' perceptions of fairness in the administration of discipline, and by their belief that they can influence what happens in their lives and that teachers have high, positive expectations of them. While principals in safe schools may be considered strict, they are not generally considered by students to be mean or authoritarian.

Finally, corporal punishment of various frequencies, durations, and intensities can result in posttraumatic stress disorder (PTSD), a debilitating emotional problem we will discuss later in this book.

So Why Do We Need Paddling in Schools?

Besides the last-resort argument, some of the most popular defenses include the beliefs that corporal punishment is needed to maintain discipline, to make kids respect teachers, and to put fear into the hearts of the worst kids so they will think before they act out. These are all hogwash! Our studies demonstrate that eliminating corporal punishment does not increase misbehavior, so it wasn't needed in the first place. The major decision to use corporal punishment is usually based on an orientation toward physical punishment by school personnel and the community and has nothing to do with its effectiveness to deter misbehavior. In fact, before the white men arrived in the New World, there were whole cultures that had no concept of corporal punishment. The following case illustrates a whole range of issues regarding beliefs in corporal punishment and the clash of cultures within American education. It is an exemplar of a school board's rejection of toxic practices.

A female physical education teacher whom we will call Ms. Snow, with nine years' experience in an Alaskan school, was alleged to have pushed, grabbed, and wrestled a rude fourteen-year-old male student, whom we will call Keith. The reaction of the school board, made up of Inupiat Eskimos, was to assert their concept of traditional cultural values.

Unlike the values of the American and Russian settlers who colonized Alaska, Inupiat family values did not include hitting children. They did not even have vocabulary to describe anger and violence within families. It was the Christian missionaries who introduced them to the spare-the-rod values of the good old days. So when the state of Alaska turned over control of the schools to local communities in rural Alaska, the Inupiat community enacted a board policy reflecting their own traditions—no hitting students. This was one of the first policies they enacted in the 1970s and it also complied with state policy when the school district was formed.

Ms. Snow assaulted fourteen-year-old Keith during and after a game called "sack-it," an indoor version of baseball. Keith was pitching a small rubber ball in a boys-against-girls contest. His erratic pitching resulted in hitting some girls and the teacher, who was batting for the girls' team.

Keith refused to follow Ms. Snow's instructions to pitch the ball properly. She became angry, went up to him and pushed him on the chest. He cursed at her as they walked away from each other. Apparently angered by his obscenities, she turned around and threw the wooden bat toward him. It slid across the floor and hit or touched his foot.

After class ended, Keith went into the locker room for a brief time. Later, he walked by the teacher, who was seated on a bench in the hall. Ms. Snow called him to come to her. He refused to comply, walked by her, and sat down at the other end of the bench. She went to him, grabbed him by his jacket and pulled him to his feet. At this point the accounts of the witnesses and the teacher differ somewhat. However, it appears that some sort of "wrestling match" ensued. It is clear that Keith ended up on the floor with Ms. Snow above him and in control. She then pulled him up and either placed or shoved him against the wall, depending on whose account you wish to believe.

I believe that Keith lost the match, since it ended with him bleeding from the mouth and crying. Although Ms. Snow neither sent Keith to the principal nor reported the event, another student notified the principal.

After appropriate due process hearings held by the board of education, Ms. Snow was fired. She appealed to the courts and at that point the school board employed me to testify as an expert witness regarding the appropriateness of the disciplinary procedure and whether it was a case of illegal corporal punishment.

At the trial, testimonies were equivocal and less clear about the events than they were as revealed in the school board hearing. For instance, Ms. Snow alleged that Keith actually jumped off the bench and charged at her when she put her hand on his shoulder in order to restrain him until she could calm him down.

The judge ruled in favor of the teacher as far as the assault, but also judged her to be incompetent in the way she handled the discipline situation. The school board appealed to the Supreme Court of Alaska, but the case was settled before it was heard. Ms. Snow accepted compensation and did not return to the district. The board could have reinstated her when she appealed their decision to the court or when the court ultimately reversed the board decision. But they had a point to make to the whole community. Educators do not hit students, even when those students are obnoxious. Professionals must keep calm and use effective disciplinary strategies.

This case, like others where I have testified for school boards against abusive teachers, shows that there are schools and administrators who will take a stand and commit sufficient time and resources to oppose toxic teaching. Unfortunately, this phenomenon appears to be quite rare in America.

• • •

Students in almost all other Western democracies do quite well without paddling. In fact, five countries even forbid parental spanking—with nothing but good results when parents use effective alternatives. The students in many of the nonswatting countries score higher on a variety of academic tests than do our students and appear to be less violent. The answer to the question is that there is absolutely no legitimate pedagogical justification for corporal punishment. The twenty-three states that still allow smacking, swatting, kicking, pinching, punching, and paddling of schoolchildren should enter the twenty-first century as civilized places for students to be educated. We find it inconceivable that policymakers in these states continue to ignore the research and advice offered by almost all experts in the field of discipline that the infliction of pain is not a proper pedagogical procedure.

We think that *Reading, Writing, and the Hickory Stick* made a contribution to the elimination of corporal punishment in many states. We are happy that this new book need only expend one core chapter on this topic. We can thus turn to the problem of psychological maltreatment by educators, a more pervasive, little studied, and often trivialized predicament for students.

Chapter 2

Psychological Maltreatment in the Classroom

Jimmy was a rather shy sixth grader in a Northeastern state that forbids corporal punishment. He was a nice-looking boy who could best be described as average. He had a few friends, played soccer, and attended church regularly with his parents and five siblings. As the next to youngest of six children, he was overshadowed by several very bright older brothers and a six-year-old sister his parents called "a real delight."

Jimmy's mother was active in the PTA and his father belonged to several civic groups. The parents were practicing Catholics, somewhat conservative in their outlook. All in all, theirs was a typical, community-minded middle-class family, hardly malcontents who would sue a teacher.

As a student, Jimmy frequently functioned below his potential, but since he never misbehaved, no one was seriously concerned. His parents and older siblings frequently helped with homework but they sometimes became impatient with his awkward writing and periodic inability to remember material from one day to the next. Despite his deficiencies, he received passing grades and seemed happy. Then suddenly, almost overnight, he changed.

Never outgoing, Jimmy began to withdraw in earnest. He lost interest in soccer, rarely played with friends, complained about nightmares and inability to go to sleep, and began to spend a great deal of time in his room. He began to complain about stomachaches, especially on Monday mornings. His stomachaches and headaches resulted in increasing visits to the school nurse's office. His grades deteriorated; he acted immature and periodically refused to do schoolwork.

Jimmy's frustrated parents became impatient and demanding. Escalating punishments led to more oppositional behavior and physical complaints. Finally, when he developed stomachaches daily, an appointment was scheduled with the family physician. Following a series of exams, the physician determined that Jimmy was becoming a likely candidate for an ulcer.

It was clear that Jimmy was having serious psychological problems, but it wasn't until a psychologist examined him that the truth came out. Jimmy's problems resulted directly from psychological maltreatment in school. Here is the story that Jimmy finally told.

During art class Jimmy was requested to make some sketches. He complained about his poor copying and drawing skills and begged for help. His teacher became increasingly impatient with Jimmy's whining and his refusal to complete the assignment, which he was required to do independently.

Finally, Jimmy's teacher said, "If you want to act like a baby, you can sit with the babies." She took him next door to the first-grade class and made arrangements for Jimmy to sit there for class sessions during the following three weeks until he completed his assignment. Anger at his teachers, fear of his parents' finding out what happened, and growing ridicule from peers resulted in the development of stress-related symptoms.

Psychological evaluation revealed that Jimmy was suffering from posttraumatic stress disorder—a diagnosis usually reserved for victims of unusual and overwhelming disasters such as wars, earthquakes, and physical assaults. While Jimmy was certainly not physically assaulted, the psychological symptoms observed were in many ways identical to those of physically abused children.

Jimmy's parents were shocked when they learned the cause of his problems. They were beset by guilt for having punished him for apparent laziness. They were angry that he had been humiliated and became infuriated when the school authorities stonewalled and refused to admit that a mistake had been made. Their suit against the school ended in a settlement that included the cost of two years of psychotherapy for Jimmy.

This case is startling on several accounts. Surely, the art teacher was not a sadist or child abuser who anticipated the psychological damage she was causing. Should teachers be expected to know the psychological profile of every child before using any punishment? How is one to know how much to punish each child? Are teachers legally liable under child abuse laws when punishments result in severe psychological stress? Before examining these issues, let us consider some concrete examples of what we believe to be psychological maltreatment.

What Is Psychological Maltreatment?

You will notice we are using the term *maltreatment* rather than *abuse*. Although the terms may be synonymous, and we use them interchangeably throughout the book, there are subtle differences. Abuse implies an overt act in which the abuser most often intends to inflict pain. Maltreatment includes crimes of omission in which the perpetrator ignores, rejects, or isolates the victim. Also, the offender may not realize or intend harm, as when verbal assaults delivered in a joking manner are taken seriously by the victim.

Broadly defined, psychological maltreatment takes many forms. Experts Stuart Hart from the University of Indiana and Marla Brassard from Columbia University suggest that it includes mental cruelty, sexual exploitation, allowing children to live in dangerous or unstable environments, encouraging or permitting children to use destructive drugs, providing negative and destructive role models, exposing children to systematic bias and prejudice, emotional neglect, and subjecting children to institutional practices that are clearly demonstrated to inhibit maintenance of basic human needs. The latter may occur when children in schools do not receive appropriate human contact and attention because they are unattractive or because teachers are overburdened or burned out.

Psychological maltreatment in schools consists of

- Discipline and control techniques based on fear and intimidation
- Low quantity of human interaction in which teachers communicate a lack of interest, caring, and affection for students through ignoring, isolation, and rejection

- Limited opportunities for students to develop adequate skills and feelings of self-worth
- Encouragement to be dependent and subservient, especially in areas where students are capable of making independent judgments
- Motivational techniques for performance that are overly critical, excessively demanding, unreasonable, and ignore children's ages and abilities
- Denial of opportunities for healthy risk taking such as exploring ideas that are not conventional and approved by the teacher
- Verbal assaults including the use of sarcasm, ridicule, humiliation, and denigration
- Scapegoating and bullying
- Failure to intervene when students are teased, bullied, and scapegoated by peers

Teachers may maltreat students by being overdemanding or perfectionistic, especially with children who are overly self-critical as a result of parental pressure. Obviously, the various practices that constitute psychological maltreatment conflict with the legal, moral, and historical obligations of schools.

The best way to really understand the essence of psychological maltreatment is to think back on your own experiences. Most people encounter some psychological assaults in their lives that trigger stress reactions. You may be among the 50 percent or 60 percent of citizens who can vividly remember some act by an educator that was abusive enough to implant a vivid memory. If this is so, as you recall the incident, you may reexperience some of the negative emotions that you felt at the time. This recall exercise is one we have used productively to determine the nature and extent of problems in the schools, and in upcoming sections we present actual examples reported by teachers and students of their own worst school experiences. The examples are divided into various categories of psychological maltreatment. Very often a verbal assault may include several types of abuse, so you may find that some examples overlap with other categories. To provide complete anonymity and facilitate clarity, we have edited many of these anecdotes.

Humiliation and Denigration

The following scenarios illustrate how a variety of teacher behaviors can result in humiliation and denigration of students' sense of worth and self-esteem. In some cases the actions were overtly vicious, but sadly, in other cases the teachers probably never knew the damage they caused.

> In fourth grade the principal made me and a friend sit in front of the class for the whole morning with gum stuck on our noses. I felt really bad and embarrassed because I could see the other children making fun of us.

> When I was in fourth grade the teacher told us to draw a pilgrim and cut it out. I couldn't draw well, but did the best I could. The teacher called me in front of the class and said, "What is this? That's not a pilgrim. It's awful." I felt terrible. She told me to take it to show to two teachers to show them how awful it was. They didn't know why I was showing it to them and they said it was good. They were kind but I never forgot it. It was so humiliating. I am Jewish and I am sure the teacher was anti-Semitic.

> A teaching sister pulled up my dress and spanked me in front of the whole class in second grade for talking in church when I was in fact reciting prayers! She did not allow me to walk in a church procession and threatened to prevent me from making my first Communion.

> My teacher noticed that I was scratching my rear end and commented on it in class. I was utterly humiliated.

> In tenth grade a teacher identified me, in front of the whole class, as someone who never does well on history tests. She then stated that if I could pass the test, anyone could.

> I did not hear that boys were called at bathroom time in kindergarten, so I went into a stall and started to go to the bathroom. The teacher came in, saw me in with the boys and dragged me out with my panties at my ankles, while she yelled and screamed about listening.

Rejection, Ignoring, and Isolation

These types of abuses are often offenses of omission rather than commission. In their subtler forms they may be hard to document. But children, probably due to both genetic programming and social learning, expect and need nurturing and support from caregivers—and suffer when they do not get it. Caregivers may be broadly defined to include adults who, by virtue of physical proximity, authority, or familial relations, can affect the health and welfare of a child.

For example, in this world of high rates of divorce and remarriage, many schoolchildren have stepparents, stepsiblings, and half siblings. Take the following situation as an example of how omissions of behavior can fall within the bailiwick of emotional abuse.

Mr. Gold, a middle-aged man with two grown children, divorced his wife, remarried, and had another child. His grown children considered it bizarre, disgusting, and immoral that a person whom they considered a geriatric case could father another child. Jealous and angry, they generally ignored Jan, their half sister, whom they did not consider a member of their family. They never contacted her, were lacking in affection when they were with her, and rarely acknowledged milestones such as birthdays and holidays.

Overtly, this type of rejection seemed to have little effect on Jan, a very bright and outgoing child. However, as she grew up she observed that most step- and half siblings she came in contact with were the recipients of affection and positive attention from their siblings. The underlying hurt Jan felt was reflected when she commented to a parent, "If they do not love me, then I will not love them. If they do not care about me, I will not care about them." Think of the implications of this statement and then translate it to situations involving professional caretakers.

While school staff are not relatives of their students, by virtue of their positions they are obliged to be professional caretakers. They are obliged to attend to every student and should never reject, ignore, or unduly isolate a student. They should be aware of children's emotional needs as they vary according to age. Preschool and primary grade children generally have strong needs for nurturing. These include the desire for lots of praise and physical contact. This latter may include holding, rocking, and hugging young children when they are distressed. Therefore, denial of touch and hugs for needy children may constitute maltreatment, despite fears of reactionaries that any kind of touching may constitute possible sexual abuse.

Did you ever visit a classroom and notice that some children, despite constant hand raising, are rarely acknowledged by the teacher? This may constitute rejection. As students get older, especially into their preteens, their need for competence and acknowledgment is very strong. The best way to guarantee alienation as they enter their teenage years is to ignore these needs.

While time out and removal from class are legitimate disciplinary procedures, teachers too often abuse these practices, as was illustrated in Chapter One.

The following is a sampling of real experiences that illustrate the point.

> In second grade, my teacher seemed to single me out to pick on. She ignored me when I raised my hand but she always called on me for answers I didn't know.

> I was very rude, immature, and defiant when I was in the ninth grade. My biology teacher put me in a corner, piled chairs around me, and told me I was being caged just like an animal.

> In second grade, my mother accidentally threw out a folder with really important papers in it. When I couldn't return these papers, which were supposed to be signed by a parent, my teacher made me throw out one of my art projects that I had worked very hard on.

Authoritarian Discipline

This category includes disciplinary techniques in which the teacher ignores basic concepts of fairness, justice, and due process, which are the cornerstone of Democracy. We have included in this category examples of scapegoating, favoritism, and situations in which teachers allow students to tease, bully, and humiliate their peers. The reasons, excuses, or rationales used by teachers to defend these behaviors often border on the bizarre, considering that they are not teaching in Nazi Germany. What do you think?

> I have Tourette's syndrome and when I was in middle school, one of my teachers always laughed when the other students called me "woodpecker." One day a student was allowed to completely read to the class a thinly disguised report that was obviously about me and the fact that they called me "woodpecker." Before he finished reading it, I objected to the teacher that the report was about me. It included other names and cruel things that the kids did to me. Without comment, she sent me back

to my desk and took his paper. The next day I got the hell out of that class and then found out that he had earned an "85" on the paper, which really upset me.

I suffered from alopecia, which is the loss of hair in patches, for which kids made fun of me. One of my teachers made light of it and never stopped the kids from tormenting me. As a result, I hated her and still do.

In fifth grade, I threw another kid's hat in the air. I was taken to the basement of the church where a nun presided over a mock court. I was sentenced to write a three-hundred-word composition on how to behave on the playground. While it may not sound like much, being in court at the age of ten scared the hell out of me.

In ninth grade I made the mistake of taking $16 from shop class. The principal could not prove I took the money so after an hour of questioning, he told me if I confessed, he would not involve the police. As soon as I confessed, he called the police and filed charges. That day I lost trust in the people in power.

In the seventh grade, a student who sat beside me wrote a note on the desk for a student who would be sitting there in the following class and signed my name. The instructor saw it and assigned me to detention, even though I had never been disciplined for anything before. I denied that I wrote it and begged the teacher to compare the handwriting to mine on previous assignments. He refused and reprimanded me without even comparing the handwriting.

Sarcasm and Put-Downs

If you have never heard a sarcastic statement by a teacher, then you probably never went to school. This is especially true in middle and junior high schools. Now we will admit that many thirteen- to fifteen-year-olds are in the throes of hormonal and psychological turmoil that sometimes renders them incapable of responses that are even remotely human. Most teachers of these children deserve all the kudos we can give them, especially if they retain their sense of humor, patience, and enthusiasm. I have worked for thirty years as a group therapist with adolescents. Many of my patients take pride in their status as their teacher's worst nightmare. Their modus operandi is to piss off every adult and authority figure they deal with, including their therapist. So I know it ain't easy. Sarcasm and put-downs are probably most frequent with this age group.

Despite the provocation, I have found that the best way to deal with these kids is to not treat them in kind. Whether or not you agree with me, the more obnoxious teenagers are, the more they are hurting. Real professionals realize this and do not use sarcasm and ridicule to deal with kids who are hurting. Here are some examples of teacher behaviors that just cannot be justified.

> One day in Spanish class, I told the teacher that I was lost and that I didn't know what was going on. In reply, he said, "There is a place for people like you to go and it's called the 'lost and found.'" The whole class laughed but to me it wasn't funny and I was embarrassed.

> In the ninth-grade English class, my teacher accused me of cheating to earn an "A" on a test about *Romeo and Juliet*. I actually liked Shakespeare and enjoyed reading him until then. I was in a class with a lot of bad students and so the teacher assumed I was just like them.

> In kindergarten class, I was told to color a picture of an umbrella. I colored mine black. However, the teacher didn't approve of my color choice or the fact that I colored outside of the lines. She called me in front of the class and then verbally upbraided me for quite a long time.

> When I was sixteen I was always behind in school because no one knew I had a focusing problem. One day my computer teacher took me out of class and lectured me and insulted me and my family. I started to cry and he said I'd never amount to anything.

Name-Calling

Name-calling is a common type of maltreatment of schoolchildren. The types of name-calling range from the mundane to the inventive.

> One day in the third grade I didn't totally understand something. My teacher loudly said, "It's easy, what are you, retarded?" Then she hit me on the side of my head. It really bothered and embarrassed me especially because one of my relatives is retarded. I cried all that day and my mother was so angry she called and yelled at the teacher.

A substitute teacher in eighth grade called me a "ditz" just because I forgot my book. I felt offended by this because a teacher shouldn't be calling anyone a name except their own.

In the sixth grade I was in a school play and put lipstick on. I tried to remove it, but some was left. The teacher yelled at me in front of the class to remove it because I looked like a "slut."

In second grade I was told to go to the back of the room and stand there for talking. When I started to cry, I was yelled at and called a "baby" in front of my classmates.

I wanted to play with the older girls who were jumping rope. They were in my brother's class. They wouldn't let me join so I bit one of the girls. The teacher then brought the whole class (including my brother) to look for the "DOG."

Ms. M. stood in her door as my first-grade class passed her on the way to the auditorium. As I passed, she chided "crybaby, crybaby" because I often cried.

My high school gym teacher ridiculed me in front of the class for being clumsy.

When I did not understand a lesson in eighth-grade English, I asked the teacher to explain it again. She yelled at me, called me stupid, and sent me to the vice principal.

In eleventh grade my French teacher announced to class that I was failing second year French, and that I was so stupid she could not understand how I had been put in her class. She raved on for at least ten minutes, then made me come in every morning and every day after school to work with her.

Ridicule Related to Intellectual Abilities

Some teachers resent students who are smarter than they are and will use any opportunity to denigrate them. Others have no patience for children with limited ability. It appears that some teachers are even equal-opportunity ridiculers who rarely miss a chance to practice their art. As the following examples show, children with learning disabilities, limited intellectual abilities, and even high intelligence can become victims of verbal assaults by teachers.

I had a teacher in sixth grade who put the "smart" kids in front of the class
and the "dumb" ones in the back. He used to pull the "bad, dumb" kids
into the hall and take his index finger and ram it under our chins until
we would "smarten up."

In third grade I had trouble telling time. For many days the entire class had to
wait for me to say the correct time until we could go to lunch.

One of my teachers looked up IQ scores of students and referred to them in
class—saying in front of everyone, you should be doing better, your IQ
is such and such; you are an overachiever, your IQ is such and such.

In first grade, my teacher reprimanded me for reading through our primer,
Dick and Jane, and advancing beyond the point where she was instructing the class.

In fifth grade I had difficulty with multiplication facts. Each day one teacher
would orally quiz us on our facts. I was chosen to relay the multiplication
tables for the number seven and had great difficulty with the exercise.
The teacher stopped the class and drew everyone's attention to me. At this
point he began to tell me how stupid I was and that I probably didn't
study (when I did). I was so embarrassed I was in tears and had to leave
the room. I never forgot it.

Performance Pressures

Psychological maltreatment occurs when teachers are overdemanding, hypercritical, and unreasonably require perfection of
students. This is often quite subtle and unlikely to be recognized
as a form of maltreatment. It is frequently directed toward children
who are already highly motivated, especially those who are considered the best and brightest. Parents and the community are frequently co-conspirators with schools in creating a culture in which
these students lead frantic, overscheduled lives.

This culture is characterized by high-achieving parents who, in
their attempts to developed well-rounded children, overschedule
them in their activities. These children's lives are a constant round
of activities that may include organized sports, music lessons, religious instruction, club membership, cultural events, and massive
amounts of homework. Their struggles to meet the expectations
of parents and teachers may result in anxiety, depression, rebel-

lion, sleep deprivation, or complete shutdown in which they refuse to do any more work.

Many children are able to organize their routines in such a way that they survive the demands for perfection. However, others become victims of this type of psychological maltreatment that may result in poorer performance and hatred of an activity that they once enjoyed.

Our research on worst school experiences did not reveal any examples of this kind of abuse. However, clinical cases too often illustrate this problem, especially with highly ambitious children. Consider the example of fifteen-year-old Michael, a gifted, straight-A student. Michael, his parents, and his teachers all agreed that he could be placed in all honors and advance placement courses. However, he found that in order to maintain his grades, he was spending five and six hours a night on homework in addition to devoting significant time during the weekends. Despite his efforts, Michael had difficulty keeping up with the extremely complex concepts in an advanced mathematics course. As he devoted increasing time to this subject, his grades began to drop in several other courses.

Michael began to have trouble sleeping; he developed a nail-biting habit, frequent headaches, and stomachaches. Medical evaluations revealed no organic cause for his problems. It finally occurred to his parents that he was under too much pressure and should drop to a regular level of mathematics. Michael's guidance counselor insisted that he had the ability and that he should continue in the program. His parents related how stressful this was for Michael. However, the counselor and Michael's teachers warned of the dire consequences if Michael dropped to a lower level. They cautioned that this action could affect his chances of admission to a prestigious university. Michael felt conflicted over the desire to remain in class with his friends, the potential disappointment of his parents, and the painful pressure to keep up with the material.

Fortunately, in this case, Michael's parents realized that the school officials were more concerned about his academic standing than his mental health. Despite the counselor's warning, they helped Michael weigh the pros and cons of the situation. They assured him that they would support his decision, which was to drop to a lower level math course. His stress symptoms decreased, he appeared much happier, and he had more time for extracurricular activities.

Ridicule Related to Physical Attributes and Appearance

We are always amazed and chagrined when teachers make fun of children's physical appearance and attributes. This is the worst! Consider the following.

When I was in eighth grade I had a substitute teacher who tried to hold the class's attention by telling jokes about dumb blondes. Since I was blonde I asked him to stop. He began to argue with me and humiliated me in front of the class by yelling at me and justifying his humor.

My fifth-grade teacher was looking over school photos of all students in the class during milk break. When he came to mine, he held it up and exclaimed, "What a face!" Students were standing all around the teacher's desk. I was horribly embarrassed. I felt my face get hot. I still feel like crying when I think about it. I am now thirty-six years old. I know he didn't mean what I thought he meant, but that doesn't change how I feel. He was one of my favorite teachers. I have always seen myself as ugly since that time.

In fifth grade a teacher called me fat and meant it in a bad way.

In fourth grade, I was severely burned on my face. When I returned to school the following year I had to wear a band on my head to keep pressure on the wound. On the second day of class, the teacher said to me, "Hey, tough guy, are you going to wear a headband every day?"

In sixth grade, I wore the wrong color socks. I was made to stand in the corner and was slapped in the head and back.

In third grade, a teacher ridiculed a fellow student who had a urinary infection for "going in his pants."

In the tenth grade my history teacher (a nun) had had my sister (a bit of a troublemaker) in a previous year. This teacher humiliated me in front of the class at every possible opportunity. One example: I was wearing the older version of the school uniform, and she made me stand up in front of the class and laughed at me, saying, "Why do you have that uniform on? Are you too *fat* for the other one?" And so on. Yes, I was!

My coach told me that I was a disgrace as a captain of the team because my hair was long and I had lost a game in overtime because the person I was guarding had scored.

I was in seventh grade and was very tall for my age. I was extremely self-conscious and nervous about giving an oral talk for my English class. My heart pounded as I walked up to give my speech, and nervously began. My teacher interrupted my speech and said, "God, you have big feet! What size shoe do you wear?"

A dental hygienist came to our class and asked me to rinse with a solution that shows where food is left on your teeth. The teacher took me in front of the class and showed the class what was "wrong" with my teeth, even though it was after lunch.

Bigotry in the Classroom

Teachers may reflect their own bigotry by both conscious and unconscious remarks. Often, subtle forms of prejudiced behavior are recognized by children.

I was observing a class in which the teacher was teaching about Martin Luther King. The children realized he was black and was fighting for civil rights. When the children were confused about the difference between black and white, she asked me (I am black) to come up and pointed out all of the supposed physical differences between black and white people.

I was the only Jewish person in the whole school. The teachers all knew this because I took off for the holidays. One day our math class was being very bad. Mr. S. stood on his chair and pointed his finger at us and said, "You kids are worse than the Jews that put Jesus on the cross!!!"

Mrs. B., my white third-grade teacher, told me that black children (I am black) "don't live like that"—regarding my written composition on my summer vacation in Florida.

An English teacher whose rule was "miss a test—take a 'C'" even when tests were scheduled on the Jewish holidays caused me to be excluded from twelfth-grade college English, because of a "C" I got on that basis. (I majored in Journalism in college.)

So What Is the Big Deal?

Do you find these anecdotes unusual or disturbing? Are not these just part of the everyday interactions that can occur in any setting?

What's the big deal? So a teacher joked about dumb blondes, gum-chewing students received a punishment that fit the crime, and a teacher was just trying to "motivate" a student who was not paying attention. After all, isn't this like real life?

If these experiences are not such big deals, how come the victims, who reported them as their worst school experiences, also said that they were traumatized by what their teachers did to them. These are all examples of psychological maltreatment, the most pervasive type of school abuse. Yet this insidious problem has received almost no attention by educators, researchers, or policymakers. This despite the fact that our research indicates that between 50 percent and 60 percent of any group of citizens will report that they had at least one experience in school that caused some trauma symptoms. While these experiences include both physical assaults and sexual harassment, the vast majority of worst school experiences are psychological assaults on the student's sense of worth, self-esteem, and competence. About 1 percent to 2 percent develop symptoms of sufficient duration, intensity, and frequency that they develop post-traumatic stress disorder as a consequence.

While 1 percent to 2 percent might not seem to be a large percentage of a school-age population, in a system like New York City, this would be about 10,000 children so traumatized by educators that they may suffer lifelong emotional problems. A good percentage of these may develop angry and aggressive responses and become a pool of students whose misbehavior is created by the school. The effects of these abuses may have a long-lasting impact on many areas of a person's life.

The following are just three examples in which the victims describe the long-lasting effects of what was done to them.

> My third-grade teacher ridiculed me in front of my reading group while I was reading out loud. It was an advanced reading group but not difficult for me. I made the mistake of pronouncing bow (as in bow and arrows) as bough. She screamed at me and made fun of me for this mistake in front of my classmates. I was humiliated and felt her reaction was unjustified. Yet it was so devastating I became more self-conscious and afraid to "speak up" for fear of making more mistakes. My self-consciousness and low self-esteem have only now, at the age of twenty-two, begun to heal. (Not that this was the only contributing factor to my low self-esteem).

> I had a fourth-grade teacher who simply did not like me (personality conflict). During the whole school year she made my life very difficult. After I was grown my mother and I discussed it and she told me how upsetting that year was for her. Until that point in my life I believed I was at fault. Not until I was a grown woman did I resolve my feelings and realize through my mother that this teacher was at fault.

> I recall spending several nights preparing and completing a composition. When I handed it in the teacher grabbed it—read it aloud and criticized everything about it. To this day I have had difficulty accepting positive recognition of my writing skills.

Excuses for Psychological Maltreatment

Few educators will openly support the kind of verbal abuse that is clearly linked to stress symptoms in students. Yet thousands of students each day are subjected to verbal assaults. Whereas physical assaults such as paddling and smacking are meant to inflict pain, verbal assaults have painful consequences that are often unrecognized by those who make them. When the real nature of the offenses is spelled out, perpetrators are often defensive. Here are some typical arguments to defend their acts.

I was only kidding.

This is the favorite defense of the name-caller. This educator loves to give students nick names such as "motor-mouth," "nerd," or "dirtball." Some names are more subtle but just as damaging. Once a teacher gives a student a label, even if it happens only once, the rest of the students may pick it up and the child is labeled for a long time.

A good example of this defense occurred while I was presenting a workshop on psychological abuse to special education teachers. One was offended when the participants, in listing abusive statements often made by teachers, included nicknames suggesting obesity. The teacher spent fifteen minutes arguing with 150 other participants in defense of her calling one of her students "Chubs." She insisted that the particular obese, adolescent, developmentally disabled student knew that the nickname was an expression of love.

Finally one of the other teachers stood up and told the whole group about her feelings of being an obese teenager. She was called names by her teachers and she just joked about it. But, she said, "I was laughing outwardly but I felt humiliated and shamed by those teachers. I will never forget what they did to me." She then angrily told the protesting teacher that she obviously was completely insensitive to such feelings on the part of students.

The major point is that we can never judge how each child accepts denigration and humiliation, especially in school where the teacher is the boss. Rather than trying to guess how a child can handle name-calling, just don't do it.

That kid needed to be put in his place.

This is a favorite defense of put-downs, one of the most numerous types of verbal assaults on children. It is also used to defend sarcasm. In most cases the teacher feels that the child deserved what was done, because the child's behavior was considered inappropriate or offensive. Unfortunately, in many cases the student's offense is to think differently from the teacher or to demonstrate the teacher's inadequacy in some academic area.

You should have heard what that kid said to me!

We believe that two wrongs still do not make a right. While it is true that students can be unruly and insulting, it does not follow that the educator should respond by demeaning the student. Very often, students who are disrespectful in school have been taught to respond that way. This may be because of a variety of reasons. Denigration and humiliation are counterproductive methods of helping chronically misbehaving students who generally already feel bad about themselves.

He is a big boy and can handle it. Everybody has to deal with some verbal abuse in their life.

This is a common defense for treating children with the same level of verbal abuse that some adults are subjected to in the workplace. Coaches and vocational education teachers too often think that they have to toughen kids up for the realities of life. It may be true that adults can learn to handle verbal abuse, but few are happy with it. Besides, children and adolescents have not yet developed their sense of self. They still need to test themselves against the demands of the adult world. This must be done in a way that supports rather than breaks down their developing self-esteem.

Can Psychological Maltreatment Be Clearly Defined and Measured?

We know that you may not be a legislator, educator, or psychologist. But face it, after reading the last few pages, do you think you have to be a rocket scientist to define emotional maltreatment in the schools? And if you can do it, what is the big deal for the experts?

Maybe education policymakers are in a position similar to manufacturers who are afraid to admit guilt about defective products. There is always the potential that a flood of litigation over these products can seriously damage or even bankrupt a manufacturer. The larger the market for a defective product, the greater the possible damage.

While public schools cannot become bankrupt, they can certainly be sued for causing harm to children. Perhaps, like manufacturers, many education policymakers fear opening the floodgate to litigation over the most widespread type of maltreatment in schools. Also, emotional abuse is at the core of all other abuses. For instance, denigration and diminution of individual worth is inherent in physical and sexual maltreatment of students. Better recognition of emotional maltreatment increases potential claims against schools when other abuses are charged. But there have been some attempts to define and recognize the phenomenon.

Educators, legislatures, judges, child protection workers, clinicians, and researchers have all attempted to define emotional abuse from their own perspectives. The 1974 Child Abuse and Prevention Act addresses the issue of mental injury but does not really define it. For discussion purposes, we have chosen our own state of Pennsylvania, which defines psychological maltreatment as "serious mental injury." It is a condition, diagnosed by a physician or psychologist, caused by acts or omissions that render the child "chronically or severely anxious, agitated, depressed, socially withdrawn, psychotic, or in reasonable fear his life or safety is threatened." An important corollary is that the child's ability to "accomplish age appropriate developmental and social tasks" is compromised. Finally, refusal to treat a child's problems can also constitute serious mental injury.

We do not know what you think, but we do not believe that these types of vague terms and descriptors are very helpful. At the same time, they are light-years ahead of guidelines generally used in education to deal with emotional maltreatment. Objective definitions of emotional maltreatment are difficult to find in guidelines by state departments of education or local school board regulations, but the concept that educators can emotionally abuse children is well recognized in case law.

To our knowledge, Connecticut is the only state that has made a serious attempt to deal with the issue of emotional abuse of students. Dr. G. Carafino, a member of the state board of education in the early 1990s, asked me to develop some guidelines.

The Connecticut State Board of Education addressed the issue of emotional maltreatment by teachers in its *Code of Professional Responsibility for Teachers*. As far as we know, Connecticut is the only state to prohibit this practice. The practical effects of this provision on everyday teaching are difficult to assess. However, its inclusion in state regulations provides parents, school boards, and state education authorities with sufficient legal backup to discourage and prosecute emotional maltreatment of students. It has been used in personnel actions against teachers who have violated its provisions.

We believe that part of the problem is that up until very recently there has been very little research on emotional maltreatment. However, within the last five years there has been quite a lot of interest and publications by scholars, researchers, and child abuse experts. This explosion of knowledge makes it possible to translate vague legislative jargon defining mental injury into objective, measurable language.

Transforming vague language into effective legislation requires consideration of three factors. The law or supporting regulation must define the act, spell out the connection between the act and negative, observable effects (symptoms) on the child (*proximate cause* in legalese), and consider whether intention should limit culpability.

Define the Act

In this chapter we have given you clear examples, written by the victims, of acts that constitute emotional maltreatment in schools. These acts are statements and actions—often claimed to be motivational or disciplinary—that overtly or covertly, by omission or commission, are recognized by both victims and experts as humiliating, degrading, rejecting, ignoring, isolating, name-calling, and ridiculing. Also included are statements and practices that reflect bigotry and overly punitive, authoritarian attitudes that undermine students' understanding of and belief in democracy.

If that definition seems too long-winded, try this one. *Emotional maltreatment is any disciplinary or motivational practice that psychologically hurts children.* How can we tell what hurts children? Setting aside general definitions, how can you as a parent discover if your child was emotionally abused? You can start by looking for sudden and unexplained changes in behavior.

The literature provides extensive data on the acts that constitute psychological maltreatment in schools, and these can be relatively easily translated into legislative language. We have already identified the major acts that we believe constitute abuse. These include humiliation, denigration, rejection, ignoring, isolation, excessive authoritarian discipline, sarcasm, put-downs, name-calling, ridicule, and bigotry.

Connecting Acts to Symptoms

The psychological effects of physical, emotional, and sexual abuse are similar, so the following discussion should be viewed within that context. In general, studies of psychological maltreatment by caretakers indicate that victims may begin to perform at lower levels than would be expected on measures of ability, academic achievement, and social competency. Therefore measures such as IQ, achievement tests, and social competency scales and rating systems, used by trained psychologists, can be good indicators that something is wrong. An experienced psychologist or other mental health professional knows that maltreated children display behavior problems including aggression, anxiety, and depression. In some cases, victims' feelings of inadequacy, alienation, and resentment may lead to violence, as we have witnessed in a rash of school shootings in 1997 and 1998.

Using psychological evaluations as a measure to screen for and identify individual acts of psychological maltreatment is quite effective. But it is unlikely that most schools will be helpful in determining the culpability of one of their own. If you suspect maltreatment of your child, you may not get a lot of help from your local school psychologist, who should be the ideal professional to aid you. School psychologists, although trained to be child advocates, may be subject to immense political pressure, or even threats to their employment, if they publicly admit that a colleague was abusive. You may have to employ an outside evaluator. However, this may be prohibitively expensive and time-consuming. We will discuss these issues in detail and offer solutions in Chapter Seven, which tells you what to do if your child was abused.

Rather than depending on individual cases to develop guidelines for defining the relation between specific acts by teachers and the damage to students, it is better to have broad guidelines. For instance, teachers might argue that they use sarcasm for humor and most students accept and understand that. So, if some students get upset by the sarcasm, it is their problem. How is a teacher to know who is overly sensitive and who isn't? Of course, our response is that if you do not know who is sensitive to sarcasm, just "say no to sarcasm." But no one gave us a license to tell teachers what to do and not do in their classrooms.

In response to reactions to defining maltreatment solely by the act itself, our colleagues and we at the NCSCPA have clearly documented the range of student symptoms that result from maltreatment. The approach we have used depends to a great extent on individual symptomology. In other words, say Mr. High-and-mighty tells his students they are all lazy no-goods who will never amount to anything. If only one student feels denigrated, scared, threatened, or humiliated, something bad happened. It doesn't matter if the twenty-nine other students in the class did not take the teacher's statements personally. The feelings of stress that result from any type of trauma, especially when it comes from verbal or physical assaults, are idiosyncratic.

Let us give you an example of how reactions to trauma differ from one individual to another. Out of a hundred people similarly injured in car accidents, only ten may develop a phobia about getting back into a car. If these ten victims develop sufficient symptoms, they may be diagnosed as having posttraumatic stress disorder (PTSD). Because the ninety other victims did not develop significant stress symptoms, should we deny that car accidents are traumatic or can cause PTSD? The same goes for emotional maltreatment in school.

Unfortunately, many educational policymakers and teachers just do not accept our argument, but it is gaining ground. If a student develops stress symptoms from any type of verbal assault, it doesn't matter if it doesn't bother other kids. The presence of the symptoms evidences the fact that the teacher's acts were traumatic and therefore abusive to the student.

We developed the *My Worst School Experience Scale* (MWSES) to measure the effects of all types of school abuses. This scale has helped us identify 105 symptoms related to all types of maltreatment in schools. Most of them are emotional. Students who develop PTSD from school abuse develop stress symptoms that may include all or some of seven symptom clusters. Related to these symptoms, the scale identifies thirty-nine specific acts of physical and emotional maltreatment that occur in schools. This information can help develop reliable guidelines for defining and measuring emotional maltreatment. (Chapter Seven returns to the MWSES in more detail, including a checklist based on it that you can use to assess whether your child may have been abused.)

A child who has been abused in school, whether physically or emotionally, will develop some or all of the symptoms we have identified. These include feelings of depression and withdrawal, desire to avoid the abuser or school, behavior that is oppositional and defiant, suspicion and unusual vigilance and alertness for fear of being further harmed by the offender or others in a similar position, somatic complaints such as headaches and stomachaches, unwanted memories and intrusive thoughts of the traumatic event, and sleep-disturbing dreams and memories.

The presence of these symptoms without any other explanation for their appearance indicates that maltreatment has occurred. The number of symptoms and the frequency with which they are felt gives us a measure of how devastating the experience was for each individual. Therefore, guidelines defining emotional maltreatment should spell out the symptom cluster and specific symptoms from the list.

Some may question a symptom-based approach to defining and measuring psychological maltreatment. They may feel that direct observation is the most appropriate way to identify and define it. However, most educators are unlikely to engage in questionable classroom practices while under observation. This is a pity—in litigation I have found that testimony by witnesses, mostly students, is quite helpful in establishing exactly what the offender did and said. Unfortunately, under pressure from many sources, these student witnesses quite frequently recant their initial descriptions of maltreatment.

Should Intent Limit Culpability?

In general, our laws recognize that intention should be one consideration in determining a person's guilt. This can cut two ways. For instance, most teachers will deny that they intended to do harm, just as do many criminals. Teachers may have their own version of the excuse to avoid the death penalty that goes something like, "I didn't mean to shoot him, judge—I was only using the gun to scare him."

Certainly a system of justice should consider lack of intention to cause harm as one of the mitigating circumstances in considering both guilt and sentencing. But teachers, when they are brought to trial, are not common criminals. They are professionals who have been trained to meet certain standards. It is assumed that they understand or at least should be familiar with the science and art of teaching. It is expected that they understand the developmental and emotional needs of their students and that they know something about the difference between effective discipline and denigration. So should guidelines defining and measuring emotional maltreatment consider intention? We do not think so.

The question of intention involves legal and psychological considerations that we believe complicate the problem of defining abuse. If a teacher claims that he or she did not intend to embarrass a student, is the teacher relieved of responsibility? There are numerous cases where the teacher claimed to have no malicious intent, but the results were nevertheless devastating. If a person takes a gun, points it, and shoots someone, intention may mitigate the sentence, but a crime has still been committed.

We believe that guidelines should clearly spell out the nature of emotional maltreatment. Further, they should spell out sources of information and training on the topic and ensure that all teachers and college education majors receive training in the topic. If every teacher understands what you have learned from reading this chapter, there will be no need to consider whether or not the teacher intended to hurt the student.

If a school district has clear guidelines regarding emotional maltreatment, it can more easily discipline, suspend, or fire an abusive teacher. I have testified and consulted on such cases. One involved a high school math teacher whose sarcasm, criticality, and unreasonable assignments were legendary in his district. While he probably put in more hours and worked harder than some other teachers, part of his downfall was his self-aggrandizing with students about his ability in comparison to other staff. But his eventual termination was based on his verbal abuse of his students who did not meet his standards.

In another case, a primary school teacher was suspended without pay for constantly criticizing her students. I am not sure whether it was the actual verbal assaults—which were done about six inches from the students' faces—or her bad breath that was more offensive to the students. I am sure that many were scared of her. I used the MWSES and found that many of her students had developed stress symptoms as a result of her constant yelling.

Do Courts Understand Psychological Pain?

Courts have recognized that the infliction of emotional stress is a basis for dismissal of school employees. However, successful litigation against schools is relatively rare. Part of the reason for this is that in almost all state education department regulations, psychological maltreatment is either absent or not well defined. Also, the victims have to prove that the educator intended to maltreat the child and that the act caused actual harm. And furthermore, the standards for winning a case for emotional maltreatment are higher than if the child were physically abused. This probably accounts for the relatively few claims made against schools.

A reasonably thorough search of case law regarding psychological maltreatment in the schools reveals little to help predict decisions. We suspect that schoolchildren do not have any constitutional protection from psychological maltreatment except for the possibility of substantive due process. This safeguards students against the deprivation of personal liberty and assures that there should be a reasonable relationship between the nature of the offense and the purpose and extent of the punishment. However, there is case law that does set precedent for students' tort claims.

In the case of *McGinnis* v. *Cochran,* Billy, an eleven-year-old special education student, misbehaved in chorus class in New Mexico. The teacher required every student in the class to write "I will kill Billy" one hundred times. The following school day, the teacher made the students wad up their papers and throw them at Billy. One paper ball had a stone or other hard object in it. Billy was then required to pick up all of the papers and throw them in a wastebasket. Following this event, his peers verbally threatened him with death and a few students physically attacked him.

Billy required psychotherapy to deal with the emotional trauma. When the parents sued, the district court supported the plaintiff's substantive due process claims. Even though this case is often cited and despite the fact that there was some physical assault involved, the details of the case are not published. However, the judge clearly indicated that psychological abuse alone is forbidden under substantive due process law.

Several other cases suggest that it is possible to claim damages for psychological abuse. As a result of findings in tort claims, teachers have been dismissed for emotionally abusive behavior such as calling children names such as "dog," "slut," "prostitute," and "dumb nigger." In one case, a teacher was fired for requiring eleven-year-old girls who used vulgar terms to write them a thousand times as a punishment. The problem with depending on constitutional protections is determining the threshold for verbal maltreatment. At what point does verbal assault of students cross the line between so-called normal disciplinary verbiage and language that violates substantive due process rights? Since courts are reluctant to expand the rights of students and schools tend to tolerate verbal assaults, litigation based on constitutional issues is difficult.

Within the framework of tort law, courts and insurance companies are familiar with the concept of long-term psychological or psychic injury, which is frequently used in litigation involving worker's compensation and disability. Schools and laws in general have not been helpful in dealing with psychological maltreatment of students. Even though at a class advocacy level we must continue to change policy in this area, we must presently rely on individual cases to litigate schools. Each tort case brings the attention of this issue to the public, school boards, and insurance companies. These activities continue to put pressure on policymakers to address this issue.

• • •

In summary, we believe that there is ample evidence that psychological maltreatment in schools can be defined, measured, and prevented. There is case law demonstrating that offenders can be disciplined. You can do your part, if you are a parent, by encouraging your child each day to tell you about school. If this habit is established on a regular basis, you will hear about events that your child finds disturbing or strange. After reading this book you will know what to do.

In the next chapter we will consider the results of a melding of police tactics and school discipline that can result in emotional trauma. This is a much more controversial issue, since the emotional maltreatment is generally caused by visitors in the schoolhouse who are sometimes invited and sometimes not.

Chapter 3

Attacks on Children's Sense of Justice and Democracy

To many, justice and democracy are abstract concepts. Throughout our history, legal scholars have attempted to interpret the true meaning of these terms as defined in the founding papers of our democracy. To get to the heart of the matter, you only have to read the second paragraph of the Declaration of Independence. The essence of democracy is the concept of equity and justice, which is enshrined in the assertion "that all men are created equal, that they are endowed by their Creator with certain inalienable rights, that among these are Life, Liberty and the Pursuit of Happiness." This is the core of democracy and should form the core of the educational enterprise: both taught in the curriculum and experienced in the classroom and the climate of the school. By graduation, every high school student should know how to participate in a democracy. This cannot happen in toxic schools.

Remember that our democracy was founded by revolutionaries seeking a form of government free of monarchies and domination by religion. By seeking liberty for every individual, our forefathers conceived a government that would be based on democracy. Their views, which were quite radical in their day and (though many may not wish to admit it) remain so in ours, were rooted in the assumption that the way to control intrusive government was to ensure a broad range of liberties for each citizen. These principles should also apply to schools.

The Constitution assured that participatory democracy would be protected by a government controlled by checks and balances. However, even this form of government could not offer justice and equity without adding a Bill of Rights. The Bill of Rights added guarantees of personal freedom to protect every citizen from arbitrary governmental intrusion into their lives. Yet history has revealed that most Americans have little appreciation for this document. In fact, for almost 130 years, the Supreme Court heard few cases based on the Bill of Rights.

Repeated studies have shown that the majority of Americans are suspicious of the freedoms guaranteed by the Bill of Rights and are only too happy to give up their rights to government authorities. For instance, Americans have tolerated clear violations of the Bill of Rights such as slavery, denial of the vote to women, internment of Japanese American citizens during World War II, McCarthyism, and segregation. Contemporary debates over topics such as school prayer and censorship on the Internet are still hot button issues. This is happening over two hundred years after our founders attempted to disentangle government from religion and fought vigorously to establish the idea of freedom of speech and press.

The war on drugs has generated a political rhetoric that emphasizes getting tough on crime while at the same time undermining the Bill of Rights. Police are given increasing powers in the area of search and seizure as employers, government officials, and school authorities have made urine screening a common experience for many citizens. Few Americans realize that, as pointed out by Ira Glasser of the ACLU, in the eighteenth century the people would not ratify the Constitution without the Bill of Rights. That was the first and last time Americans refused to vote for politicians unless they supported the Bill of Rights.

Now, why is this little history lesson important in a book about toxic schools? Because even many of those who do understand history have difficulty comprehending how the Declaration of Independence and the Bill of Rights relate to schools and students.

Since justice and equity are at the roots of our democracy, they should be taught as both content and process in the schools.

Schools should be just communities. By this, we mean students should be taught the rights, duties, and obligations implicit in our society. This should be done both by lecture and readings and—even more important—by example. Teachers should strive to exemplify democracy in their teaching styles. Democratic teaching includes modeling justice and equity by treating all students fairly, allowing students to make developmentally appropriate decisions and choices, displaying open-mindedness, encouraging free speech and expression of unique or different ideas, enhancing self-confidence, teaching cooperation and consensus building, encouraging respect for facts, inoculating students against propaganda and false advertising, instructing students to be wary of hierarchical organizations and authority, and teaching appropriate skills of dissent within the system.

In a just school that promotes equity, there should be little need for retribution and punishment. Students learn the rights, duties, and obligations they have for each other and for society. They also learn society's responsibility to provide for their rights. Teachers should be mandated to provide for the safety, security, and privacy rights of students. In other words, the Declaration of Independence and the Bill of Rights provide a pedagogical model for just and equitable schools.

Why is it, when we include these principles in a speech, many react as if we are some sort of idiotic idealists? This is only idealism if you do not believe schools should be the torchbearers of democracy. There is lots of research to show that democratic teaching works much better than the more frequent authoritarian model in education. Nonetheless, all too many schools treat students as the enemy, to be controlled and contained at every turn. Despite the toxic climate it creates, such schools find it all too easy to set aside their obligation to be bastions of democracy, and to introduce police tactics into their routine administration.

Search and Seizure in the Schools

Our schools have become a major battleground in the war on drugs and school violence. The weapons used in this battle are destroying students' sense of justice and equity by undermining basic constitutional protections that are assured to adult citizens. Police tactics are replacing the traditional school disciplinary procedures that were based on an understanding of development, education, and learning. Despite the intrusion of this new philosophy into education and the concomitant resources being expended, we think we are far from winning the war on drugs or school violence.

Considering the time, expense, and dismal success rate of increasing police tactics and presence in schools, we believe there is a good case for reexamination of where we are going. We are especially concerned about the wholesale assault on the Fourth Amendment to the Constitution, which states, "The right of the people to be secure in their persons, houses, papers, and effects, against unreasonable searches and seizures, shall not be violated and no Warrants shall issue, but upon probable cause." To conduct a legal search, police must believe that there is probable cause that a crime has been committed and that evidence will be found in the search. These concepts are cornerstones of our democracy. The Fourth Amendment is what separates us from dictatorships and totalitarian governments. It is crucial that citizens, starting from childhood, begin to learn the rudiments of this basic protection of democracy.

In Loco Parentis

Despite what many may think, students are citizens, even though they cannot vote. The Supreme Court in the case of *Tinker* v. *Des Moines Independent Community School District* in 1969 stated that students do not "shed their constitutional rights . . . at the school house gate." But there is a caveat, since school authorities act "in loco parentis." This legal concept is rooted in old English law and applied to the disciplinary powers that the nobility and the rich gave to their children's tutors. In those days, the tutors were employees who could be easily fired if they abused the power of "in loco parentis."

In contemporary bureaucratic schools the power of "in loco parentis" is controlled by the schools rather than the parents and can be abused. Today, parents cannot fire teachers for maltreating their children. In fact, "in loco parentis" has been used as a mechanism for stealing parents' rights to assign parental privileges to teachers. For instance, in the case of *Baker* v. *Owen,* the Supreme Court decided in 1975 that schools in North Carolina could override the parents' previously expressed objections to the paddling of a schoolboy.

However, lower courts in several other cases decided that schools could not paddle children if the parents previously objected. Given the current climate of emphasis on parents' rights to control the education of their children, we believe that eventually courts will recognize that "in loco parentis" is a legal concept that is outdated and invariably abused. Schools should not be given the ability to overrule parents' constitutional rights to prevent disciplinary procedures that are perceived by the parents to be abusive.

It is disturbing that "in loco parentis" can be used as justification to punish children in ways that would be abhorrent to their parents. Parents realize that their children make mistakes. As they watch children grow they are aware of their capacity to change and mature. Most parents want their children to learn from their mistakes, not go to jail for them. Many American parents understand that the core of the Judeo-Christian ethic is forgiveness. Psychologists and educators understand the need to forgive children and help them grow. These concepts are not inherent in law enforcement. Therefore, it is a mistake to introduce a police culture into the schoolhouse where professional educators should act as parents rather than as enforcers. For instance, most parents would not invite police into their homes to search their kids for drugs.

In a somewhat confusing opinion, the Supreme Court decided that "in loco parentis" does not apply to school officials when they are searching students. School officials are theoretically constrained by the Fourth Amendment, which protects citizens from unreasonable search and seizure. Yet a warrant is generally not obtained to conduct searches in schools. This is puzzling, since school officials and police act as government agents rather than parents under the Fourth Amendment. This is even more confusing since almost all other legal precedents, other than search and seizure, define educators within the parameters of in loco parentis. Let us examine the case that set this odd precedent.

The Standard of Reasonable Suspicion

In 1985, the Supreme Court, in a decision on *New Jersey* v. *T.L.O.*, lowered the standard for searching students. Rather than using a standard of probable cause, schools may now apply a less strict standard called *reasonable suspicion* to determine whether to search a student. The standard for probable cause in the real world is higher than what would be considered reasonable by school officials. This means that in the context of the school, where officials have immense power over the lives of children, student searches can be triggered by such flimsy evidence as rumors, hearsay, or even the student's appearance.

School personnel must balance children's liberty rights with the need to maintain discipline in the schools. Therein lies the dilemma. If you really want to understand search and seizure in the 1990s and beyond, you have to know about the 1985 Supreme Court decision in the case of *New Jersey* v. *T.L.O.* Here is a brief summary of a complicated case.

In 1980, Terry Lee Owens (T.L.O.), a fourteen-year-old girl in Piscataway High School, was reported to the principal's office for smoking in the lavatory. When confronted by the principal, she denied ever smoking. He then asked for her purse, opened it, and discovered a pack of cigarettes. He also found rolling papers, a metal pipe usually used for smoking pot, a packet of what appeared to be marijuana, and note papers that suggested she might be dealing. When taken to police headquarters, Terry admitted to selling marijuana at school. She was suspended for ten days and remanded to the juvenile court.

Now, the simplest way to look at this is that the school did a good job of catching a pusher. Why should any student be protected from having her purse, pockets, locker, or body searched? After all, in cases of search and seizure, innocent people have nothing to worry about, right? Wrong, if you believe in our Constitution and the decision of the New Jersey Supreme Court. The court held that there was no reasonable cause to expect that Terry's purse would reveal drug paraphernalia. They claimed that the search was unreasonable and therefore the results were inadmissible at juvenile proceedings.

The United States Supreme Court disagreed in a major decision, which lowered the standard for search and seizure in schools. They claimed that since Terry had been reported for smoking, it was reasonable to search her purse. It was further reasonable, as part of that search, to discover the contraband.

If you read the whole decision you will be mystified. In lowering the standards, the Supreme Court gave very vague guidelines and not very much guidance to school officials. This vagueness opened the door to a lot of beliefs and misbeliefs of school authorities regarding how far they can go to discover guilt. The Court indicated that searches should not be "unnecessarily intrusive," but never defined or directly addressed intrusiveness, including the personal invasiveness of strip searches.

Dissenting opinions by Stevens, Brennan, and Marshall warned about the dangers of allowing educators to balance children's Fourth Amendment rights as citizens against school safety and discipline concerns. When administrators cross the line of the Fourth Amendment, they begin to think and act as law enforcement officers. They are neither police officers nor lawyers and really should stick to their roles as educators, as the cases in this chapter suggest. Further, in his dissenting opinion, Justice Stevens warned about the undesirable consequences of "the shocking strip searches that are described in some cases [that] have no place in the schoolhouse."

Are our fears of drugs and violence in schools worth the erosion of civil liberties of students? Will lowering the standards on search and seizure result in the apprehension of more drug pushers in schools? We doubt it. Given the expense and the assault on civil liberties, we are paying too high a price for an unsuccessful war on drugs and school violence.

Now, before you accuse us of being soft on drugs and crime, let us assure you that we do not endorse students getting high on pot, getting drunk, or fighting in school or in any other setting. Nor do we accept the presence of pushers, vandalism, or attacks on teachers in or around schools. We have worked with delinquents, addicts, and casual users and we know firsthand the damage that illegal activities can cause. This is discussed extensively in *School Discipline and School Violence,* a text I developed with several colleagues in 1997. But the criminalization of substance use and abuse by adolescents should not encourage the use of police tactics in schools.

Patterns of arrests and sentencing of adolescents tend to reveal that children of poor and minority families do not fare as well in the criminal justice system as do their wealthier peers. Being victimized or being a witness to this system undermines students' faith in liberties promised by the Bill of Rights. This enfeebles faith in guarantees of equity and social justice that are at the heart of democracy. In this climate students become the adults who accept increasing infringements upon their rights as American citizens.

When toxic educators use police tactics, relatively few families fight back. Some may just be deferential to all authority and be unwilling or afraid to challenge the school. Some may feel that their kids are out of control at home and therefore deserve any punishment the schools can deliver. Others may believe that if they complain, school staff will further victimize the child and his or her siblings.

Many families who do fight back tend to be unfavorable toward punishment in general and especially toward excessive punishment. Those with whom we have worked who do take on the system are usually quite cohesive as a family and often have a good support network. They often have an abiding belief in our system of justice and that the little guy can prevail. They refuse to accept injustice and they have the guts to go all the way if they have to. The following is a good example of this type of family.

Hell in Hawaii: How a Strip Search Nearly Destroyed an Innocent Student

On October 26, 1992, thirteen-year-old Stephanie Lum was sitting near her friend Raejean in class in King Intermediate School. Her friend noticed a wallet on the floor and picked it up. It belonged to Donald Elsas to whom it was returned. However, Donald complained to the teacher that Raejean had touched the wallet and must have removed the $10 that was in it.

The girls were marched off to the office by the guidance counselor, Ernest Hamai. Since the principal and vice principal were not present, he turned them over to a brand-new security guard, Ms. Kaluhiwa, to continue the investigation. Depositions of the defendants differ about who decided what to do to uncover the missing $10. Without going into all the details of whether or not Mr. Hamai suggested what she should do, Ms. Kaluhiwa acted. She strip-searched both Raejean and Stephanie. Perhaps she thought this would be a real coup if she and Mr. Hamai broke this case without the help of higher officials.

Now, there are many types of strip searches ranging from removing shoes and socks to cavity searches. But no matter what is done, it is a terrible and frightening invasion of privacy for almost any child or young adolescent, especially if the parent doesn't know about it or is not present. As with the majority of school strip searches, no contraband was discovered on either girl after making them take off their clothes and looking into their panties and bras.

How would you feel if your thirteen-year-old came home and told you about being stripped by a school security officer for a lousy $10? Like the Lums, you would have been pretty upset and angry. After all, the imagery of strip-searching is one of hardened criminals being searched for contraband before incarceration. Are not strip searches used to find deadly weapons, drugs, and even valuables such as diamonds that can be hidden in body cavities? Whoever heard of making someone take their clothes off to find a pittance such as $10?

For the next few months, the Lum family went through hell. Their experience with school authorities, the emotional impact on their daughter, and the disruption to the family are familiar scenarios. The Lums angrily demanded that school authorities explain how their daughter, an honor student with no history of behavioral problems, could be treated in such a draconian fashion as a result of such an insignificant charge. Par for the course, the school stonewalled, trivialized, and evaded. The Lums discovered that the school's own rules ban the use of strip searches unless the purpose is to discover a deadly weapon.

The Lums knew there would be trouble when Stephanie, crying bitterly, refused to go back to school the next day and stated that she did not ever want to go back. Every day it was a struggle to get her to go to school. Finally, they enrolled Stephanie in a private school where her behavior continued in a downward spiral.

Two years after the event, I was contacted to evaluate Stephanie to determine the emotional impact of the strip search. Her reaction to being victimized in school was not unlike those of students who had been physically and psychologically maltreated in other ways.

In order to understand Stephanie and her family, I obtained a family history, which revealed a transgenerational pattern of stable, nurturing, and hardworking families. Stephanie's history before the strip search revealed a happy, active, outgoing child who was consistently described in reports by teachers as cooperative, enthusiastic, confident, and conscientious. She had excellent grades and was active in hula lessons.

The Stephanie I met was a slim fifteen-year-old. She was a child of striking beauty, reflecting a melding of the best features of Polynesian, Chinese, Japanese, and Caucasian ancestors. Unlike the upbeat child described in reports, however, she appeared depressed, moody, resistant, and avoidant.

Comprehensive evaluation, including administration of the *My Worst School Experience Scale,* revealed that Stephanie was suffering from PTSD. She was in denial about her problems and, as with many adolescents, refused the type of therapy that could help her. This formally complacent and obedient child had become rebellious at home and school.

After completing the evaluation, I was somewhat depressed and angry. Why, for a lousy $10, would any caregiver think that it was worth it to strip-search a young adolescent female? The answer is that once security guards, police, and police procedures are invited into the schools, there is always the potential for emotionally catastrophic impact on students.

The families of both Stephanie and Raejean settled out of court. But do you think the money was any real comfort? I recently called the Lums to see how they were doing. As the title of this section implies, Stephanie went through a special type of hell devised for adolescents who are victimized by caregivers and develop PTSD. Fortunately, because of her strong family ties and nurturing parents, now—at nineteen—she is beginning to get her act together. But Stephanie is more fortunate than some other victims of strip-searching, especially those from impoverished backgrounds.

The Case of the New Castle Six

On December 18, 1992, Amen Hassen, principal of Ben Franklin Middle School in the New Castle Area School District in western Pennsylvania, thought that he had benefited mightily from the efforts of a student undercover agent. In the best tradition of secrecy, we do not know who the student snitch was. But we do know that he reported to the principal that he had seen six boys on the practice field smoking marijuana. It was not startling to receive reports about marijuana in the school. However, Hassen was surprised about the allegation that one of the boys, whom we will call Curtis, had a vial of crack cocaine.

Hassen rounded up his guidance counselor, Warren Williams, and began a strategic operation of interdiction, search, and seizure. A series of phone calls to upper-level personnel ended with the advice of school solicitor Dominick Motto that Hassen and Williams could legally search lockers, have students empty their pockets, and do "other things of that nature." As in the case of Stephanie, our intrepid investigators ignored the fact that none of the students had previous drug problems. They did not conduct visual inspections of the students or have the school nurse evaluate them for evidence of drug use.

The lockers of all six suspects, whose ages ranged from thirteen to sixteen, were searched, as were their pockets. Five hours after the informant's information was received, the six potential perpetrators were told to remove their socks and shoes, lower their pants to their knees, and raise their shirts. Octavius Tipper and Dayna Griffin testified that the principal placed his thumb inside their underwear and ran it along the waistband after telling them to lower their trousers. After dropping his pants Dayna testified, "I wanted to know what was going on. I told [Mr. Hassen] that's why black kids don't want to come to school."

When the students asked if they could call their parents, they were informed that school district policy required the officials to summon the police if parents were notified. They were also told that even if the police were notified, the parents would not be called until after the search was over.

Guess what? Our detective wannabes found no contraband. But they did find lots of trouble. The parents, all African Americans, were outraged and believed that—among other things—this treatment of their children was a violation of their civil rights. The case was taken up by the Greater Pittsburgh chapter of the American Civil Liberties Union in cooperation with Alan K. Sable, a local attorney.

When I received a call from Witold Walczak of the ACLU, he began by describing what had been done to the students. I then said, "Wait, let me tell you what happened when the parents objected to the victimization of their children." Now, let me assure you, I do not think I am a psychic. But I have evaluated so many cases of student victimization that I can generally predict the scenario. Of course, when the parents objected, the school district stonewalled, trivialized, and prevaricated. One school official was quoted as saying, "I will strip-search any child in this school if I want to, even kindergarten children."

Unlike other cases I have described, the parents in this situation were generally poor and probably considered powerless by school authorities. An added dimension was that several of the students were threatened by school staff. One of the kids reported that a teacher had told him, "I'm not through with you yet, Darren."

I spoke by phone to all the parents and most of the six boys. As might be expected, all of them had some stress symptoms. They were angry that they had been treated unfairly and most were alienated from the school administration. Several were very upset that Mr. Williams, an African American whom they had trusted, had betrayed them. One of the boys became seriously withdrawn and refused to go to school. The two boys who seemed most disturbed were evaluated through use of the *My Worst School Experience Scale* and another instrument. Based on phone interviews and test results, these two boys were victims of PTSD. I never got the chance to conduct individual evaluations in person or testify in court because after several days of testimony, a settlement occurred.

The school authorities' arrogance was noted by the plaintiffs' lawyers and apparently by the judge. In December 1992, Judge Alan Bloch, stated on the record that he believed that the strip search violated the students' Fourth Amendment rights, that the school district's strip search policy was unconstitutional, and that he would issue a temporary restraining order unless the defendants consulted with the ACLU to craft a constitutionally acceptable policy.

The New Castle Six fared well compared to Brian Cornfield, a sixteen-year-old student enrolled in Carl Sandberg High School in Illinois. Brian, a young man in a behavioral disorder program, was observed by several school staff as having an "unusual bulge" in his crotch area. Richard Spencer, Cornfield's teacher, and Dean Richard Frye, believing that Brian was "crotching" drugs, informed him that they wanted to investigate whether or not he was hiding drugs. At Brian's request, they called his mother, who refused to allow a strip search. This refusal was ignored and Brian was escorted to the boys' locker room where he was instructed to remove his clothes.

Spencer and Frye observed Brian's naked body and physically inspected his clothes, finding no evidence of drugs or contraband. Court records do not reveal whether the bulge in Brian's sweatpants was the result of generous endowment. In any event, Brian and his mother were angry at the school and sued.

The United States Court of Appeals for the Seventh Circuit ruled that Brian did not have a case. They felt that because Brian had a past history of alleged but not confirmed involvement with drugs, there was reasonable cause to search him. Further, he was found at one time to have a live bullet in school. Particularly bothersome was the school's assertion of suspicion because Brian had not successfully completed a drug rehab program. However, they had no records attesting to this and, in fact, Brian's mother asserted in an affidavit that Brian left the program because the professionals concluded that he did not have a drug problem but had an attention deficit disorder. It is very troublesome that all these allegations that were used as the basis for "reasonable suspicion" evaporated when investigated. Yet the judges ruled in favor of the school.

These two cases illustrate the use of police tactics and flimsy evidence to meet the low standard of reasonable suspicion in school-related searches. We believe that this standard is toxic and dangerous to students. The use of student informants, strip searches without adequate training of school personnel, and lack of written guidelines can not only cause serious emotional harm to the victims but can have a ripple effect throughout the school. Most educators, students, and parents can quickly learn not to trust school authorities in any sphere. What is especially scary is what can happen when a student or parent complains about overly intrusive searches of any kind, especially when the police are involved.

One school in Savannah, Georgia, embraces police tactics to ensure that students are drug free. School officials, armed county officers, and dogs routinely search common areas and classrooms. Students are herded into the halls, where they are scanned with metal detectors while dogs sniff their book bags and purses in the classrooms. One teacher objected and stated that it is degrading and humiliating to the students who are being treated like criminals. In apparent retaliation, her son was singled out—of fifteen hundred students—for an individual search.

We believe that we have gone too far in tipping the balance in favor of police tactics of search and seizure in schools. By constantly lowering the standard for the excuses used to mount massive searches in schools and on the bodies of students, we are doing terrible long-term damage to our youth's developing sense of the essence of democracy. We are undermining their understanding of their constitutional rights to be free from unreasonable search and seizure by government officials. This may be due in part to educators' confusions and downright ignorance about the Constitution and how far they can go in searching for contraband.

What School Administrators Believe About Strip Searches

After my first few strip search cases I realized that there are virtually no social science data on the topic. Fortunately, one of my colleagues at Temple University, Jacqueline Stefkovich, is one of the few experts in the country. She helped me and graduate student Jessie White conduct a statewide survey of administrators in Pennsylvania. Here is what we found.

Twenty-nine percent of the respondents indicated that their schools allowed strip searches and they reported eighty-nine cases during the previous year. The major reasons given were to find drugs, followed by searches for money, jewelry, and other reportedly stolen items.

In determining what was appropriate in a school setting, 52 percent indicated that it was OK to require removal of shoes and socks. Approval rates went down as more clothes were removed—but about 3 percent approved of removal of all clothes. Most respondents were clearly confused about constitutionality and personal liability involved in searches.

While 90 percent of the respondents agreed, in the abstract, that students should be protected from unwarranted invasions of privacy and 50 percent felt that strip searches were an invasion of privacy, only 50 percent of all respondents saw the practice as potentially emotionally damaging. Most of the uncertainty seemed to be related to legal and procedural issues regarding liability.

As far as we know, there are no data available regarding the success of strip searches. Our respondents reported an average of about 13 percent successes for drugs and about 50 percent for weapons. The search for weapons is generally the least intrusive, since most are easily seen or felt, especially if they are in the student's pockets. However, small amounts of drugs may be easily concealed in underwear or even body cavities, thereby requiring very intrusive searches. Of course, searches for less dangerous items such as drugs or money may require removal of most or all clothing. We believe they are generally the least successful and tend to cause the greatest emotional damage.

Undercover Agents in Schools

Until 1994, I had never thought much about undercover agents in schools. I do not believe I had ever seen an article about this topic in either professional journals or the media. Then, I met Tammy (not her real name), a young woman from Wyoming, who had been sexually victimized by an undercover agent in her school. She and her mother appeared on the *Geraldo* show with me. This episode revealed another potential poison being covertly introduced in the schools.

Undercover tactics have a long history within the criminal justice system. The use of undercover agents is quite seductive in terms of the potential for gathering intelligence, monitoring illegal activities, and apprehending criminals in the act. Despite this appeal, covert measures pose a real threat to justice and equity in a democratic society. The Constitution bars the government from unbridled and inappropriate covert activities, especially those that abridge the First Amendment rights to free speech, assembly, and religion.

George Orwell's prophetic book *1984* documented the dangers of "Big Brother" surveillance. However, in recent decades, increases in undercover operations related to criminal investigations have been illegally paralleled by political surveillance that confirms the prescience of Orwell. Undercover agents have a history of illegally infiltrating the Civil Rights movement, the anti–Vietnam War movement, and college campuses. As recently as the last decade, prohibited FBI undercover operations were used to spy on critics of the administration's Central American policies. The lure of covert tactics was bound to spill over into the schools as the war on drugs heated up.

Undercover operations have tremendous potential to undermine students' sense of justice and fairness and their trust in school authorities. There is always the danger that undercover agents will use their tactics to entrap and incite students to buy or sell drugs. Agents may encourage rather than prevent crime and allow crimes to continue to a point that may endanger the health and safety of students. To justify the amount of money spent, agents may act in unethical and illegal manners in their efforts to arrest students.

Not infrequently, these toxic cops become loose cannons because of lack of supervision. As a result, they may unconstitutionally coerce confessions from students who are denied the presence of parents or attorneys. Finally, in terms of expenditure of resources, these techniques may not be cost-effective since, according to the majority of news accounts we have reviewed, they rarely result in significant arrests that make a dent in drug use in schools.

For instance, a number of undercover efforts in the twelve high schools in Wake County, North Carolina, resulted in little effect over a twenty-year period on students' reports of marijuana use. Kevin Davis, one of the seventy-five students arrested and expelled in the most recent sting operation, claimed that he was lured into selling marijuana by an undercover agent. The State Court of Appeals decided that the 1995 investigation was constitutionally legal and rendered the astonishing decision that expulsion is not punishment in the eyes of the law. The court claimed that this action, which generally denies students an adequate education, is a "remedial measure."

This paradoxical opinion by the Court of Appeals exemplifies the problem when people accept the use of police tactics in schools. While we certainly do not condone pushing or using drugs in schools, we remind you that we are talking for the most part about alienated, disaffected, and often failing students who need real remediation, mental health services, and often vocational guidance. However, these large school drug busts impress the public, increase the political opportunities of prosecutors, and often enhance the reputation of local police. We have grave reservations about the use of intrusive undercover procedures in schools. Historically, they have too often been used illegally in our society to undermine the Bill of Rights.

The Cases of Tammy and Pammy

Let us return to the case of Tammy, which well illustrates some of the problems we have mentioned. Several weeks after the *Geraldo* show, I received a call from her attorney and an attorney representing another victim of the same undercover agent run amuck. The stories of Tammy and the other girl, whom I will call Pammy (because their real names rhymed), were so similar and tragic that I immediately offered my services.

Kevin Carter, a twenty-three-year-old freelance undercover agent, was employed by law enforcement officials in Wyoming to infiltrate high schools in Lyman and in Pinedale, both small rural communities. Data indicated that the drug problem among students was no better or worse than other similar areas in the country.

The story of Kevin Carter, alias Craig Madsen, has all the elements of a successful movie—sex, drugs, and intrigue. Carter began to establish his infamy while working undercover in Lyman. His modus operandi was to move in with a make-believe father with whom he was supposedly in constant strife. Enrolled in high school, he took on the persona of an alienated druggie. It did not take long to connect with the disaffected youths of the community.

While Carter was infiltrating the student body, he was alleged to have been involved with teenagers who stole beer from the American Legion and threw an oil drum off of an interstate bridge. He apparently had no trouble being accepted as a certified hell raiser. Here is a good example of a toxic cop aiding and abetting crime.

Despite his involvement with the drug culture of the high school, Carter's efforts and taxpayers' money yielded little in terms of criminal prosecutions. But, all in the line of duty, he did have fun, especially with one young female. His romantic involvement with Tammy, a fifteen-year-old pregnant student, resulted in litigation against the school, his supervisors, and other law enforcement authorities. This is an example of invasion of a student's privacy rights and concomitant undermining of her trust in government. This also illustrates the loose cannon phenomenon among undercover agents.

After Carter's dismal failure to obtain any meaningful convictions in Lyman, he moved on to another assignment in Pinedale, where he followed a similar M.O. This time, the new victim of his sexual predations was seventeen-year-old Pammy. Like his earlier victim, Tammy, she was tall, blond, slim, and attractive. An expert in finding vulnerable girls, Carter had managed to endear himself to two girls who had low self-esteem and were ripe for plucking. In 1993, Carter pleaded guilty to fondling both girls but denied having sex with either of them.

Pammy's family, when they found out about the duplicitous Mr. Carter, sued seventeen defendants, including school staff, the school board, the State Division of Criminal Investigation, and the attorney general. As reported in *Education Week,* Donald Wright, the superintendent of schools in Pinedale, said that the schools had not asked for an undercover agent. He claimed that he was snookered by the State Division of Criminal Investigation, who exaggerated the drug problems in his school.

I conducted extensive psychological evaluations of Tammy and Pammy. Both suffered from PTSD, depression, and lowered self-esteem as a result of the betrayal by their supposed boyfriend. They were angry and distrustful of all government authorities. Here is an example in which attacks on the protections guaranteed in the Bill of Rights can permanently undermine a whole family's trust in any government officials.

Tammy and Pammy both went through periods of depression and self-destructive behavior as a result of the duplicity of school and police officials and of hostility and mistreatment by peers, neighbors, and former friends. They and their families suffered from actions taken against them because of a stream of rumors of illegal or immoral activity that were provoked or at least encouraged by Carter. The fruitless activities of Kevin Carter resulted in an undermining of the morale of the targeted victims, the schools, and the community.

Needless to say, many students and staff in both schools were angry and disheartened by what had occurred. Hostile public meetings sowed dissension and mistrust in the communities. The feelings of many school staff were expressed by an educational leader in Wyoming. In the October 5, 1994, issue of *Education Week,* Jean Hayek, president of the Wyoming Education Association, stated, "In our eyes, when kids come to school, the school becomes the parent. What parent would willingly entrap their own child?" Others who were interviewed indicated that they thought the use of Carter was overkill and that only local authorities and parents should decide if police should be allowed in the classroom.

Both women prevailed in their litigation and received settlements from the defendants, but they and their families paid a terrible price. Pammy's family moved out of the state. Tammy's parents, who had deep roots in their community, stuck it out but went through hell. Despite the financial settlements, both families would much rather have skipped the experience of being seduced by a lying, cheating undercover agent.

Now, you might ask, aren't Hyman and Snook going overboard about these two isolated incidents? After all, everyone knows that we have a major drug problem in our schools, because data show that about 20 percent of schoolchildren use drugs or try them at some level. Besides, how many undercover agents are there in schools? We need to use standard police procedures such as covert operations to bust drug gangs, catch distributors, and save our children.

Critics of our alarmed reaction maintain that better screening and supervision of Carter would have prevented problems. Thomas R. Rardin, former legal adviser to several FBI undercover teams, criticized Carter's supervisor for not keeping a tighter rein on him. If the supervisor had done his job, Carter might not have turned his apartment into a party house for kids who knew he would get them booze and drugs, as alleged in the suit. While Carter may have been one source of supply, he never did catch the drug dealer in Denver who was supposedly providing the kids with LSD. But Carter may have mirrored the undercover industry, where substantial or meaningful convictions seem to be rare. In fact, I don't believe anyone really knows how successful these school operations are in catching anyone but low-level users and pushers who sell to their peers to feed their own habits. My lack of information led to an interesting turn of events.

After I evaluated Pammy I was deposed by the defendants— who, it seemed to me, represented all the law enforcement agencies in Wyoming. Five lawyers submitted me to ten hours of grueling attacks, including criticism of everything from the letterhead on my stationery to my credentials for testifying about discipline and undercover agents. They brought in a psychiatrist to shoot holes in my testimony. His attendance, which I found quite unusual, delayed the deposition until a judge ruled that he could sit in on it. However, he was instructed not to intimidate or challenge me. Instead, he sat and sneered frequently, offered smiling asides to defendants' attorneys, and generally tried to intimidate me through facial expressions and smirks. It did not work—one look at his credentials told me he was a lightweight.

Even though my brain turned to mush after nine hours of attempted intimidation, the lawyers for the defendants could not shake my belief that Pammy suffered long-term emotional damage from her experience with Carter and the law enforcement community. They then decided to attack my expertise about undercover agents.

Representing one of the defendants, attorney Ann Rochelle belittled me for not knowing that states such as Utah, Oklahoma, Texas, South Carolina, North Carolina, and Virginia regularly used undercover agents. She pointed out my ignorance about training groups that travel around the country to promote the use of undercover tactics. Based on her comments, I was willing to believe in the existence of a national cabal directing a shadowy world of police spooks who promote undercover work in school. It was kind of scary to me and I admitted my ignorance.

A Survey of Undercover Activities in American Schools

When I returned to the world of light and reasonable normalcy, I enlisted the aid of twenty graduate students in school psychology to help me become an expert in an area unfamiliar to every educator I knew. After an exhaustive search, we could find almost no literature or data on the topic. Perhaps this is consistent with the secret nature of covert operations. So we were driven to conduct a survey of federal agencies and officials in all fifty states.

We surveyed relevant federal agencies and local police and school officials in the forty-two responding states. Fifty-six respondents reported familiarity with, or use of, undercover agents in schools. At the federal level, most officials had little or no information about covert police activities in the schools. At the time, none of the national reporting agencies we contacted had any data.

At the state level, most respondents reported that their agencies were not involved in covert operations in schools. Those who had experience with undercover operations were generally evasive about providing information, especially about success rates. The head of the police operation in Los Angeles suggested a 30 percent success rate, but could not cite actual data. And even this alleged success rate is most likely based on arrests of users and low-level pushers in targeted schools. There are no data to indicate that these activities are successful for anything more than a short-term cessation of drug use or that they result in the arrest of high-level distributors.

Supporters of undercover operations claim they help round up many students at once, sometimes lead to the arrest of others in the surrounding community, and—if successful—slow down or prevent drug use by those arrested. Experienced officials in big cities claim that agents must be highly trained and closely monitored, must not allow or invite students into their homes, and should not act as provocateurs. These officials believe that when officers are carefully screened they are generally successful. But the officials could not (or would not) provide any data to support their contention.

Most law enforcement officials, especially those who did not believe in using agents in schools, were leery of placing young, virile officers in a potential sexual hothouse. Just imagine involving a twenty-something young officer with a bunch of young, disaffected, rebellious, sexually active adolescents. How tempting!

Many officials interviewed did not support undercover work in schools. They understood students' feelings of betrayal when they discover that they have been scammed by police and school authorities. There was concern that these operations are generally ineffective, especially because of problems with monitoring agents.

It is difficult to recruit youthful-appearing, trained, and reliable officers. Though it is not uncommon to recruit students to spy on their peers, most of the interviewees suggest that this is a bad idea, because of unpredictability of adolescents. These officials pointed out a general failure to arrest anyone but students who are small-time pushers (and often users themselves), lack of cooperation from school principals, public suspicion of covert operations involving students, and temptations by agents to "go native" by identifying with the student culture.

Educators who would not allow undercover agents in their schools indicated the potential for creating a climate of student paranoia and distrust of school staff. Such a climate, they felt, would have a negative impact on the learning atmosphere. Some expressed concern that blurring the boundaries between education and law enforcement might undermine traditional democratic ideals protected in the schools. Their views were reflected in statements by civil liberties experts, who were especially concerned about compromising the authority and autonomy of schools. The schools' mission is to promote learning in a safe atmosphere where authorities are familiar with the vulnerability and the unique problems of each age group.

Historically, policymakers, judges, and educators have been reluctant to allow police and police procedures to operate in schools. This has been a wise decision because children and adolescents are known to misbehave and make many mistakes as they grow up. Educators and psychologists have recognized that children can learn by their mistakes and it does no good to criminalize their misbehavior. Many of these misbehaviors are the result of environmental factors such as poor parenting, poverty, and racism.

While some would say that these factors are no excuse, we believe that they offer an explanation of why misbehavior occurs. Educators should attempt to prevent and remediate misbehavior rather than punish it. Punishment, the least effective way to change behavior, is easy and requires little brain power. That is why most police officers are not required to have a college degree, a minimal credential for teachers. We do not mean to demean the law enforcement profession, but we want to emphasize that cops are not trained and perhaps not inclined to understand and remediate children's problems. Their job is to enforce the law.

After our initial study, I have kept track of clippings of cases of undercover agents in schools. I don't have a lot of stories to tell, but there are enough that I continue to be worried. For instance, a school in a Milwaukee suburb employed an undercover police officer, Clint Carson, to pose as a student in search of drug dealers. Carson targeted students he suspected of using drugs and turned them into dealers by encouraging them to sell him small quantities of marijuana. He became so ingrained in the culture that he drank with underage students and once drove a car while intoxicated. After two months, sixteen students were arrested for possessing minute amounts of marijuana and faced fines of $500 to $25,000 and even prison terms up to three years. As in many cases we read about, an expensive and ultimately useless entrance of police tactics did not uncover one drug dealer in the entire school. The users who were caught could probably just as easily have been caught getting high at any party or place where they usually hung out.

Here is another example of covert operations in schools. The sheriff's department in a small town in Georgia developed a program to employ students as undercover agents. Students were paid $20 each time they turned in fellow students suspected for using or dealing drugs. Many students were happy to earn a good day's pay as the police received 224 tips.

In conclusion, review of the literature and our small national survey suggest that the use of undercover agents in schools can only be justified in extreme situations where there is a strong likelihood of significant arrests for major crimes. It is likely that well-informed school staff, especially school psychologists, usually know who is using drugs and have information about much of what undercover agents want to know, without having to resort to covert activities. Counselors and psychologists can be much more effective in the long run when provided with sufficient resources to implement programs of prevention, intervention, and treatment for at-risk students.

While the inherent problems with undercover agents are obvious, there are more subtle ways of spying on students that also serve to undermine the sense of community, equity, and fairness that are the underpinnings of democracy. Consider the following case.

Student Spies: Can CIA Tactics Help Teachers?

Lynn was a bright, outgoing, and thoroughly delightful fifth grader. She was always well behaved and respectful to her teachers. From the time Lynn was in preschool, her family would sit down in the evening and discuss her school day. When many children are asked about their school day, the conversation ends with a brief reply—"fine," "OK," "terrible." Not Lynn. She loved to describe her daily adventures in school. While Lynn's parents' intentions were not to spy on the teachers, they were accustomed to daily debriefings. Little did they know that spying would become a topic of concern.

One day when Lynn was in fifth grade, she reported a practice that deeply disturbed her. She said, "Today, while we were lining up for lunch, Mrs. Smith whispered to me that I should watch the other kids and tell her if any of them talked in line. I had heard that she sometimes did this, but she never asked me to tell on my friends. I said OK, but I did not want to. What do you think I should do?"

Lynn's father, a lawyer, was at first amused. His reaction was, "You mean that Mrs. Smith is setting up a system of spies. Maybe she is preparing you to work for the CIA."

However, as the discussion progressed, he became incredulous about the facts. He then determined that this matter required further investigation. He told Lynn to discuss the matter with her friends to discover how they felt about it. The next day Lynn realized that she was not the only one who was angry about being asked to betray friends. Several of her friends revealed that Mrs. Smith had asked them to tell on their friends, but they were reluctant to do so. One student had obediently complied with her teacher's request.

Before confronting the teacher, Lynn's father decided to confirm his daughter's report. That evening he called the parents of children who were asked to be informants. None of the parents knew about it, nor were they amused. In each case the parents questioned their children and discovered that their children were being recruited without their knowledge as undercover agents. When the parents called Lynn's father back, they were all disturbed.

The parents' comments included "It's the teacher's job to discipline the kids, not my son's" and "I did not send my son to school to learn to be a spy." The most indignant parent stated, "Isn't that the way the communists and other dictatorships work? Before you know it they'll be asking the kids to spy on us!"

The parents agreed that Lynn's father, because of his legal training and experience in school law, would speak to the teacher. Here is how it went.

Father: Mrs. Smith, I was talking to my daughter the other day and she told me you had asked her to watch other children in line and to tell you if they were talking. I have never heard of this procedure used in school and I wonder if you could tell me about it.

Mrs. Smith: That's right. I have been doing this for years. I heard about it in a workshop. It really gives the children a sense of responsibility.

Father: Gee, I never heard of that approach to discipline. I have done some legal work in the area of school law and I was wondering which particular discipline theory this practice is associated with.

Mrs. Smith: Well, I don't really know that, but the system works. That's the most important thing.

Father: I wonder if you could provide me with any books or materials that describe this technique. I'm really interested in the underlying theory of why this approach should be used.

Mrs. Smith: I really don't know about anything in writing about this. I can tell you two other teachers do the same thing.

Father: Well, I would really like you to think about the consequences of this approach. While it may be useful, I am wondering about its effect on the children. My daughter was conflicted about her loyalties. On one hand, she has always been a respectful and obedient student, yet, on the other hand, she also prides herself on her loyalty to her friends. This presents a real conflict. Should she betray her friends because you are the teacher or should she lie and tell you that

none of her friends talked, even though she saw
them talking?

Mrs. Smith: You certainly do raise some good points and I will
think about them.

Mrs. Smith must have thought long and hard about how to justify her spy system. The next day she announced to her class, "Children, I have decided to change my method of making sure that
you are quiet in line. From now on, each day I will announce the
name of a monitor. That student's job will be to watch the rest of
you and tell me who talked in line on the way to lunch."

Mrs. Smith appeared to see no relation or conflict between her
discipline method and democratic ideals of justice and equity. She
could not comprehend that her informant system did not teach
each child to take responsibility for not talking in line. What it did
teach students was to fear talking in line because a friend might
tell the teacher.

Mrs. Smith's inability to recognize the ramifications of her
covert operation represents a minuscule attack on the essence of
democracy. She failed to realize that the use of undercover agents
in the classroom contributes to students' beliefs that it is appropriate for students to spy on each other. As adults, will they believe
that it is OK to tape conversations without permission and video-
tape employees for possible drug use in bathroom stalls? Pressure
to tattle on friends strains relationships, fosters a climate of distrust, causes loyalty conflicts regarding teachers versus peers, and
encourages children to lie to protect their friends. This concept
is anathema to both the spirit and the letter of democracy. These
are the techniques of totalitarian governments, or have we for-
gotten that?

Why should we have to remind a teacher that our nation is
founded on the concept of individual liberties and freedom from
unfair and unjust government intervention in our lives? Our
founders were quite reluctant to give government authorities, especially the police and military, any power to spy on citizens or control their lives, except when criminal acts were committed. So how
could Mrs. Smith teach these principles as content and not model
them as process? Why should we even have to write about this? If
schools cannot show children how a just community operates, how

can children learn to believe in the principles of justice that are the cornerstones of democracy?

• • •

Our belief in the right to be free of intrusion in our lives explains why the military and the CIA are not supposed to spy on citizens. That is why the FBI and police are not permitted to use wiretaps and other spying techniques unless they can show good reason. It is difficult enough to control various law enforcement agencies' proclivities to gather as much information as possible, whether legally or illegally, without having to worry about covert operations in our public schools. But we must worry. As we have already seen, our fear of youth crime has panicked us into much more intrusive acts than Mrs. Smith's introduction of Big Brother into the fifth grade.

Recent court rulings and fears about drugs, weapons, and theft in school have resulted in increased willingness by school authorities to conduct intrusive searches that were previously taboo under the Constitution. Our war on drugs, fear of youth crime, and the potential for easy arrests in schools have resulted in a perceptible shift in what increasing numbers of educators, law enforcement officials, and citizens find acceptable. This insidious relinquishing of privacy is toxic to the Bill of Rights, especially in the face of modern techniques of information gathering and surveillance. For instance, government, corporations, and hackers can easily access educational, medical, and financial information about most individuals.

If schools do not become bastions for teaching and modeling the precious principles and rights embodied in the Constitution, who will? Authoritarianism, arbitrary disciplinary practices, covert operations, massive searches and seizures, strip searches, and other police tactics have little place in the schools of a democracy. Not only do these practices do grave harm to students' sense of justice and equity, violations of students' rights clearly may affect their emotional health.

We admit that there is a relatively low incidence of police tactics in schools that attack the previously sacred wall of separation between law enforcement and education. However, how many abuses must we witness before they reach a critical mass? At what point will policymakers look at the real data on school crime and realize that we are treading on dangerous ground? Finally, how can we convince the current Supreme Court to support the principle that was established by their predecessors in *Tinker* v. *Des Moines Schools* in 1969 when they said that the Constitution does not stop at the schoolhouse gate? Is a continuation of the failed war on drugs in the schools worth derogating the Court's statement that students do not shed their Constitutional rights at the schoolhouse gate?

Chapter 4

Drugs, Dogs, and Discipline

Double Messages in the Schoolhouse

"Smash, bang, swat!" The bad guys were definitely getting the worst of it as they were violently smacked around the room by Chet's Power Rangers. Six-year-old Chet initially appeared quite normal as he sat in my office playing with his action toys while I was obtaining background information from his parents, Mr. and Mrs. Jones.

They explained to me that Chet's kindergarten teacher saw him as a six-year-old Jekyll and Hyde. Sometimes he was endearingly lovable and affectionate, yet at others he was stubborn, egocentric, and determined to get his own way. He seemed at times to be unable to concentrate. When thwarted, he would have temper tantrums, crawl under a table, and refuse to come out. Or he would run out of the classroom.

Chet's teacher, Ms. Sweet, a very patient and caring person, was concerned that he would not make it in first grade. She had taught other kids like Chet and they were all diagnosed as having ADD (more accurately called attention deficit hyperactivity disorder or ADHD). She was sure he would be able to manage with the help of Ritalin. Mr. Wright, the principal, concurred and recommended a local pediatrician who worked closely with the school on problems like this and always prescribed Ritalin. He said, "In almost every class in this school, at least one kid is taking Ritalin. It really calms them down, helps them study, and makes them behave better."

Mr. Wright mentioned that if Chet wasn't on Ritalin when he began first grade, he could be classified for special education as a behavioral problem. If so, he would be placed in a "special class" in another—far less prestigious—school district. Well, that ominous warning certainly got the Jones's attention!

Mrs. Jones called her family doctor, describing the problem and her concerns about "drugging" her six-year-old. He recommended that she consult with me about the problem. After obtaining a family history and school records, I did not rule out ADHD. However, I suggested an alternative hypothesis for Chet's hyperactive, impulsive, and disobedient behavior. Chet had learned to get his way by whining, weaseling, charming, and laying guilt trips on his hardworking, often absent parents and his overindulgent nanny. He was expert at manipulating them against each other. Interestingly, when he was alone with his father, who could be stern and consistent, Chet behaved quite well.

I decided to teach the Joneses more effective parenting skills. During the summer, I taught Mrs. Jones how to set limits and enforce rules. She learned how to ignore Chet's temper tantrums and physically restrain him if he tried to hit her. By the end of the summer Chet's behavior had improved dramatically. Unfortunately, it looked like it all went down the tubes the first day of school. Chet had a fight on the school bus with a classmate. They continued to taunt each other in class. His new teacher, Mrs. Stern, was really angry near the end of the day when Chet refused to stop talking, then ran out of class and would not return.

When Mrs. Jones came to retrieve her son (at the request of Mr. Wright), he inquired about Chet's dosage of Ritalin. When he found out that Chet was not taking Ritalin, he was quite upset. He informed her that she would receive a call from the school psychologist to initiate an evaluation.

Mrs. Jones called me and I volunteered to immediately consult with Mr. Wright and Mrs. Stern. I assured them that we could all work together, especially since the Joneses were so cooperative and Chet had responded positively to a reward system and consistent disciplining at home.

Chet improved, but by November the improvement was not enough for the school, which insisted that he needed Ritalin to stay in their school. Chet's parents, his pediatrician, and I agreed to try

Ritalin. But the caveat was that he would be a subject in a series of placebo studies I had been conducting to determine the efficacy of Ritalin for each child. This would require Mrs. Stern and the Joneses to complete daily recordings of Chet's behavior for six weeks. But before I tell you what we did and found, let me give you some background on ADHD and Ritalin. In a way, this is a morality tale about the contradictions and hypocrisy in our country concerning drugs and children.

ADHD and Ritalin

The official diagnosis of ADHD is based on a description in the *Diagnostic and Statistical Manual,* Fourth Edition (1994) published by the American Psychiatric Association. There are three types of ADHD. The first type is a combined syndrome in which the child has both hyperactive behavior and attention problems. The two other types involve either attention problems or hyperactive behavior alone.

In order to be diagnosed ADHD, a child must have at least six symptoms of inattention or hyperactivity. Inattention symptoms include not listening when spoken to, inability to sustain attention on tasks, frequently losing things, and having difficulty organizing tasks and activities. Hyperactivity-impulsivity symptoms include frequent fidgeting, leaving one's desk, and blurting out answers before questions have been completed. These symptoms must occur before the age of seven and be present for at least six months.

The symptoms of ADHD overlap with excesses of normal behavior and with other psychological disorders. Overdiagnosis of ADHD is particularly problematic because Americans are susceptible to the lure of quick fixes with drugs. It is obvious that an accurate diagnosis is crucial to determine whether a child should be put on medication.

A Brief History of ADHD

What should you know and what should you do if you suspect your child has ADHD? You need to know about the history of this diagnosis and the contradictions in our country about drugs and children. You should also know where to obtain a proper diagnosis so that schools cannot bully you into unnecessarily drugging your kids.

It is cheaper to use drugs on our schoolchildren than to spend the time and energy to change parenting and educational procedures and attitudes. How have we arrived at this paradoxical position in which the war on drugs impels us to unreasonably *punish* use of certain drugs and just as unreasonably *push* the use of other drugs?

The answer lies in understanding the interactions among science, politics, and economics. From roughly the early 1950s until the mid-1980s, mental health research and practice focused on environmental influences on behavior. Most scientists emphasized understanding a host of environmental and behavioral factors such as family influences, early experiences, quality of education, and socioeconomic status as explanations for deviance and misbehavior of children and youth. Behaviorists came into ascendance and promoted programs of prevention and remediation by manipulating and changing environmental influences. For example, research has shown the effectiveness of Head Start and the use of extensive behavior modification programs for delinquents. Psychotherapy, though sometimes lengthy and expensive, has been proven to help people change their attitudes and behaviors.

Beginning in the mid–1980s, the biological basis of behavior came into ascendance. Research on the brain has demonstrated the powerful effects of both genetics and chemistry on brain behavior. New classes of drugs can alter mood, stop hallucinations and delusional thinking of seriously disturbed individuals, and change personality with minimal side effects. However, some scientists have ignored the fact that thoughts and feelings can also change the chemistry of the brain. Although advocates for the biological basis of behavior tend to minimize the effects of environment, research shows that the most effective treatment methods include a combination of medication, psychotherapy, and environmental changes.

Parallel to the influence of neurobiology was the election of Ronald Reagan, which heralded the beginning of a new era of fiscal and social conservatism. This movement has unremittingly undermined the environmental approach to solving behavioral and social problems. There have been drastic and continuing cuts in programs of "social engineering," especially those in corrections and education that focus on prevention, rehabilitation, and treatment. The "new" approach to social problems such as delinquency, poverty, and inadequate schools has been based on quick fixes such as punishments and drugs designed to alter behavior.

For instance, various studies suggest that anywhere from 30 percent to 70 percent of delinquents are diagnosed with both learning disabilities and ADHD. These diagnoses suggest to some that medication can cure the complex problems that underlie delinquency. The current vogue is to ignore the mountains of data supporting the efficacy of social programs while overstating the usefulness of drugs. This analysis helps us understand the epidemic of medication for solving behavioral and social problems in the schools.

Psychostimulants such as Ritalin are not the only overused drugs that are pushed by physicians, schools, and parents. Since the 1960s, after the successful introduction of psychostimulants, other drugs have increasingly been used for childhood behavior problems. These include tricyclic antidepressant medications with brand names such as Norpramin, Tofranil, and Pamelor for the treatment of depression, anxiety-related disorders including school-phobia, ADHD, enuresis, sleep disorders, lack of motivation, and obsessive-compulsive disorders. Although almost all the research on these drugs was with adults and the evidence regarding their efficacy with children has been inconclusive, they are widely pushed on schoolchildren by manufacturers and physicians.

More recently a new class of drugs developed for adults called seratonin re-uptake inhibitors, such as Prozac, Paxil, and Zoloft, have been used for many of the problems described. Antiseizure medications such as Tegretal and Depakote, and blood pressure–lowering drugs such as Inderal, are also widely used for children with behavioral problems. These powerful drugs are used despite the fact that there is little research evidence for their efficacy with children and adolescents. Further, prescribing physicians have no idea why these drugs work when they do. So who are the real pushers and druggies in schools?

Somewhere between 30 percent and 40 percent of adolescents have a difficult transition to adulthood. Symptoms may range from mild withdrawal, depression, or rebellion to suicidal ideation and raging anger. These difficult transitions can generally be handled with good environmental and psychological interventions when needed. Do the normal problems of adolescent angst require heavy-duty medications? Does the normal obnoxious behavior of a teenager require a potentially toxic remedy? Experts estimate that at least 3 percent of all schoolchildren in the nation are being drugged with the medications discussed here. We don't really know how many of these kids could function well with more expensive and lasting solutions that require environmental interventions.

We do not question that in some cases, especially when children are psychotic, medication is mandatory. While medication can be helpful when used after careful diagnosis and with appropriate monitoring, we fear that many believe that it is a panacea.

ADHD in Contemporary Education

In the early 1990s, teachers, parents, pediatricians, and others suddenly discovered an epidemic of ADHD. Most experts estimate that 3 percent to 5 percent of school-age children may have ADHD, but some think it is even higher. The truth is, because of faulty diagnoses, nobody really knows the numbers. But we can tell you, a lot of educators and physicians think that ADHD cases are legion. However, this belief is misguided. ADHD shares many symptoms with other behavioral and learning disorders. Because of this it is easy for untrained school personnel or poorly informed professionals to confuse it with anxiety disorders, obsessive-compulsive problems, conduct disorder, learning disabilities, and other syndromes.

Testing for ADHD

Despite what anyone tells you, there is no single medical or psychological test for ADHD. Rating forms filled out by teachers and parents are good for screening for symptoms, but should never be the sole criterion for diagnosis. Frequently there is a genetic basis for ADHD, therefore diagnoses should always include the family and child's medical, developmental, educational, and social history. Psychological testing normally includes measures of intelligence, personality, and neuropsychological functioning.

Despite this fact, too many psychologists and physicians make the diagnoses by observing the child once or twice and relying on the rating forms. Most ADHD rating scales measure attention, hyperactivity, aggression, oppositional behavior, and social interaction. If the student's score matches those of children diagnosed with ADHD it should not in itself be the basis for a definitive diagnosis.

Another diagnostic procedure for ADHD uses a computer. This approach, continuous performance testing, requires a child to press a key depending on whether or not an image appears on the screen. This task becomes quickly boring and tests the ability of the child to attend and concentrate. But do not be fooled by exaggerated claims about these high-tech gadgets. They are very helpful but should never be relied upon as the only test for ADHD.

Various neurological tests, such as EEGs and BEAM tests, are usually useful only when identifiable parts of the brain have dysfunctional electrical impulses, as in seizure disorders. The diagnosis of ADHD is based on behavioral symptoms which are usually not identifiable by these electrical tests. However, they should be used if the child demonstrates behaviors that may be caused by other neurological disorders with symptoms similar to those of ADHD. Therefore, ask your health professional to describe why one of these expensive neurological tests is required.

ADHD and Associated Syndromes

Studies indicate that anywhere from 30 percent to 60 percent of children with ADHD also have learning disabilities. Also, around 60 percent of children with ADHD are diagnosed as having oppositional defiant disorders (ODD) or the more serious designation of conduct disorder (CD). Children with ODD are oppositional, defiant at home and school, and often refuse to follow school rules. They may get revenge on parents indirectly by getting poor grades and always avoiding responsibility. Or they may be openly aggressive with adults and peers. Children with CD are graduates of the ODD school. In addition to breaking rules, they violate the law. Some frequently get into fights, steal, and run away from home. A high proportion of children in both groups also have ADHD and learning disabilities. Also, children with CD frequently have backgrounds of abuse.

Considering the complications of multiple syndromes associated with ADHD, it is tempting to believe that something is wrong with children's brains. While this may be true, the conclusion that the solution lies in altering their brain chemistry with medication is not necessarily accurate. There is little evidence that any medication has been successful in curing these other disorders associated with ADHD.

By adolescence, after a history of repeated failures in both school and interpersonal relations, many children with ADHD and learning disabilities develop symptoms of depression and anxiety. They frequently self-medicate with caffeine, nicotine, alcohol, marijuana, and other illegal substances. There is little evidence that these "self-medications" are effective—but they do provide entry into peer support groups that share delinquent values.

Diagnosis of ADHD is complicated because the symptoms overlap with so many other syndromes. Thus a final diagnosis, before shoving Ritalin into kids, is best made by a team including a skilled psychologist working with a pediatrician, psychiatrist, or neurologist. Careful, objective teacher observations over time are invaluable in making this diagnosis, but cannot be the sole criterion. More important, a child's improved behavior after beginning to take Ritalin should never be used to judge whether the ADHD diagnosis was correct. Let us explain about Ritalin and other psychostimulants.

Psychostimulants: Panacea or Problem?

Psychostimulants such as Ritalin, Cylert, and Adderall have become for educators and parents wonder drugs that will calm kids down, make them compliant, and facilitate teaching. Yeah, but so can marijuana. Also, if you want to stay up all night to study for an exam, you may have discovered that taking speed or concentrated doses of caffeine will help enormously. But we do not push pot, speed, or caffeine in schools. Yet, with the same enthusiasm and unreasoning fervor that we battle against these drugs, we push Ritalin. This makes schools chemically toxic for some children.

Ritalin, generic name *methylphenidate,* is not an innocuous drug. It is a controlled, Class II psychostimulant ranked with amphetamines, which are known in street language as speed or diet pills.

The production, distribution, and use of Class II drugs, which are considered addictive, is carefully controlled by the Federal Drug Administration.

While Ritalin taken orally is not considered addictive, we can tell you that for years kids have pulverized it for snorting. It can give a real rush to a kid who does not have ADHD and therefore it is available as a street drug. We have known kids who do not really need Ritalin who hoard their prescription. When they have enough pills they grind them into a powder for sale in school. So in some cases, inaccurate diagnosis can create pushers.

It is estimated that 1 percent to 2 percent of all children are prescribed some type of psychostimulant medication. In this past decade, methylphenidate has been most popular, followed by dextroamphetamine (Dexedrine), and pemoline (Cylert). Ritalin is so popular that during one period in the early 1990s, demand doubled and outstripped the supply. However in the past two years, Adderall—a newly rediscovered psychostimulant—has become quite popular because it has fewer side effects and lasts longer in users' systems.

I have tried placebo protocols with at least ten adolescents who have been on psychostimulants for years. Surprisingly, even though all these kids felt dependent on Ritalin, I found that about two-thirds could function well on a daily basis without it. Some of those still took it to help study for exams. Research shows that only a small minority who do respond positively to psychostimulants significantly improve their behavior. The rest improve, but they usually need other treatments such as behavior modification programs, family therapy, and classroom modifications. A good way to think about this is to consider that Ritalin is the glue that will help the student stay seated and concentrate. But it alone will not increase motivation—the desire to learn. Many ADHD students do learn even while hyperactive and without drugs, but most teachers won't allow that kind of behavior in class. So some schools encourage drug use to accommodate teachers by gluing kids to their seats so they won't be a bother.

Now here is a most astounding misperception. Many professionals still believe that improved behavior following dosing on Ritalin is confirmation of a diagnosis of ADHD. Wrong! Contrary to this belief, "normal" children and adults can benefit in terms of improved concentration and more controlled behavior on psycho-stimulants, as mentioned previously. So, unless each child is systematically tested on different doses of psychostimulants and a placebo, performance improvements should rarely be used as a diagnostic indicator of ADHD.

We now have reached the nub of the problem. Lots of kids are dutifully popping their Ritalin when they don't need it. They, their families, and their teachers have become true believers and often proselytize to others. We are sure that the pharmaceutical pushers—oops, we mean producers—of Ritalin do little to discourage these true believers. We are also sure that Principal Wright, a methylphenidate missionary, was unaware of his role in this problem. Let us now turn back to Chet to see if he needed to be a Ritalin druggie.

How to Determine If Ritalin Is Necessary

We have no problem with the use of necessary medications with kids when there is competent diagnosis and demonstrated benefits. If a kid truly has ADHD, psychostimulants can have miraculous effects. That is why many years ago I embarked on a series of studies to determine if, in individual cases, medication is really helpful. Over the years, through the use of placebo protocols, I have demonstrated that some students who have taken Ritalin for years really did not need it. However, I have also found clear effects of specific dosages that make dramatic differences in the lives of some schoolchildren. One thirteen-year-old said to me after a six-week evaluation of different dosages of Ritalin and placebos, "I can't believe it, Dr. Hyman. That Ritalin's terrific! I actually did my homework last night. When I take it I can sit for two or three hours at a time and actually study." However, if it does not work, why unnecessarily drug a child and have to worry about side effects and other consequences?

In Chet's case, Mrs. Stern and the Joneses filled out a short rating scale daily for six weeks. The scale included items they selected from a menu of statements describing symptoms of ADHD, such as "can't sit still," "can't wait his turn," and "does not complete assignments." Depending on the week, and unknown to anyone except his pediatrician, pharmacist, and me, Chet received a 5, 10, or 15 milligram dose of Ritalin or a placebo pill twice a day. This meant that neither the teacher, parents, nor Chet himself knew whether the pills contained Ritalin or placebo, or which dosage was being tried during any week.

After all this, guess what we found? Chet's behavior was no different on Ritalin than when he was on the placebos! Now this did not mean that he did not have ADHD, but if he did, this particular drug had no effect. The following fall, Chet again had some minor problems the first few days of school, but he survived. Unfortunately, his new teacher was quite different from his last two. Mrs. Despot could easily have been the wife of Hitler. She had absolutely no patience, was hypercritical, and demanded reflexive obedience. It wasn't long before Chet decided to take her on.

The situation culminated when, after refusing to accept a punishment, he tried his old escape trick. He ran from the classroom and when Mr. Wright grabbed him, the principal received a few smacks in the face as a result of Chet's flailing arms.

Mrs. Jones was summoned from work. She was told that either Chet would be put on Ritalin or he would be suspended for ten days, classified as emotionally disturbed, and sent to the dreaded "special class" in that lesser school district. I volunteered to meet with the Joneses, Mr. Wright, and Mrs. Despot. After reviewing all the data, I reminded the school staff that Ritalin had not been effective with Chet and that he responded well to a more time-consuming behavioral intervention.

Mr. Wright retorted, "Well, that may be. But this kid is out of control again. He needs to be medicated. This is a well-run school and most of our kids come from good homes. Our parents don't appreciate these types of things happening here. I don't care what you say. This kid needs Ritalin. I described him to Dr. Pillman, the pediatrician who consults with us, and he agrees with me."

Mr. and Mrs. Jones felt utterly defeated. They would just go along with the school. Since Chet was doing well at home and my status with the school was not too great, I agreed there was nothing else I could do unless they decided to fight a long battle, which I assured them they could win. They did not have the stomach to take on this very popular principal, so we agreed that I should bow out. Sad to say, Chet was placed on Ritalin, and still may be taking it, even though he doesn't need it.

End of this story, but what about all the other cases in our country?

The case of Chet is repeated in various forms every day and all over the country. This pushing of Ritalin demonstrates a bizarre paradox in our country when it comes to the use of drugs on schoolchildren. Ritalin is a Class II drug, a controlled substance. Production is regulated and prescriptions are monitored. Because it is related to amphetamines, it is not available in powdered form, which can be snorted for a quick high. So how come schools are so eager to push this controlled substance, while they are so irrationally punitive about other drugs that are chemically less harmful, such as marijuana and Midol? How come the "Prozac generation" models the overuse of all types of antidepressants and antianxiety drugs while marshaling immense resources to prosecute schoolchildren for substance abuse? Finally, what does all of this do to children's sense of how a democracy should work?

Massive Searches for Drugs in Schools

In the last chapter we discussed some of the problems of search and seizure. In the cases of Stephanie, Tammy, Pammy, and the Newcastle Six, the abuses occurred from overzealous and improper use of police tactics in schools. The victims described were often targeted because of specific although unsubstantiated suspicions. In this chapter, we want to talk about generalized procedures that involve large groups of students for whom there is no reason to justify intrusive searches. Both of these abuses result from policies flowing directly from our war on drugs.

About 75 percent of kids at any given time have not used drugs during the past month, according to government-sponsored surveys. Of the 25 percent who do use them, most use marijuana or alcohol, or both. The more intelligent drinkers and pot smokers are not stupid enough to use and store their drugs in school. Most drug and alcohol users indulge at parties, going to and from school, at home, and in clandestine neighborhood locations. In other words, we don't believe that in most cases there is probable or even reasonable cause to think that large numbers of students in schools should have their lockers searched for drugs or that all candidates for sports should have to pee in a cup for school officials.

However, procedures such as use of police dogs to sniff out drugs, wholesale locker searches, and massive urine screening are on the rise. What is the message to students when scary-looking police dogs run rampant through their school, a place many consider a home away from home? How do they feel when trusted administrators, counselors, and teachers permit police dogs to enter the school and slobber over their clothes, backpacks, and notebooks? What is their sense of violation when an administrator or police officer goes through their lockers, reads their love letters and other personal notes, paws through their lunch bags, opens packets of Tampax, or investigates the content of pills in a Midol container? Here is how one particular articulate and courageous high school student responded when he was told that the Fourth and Fourteenth Amendments to the Constitution, which he had learned about in school, did not apply in the very school and class where he had learned about them. It is another example of toxic schools that teach the content but not the process of democracy.

Content Versus Process:
A Real-Life Example in a Criminal Justice Class

In preparing to write this book we have found unending examples of abuses of democracy reported in the media and on the Internet. We came across a particularly interesting case that really illustrates all of the problems we discuss in this book. The following account was written by Jacob Reed, a high school student in California. It describes an experience that occurred while he was attending a class about the Constitution and the criminal justice system in America. This is a paper he wrote for the class, after the series of events he describes. We have made minor editorial revisions for publication.

> In February 1996, the Galt Joint Union High School District Board of Trustees adopted a new search and seizure policy. This policy called for the use of trained dogs on campus. These dogs would search for gun powder, illegal drugs, and over-the-counter medications such as Tylenol, aspirin, and Midol. The dogs would sniff cars in the parking lot, lockers, and personal belongings of students during classroom searches.

On Thursday February 6, 1997, during 6th period, one of the vice principals came into the Galt High School Criminal Justice class and told the students that they were going to do a search with the drug dogs. She said "leave your backpacks, binders, jackets, and hats, and step outside."

As the rest of the class stepped outside, leaving their belongings behind, I picked up my binder, and without removing my jacket or hat, made my way toward the door. Before I reached it, the vice principal told me I had to leave my stuff in the classroom. I told her, "I don't agree with what's going on here. This is wrong and I don't want to leave my stuff." She said, "Well, it doesn't matter what you think is right or wrong. We can search your stuff because it is on our property." I told her I wasn't going to leave my belongings behind. She said that if I didn't that they'd just call the Galt police department to come search me. I said, "Well, if you feel you have to do that, OK."

She called the office on her walkie-talkie and told the other vice principal to come escort a student to the office to be searched by the police. The other vice principal arrived and escorted me to his office. The principal was called into the room as I sat down. The two began to tell me that there is a difference between the cops and the school. That is, the cops need probable cause to search, but the school only needs reasonable suspicion. The vice principal turned to me and instructed me to stand up. I said, "I have a problem with this. I don't see why you need to search me."

It was explained that their reasonable suspicion was that I was refusing to leave my stuff in the classroom. I then said, "I don't think that's reasonable suspicion. The reason I didn't leave my stuff in the classroom was because it's my stuff. I don't want my personal belongings somewhere where I can't see them. You tell us to leave our stuff there, you kick us out and then you close the blinds so we can't see what's going on with our stuff. The students have no representation. There's someone from Interquest, the company that does the searches, and there's someone from the administration. But we don't have any idea what happens to our stuff behind the door."

After a lengthy conversation, the vice principal convinced me that he might have the right to search my stuff because I refused to leave it in the classroom. That's when I told him, "From what I understand you might have the right to search my binder, my jacket, and my hat, but that's it, because that's all I refused to leave in the classroom." He said they don't do "half searches" and because I refused to leave my stuff, they now had the right to search me fully.

I sat there thinking for a while, trying to decide what I should do. I said, "I know of too many people who have been screwed over by administration at other schools I've been to and even this school. The administration talks to them and everything they say makes sense and sounds perfectly legal and then they think they have no choice but to cooperate. Then, when they find out their rights were violated, it's too late to do anything about it. I just don't want that to happen to me."

The vice principal then replied that it was terrible for administrators to do that sort of thing and if I knew about that kind of thing going on anywhere to let him know about it. He also told me how much he hates the disciplining part of being a principal. He told me that if I still didn't let him search me, then the cops would come down and they would do it for him. He said, "It's up to you." He left the room to get a witness for the search. I felt as though I had no choice.

When he came back with an office worker as a witness he asked me what I wanted to do. I said, "I'll let you search my stuff but if I find out my rights were violated, there could be a lawsuit." The vice principal told me that if I found out my rights were violated, it was OK if I sued him.

I felt as though I had been backed into a corner and wanted to get out any way I could. I handed the vice principal my binder. He searched it. He told me to give him my jacket. He searched it. He told me to give him my hat. He searched it. He told me to empty my pockets and I did. He felt inside my pant pockets to make sure they were empty. Then he told me to show him my socks. I did. He did not find anything illegal on me.

I sat back down and the principal came back in. The two administrators explained to me why they felt they had to search me. One explained of the possibility that a person could bring a gun to school and that because of a few people they had to have this program.

After this incident, I went back to class and with the help of Mr. Millet, my teacher, contacted the ACLU. On February 14, 1997, the ACLU sent the school a letter. The letter explained in great detail why it was their position that what the school was doing was a violation of the Fourth and Fourteenth Amendments to the Constitution. They also cited precedent cases that supported their claim. The letter asked the school to abandon the policy.

Two weeks later, on February 28, the school responded to the letter. In it, they stated that they believed their policy was lawful and in accordance with the Fourth and Fourteenth Amendments. They also cited case law that supported their side. It was obvious that the two sides would not be able to agree on a solution. As a result, on March 20, 1997, the ACLU filed a lawsuit on behalf of me, Michael Millet, and Chris Sulamo. John Heller, a San Francisco attorney, represented us in cooperation with the ACLU.

I filed the suit in hope of getting the court to rule that forcing students to leave their belongings in the classroom is an illegal seizure and a violation of the Fourth (search and seizure) and the Fourteenth (equal protection) Amendments.

Michael Millet, the teacher of the Criminal Justice class, was also forced to leave his belongings in the classroom to be subject to the search. He filed the suit in order for the courts to declare that forcing teachers to leave their belongings in the classroom is an illegal seizure and therefore in violation of the Fourth Amendment.

Chris Sulamo, another student in the class, left his belongings in the classroom and the dog "alerted" on his jacket. The vice principal searched the jacket and found nothing. She then proceeded to search his backpack and other belongings. He too had nothing illegal on him. After the search, Chris voiced his objection to the search in somewhat vulgar terms and as a result was suspended for three days. Chris filed a lawsuit hoping to get a ruling stating that his suspension was a violation of his First Amendment right of free speech. He later dropped the suit.

On May 14, 1997, the school board voted 5–0 to repeal the "use of trained dogs" section of their search and seizure policy. This was a major accomplishment for all the plaintiffs, but the school, as of June 1997, had yet to address the issue of Chris Sulamo's suspension. That is where the case now stands.

In addition to his account of the litigation, Jacob reports massive intrusions of schools using canine cops in Texas, Massachusetts, Kentucky, and California, which add to the many cases we have found through our research. Now do not get us wrong. We love dogs, even drug-sniffing dogs. I am a dog owner and appreciate how dogs can help people. So, before we are attacked by animal rights activists, we want to make it clear that we are not blaming dogs. It is not the dogs who are poisoning the stream that should water and nourish the seeds of freedom and liberty that must be planted and cultivated within our schools.

What is the effect—in a country that claims to be the freest in the world—on a generation of children who become acclimated to sheriffs and police periodically conducting massive searches with police dogs? How does this teach civic responsibility and a belief in the Constitution?

Jacob ends his report with Supreme Court Justice Stevens' dissenting opinion in *New Jersey* v. *T.L.O.*, which we have already discussed in the last chapter: "The school room is the first opportunity most citizens have to experience the power of government. Through it passes every citizen and public official, from schoolteachers to policemen to prison guards. The values they learn there, they take with them in life. One of our most cherished ideals is the one contained in the Fourth Amendment: that the government may not intrude on the personal privacy of its citizens without a warrant or compelling circumstance."

A New Type of Pop Quiz: Peeing in a Cup and Other Indignities

By now you either agree with us that attacks like these on children's civil liberties are outrageous or you find us to be hopelessly liberal crybabies. If you are in the latter group, you may not agree that it is an indignity when students who have given no reasonable or probable cause for suspicion of drug use are marched to the lavatory and, under supervision of an adult, are told to pee in a cup. Now remember, we are not only talking about long-haired, sallow, suspected druggies wearing baggy pants. Even though children like these also deserve constitutional protection, many school personnel believe that their very appearance is probable cause for searches. We are talking about any kid, in any American school, who looks suspicious to an administrator.

Legal Implications of Urine Screening

As a result of our national frenzy over drugs in schools, all kinds of schemes have been devised to test students for drug use. Any student may be subject to urine screening, whether the testing appears constitutional or not. As the law now stands, the urine donor may be a suspected user, a victim of random screening, or a candidate for school athletics. Now, before going further, visualize what we are talking about. To completely assure that the urine sample is genuine, the adult supervisor ideally would observe the urine leaving the student's body and entering the cup. During the early days of drug screening, some educational policymakers failed to acknowledge or even understand the indignity of this process. Their reasoning is difficult to follow, when even medical professionals—who take naked humanity for granted—do understand the loss of dignity to individuals who are being observed as they urinate.

In the case of *Anable* v. *Ford* (1985), a federal court in Arkansas recognized that there are some constitutional protections of personal privacy of students. In this case, an Arkansas school board routinely tested any student suspected of drug or alcohol use. Rather than using the findings to help addicted students, positive results were used for expulsion from school. The court said this practice was "repugnant to the Constitution as well as to our common sense of students' integrity."

The court also found that the test was useless in determining where the student had used a substance. If use occurred outside the school, it was "irrational, arbitrary and capricious" to expel the student since the student's behavior was beyond the scope of the school's disciplinary authority. This case set a precedent that forbids educators to observe the student's genitals during urination.

The problem is that a student who is in a stall and out of sight has a chance to alter the sample. Six years after *Anable,* the Supreme Court stripped students of potential genital privacy in the case of *Vernonia School District 47J* v. *Acton et ux.* Here is a brief summary of this important case, which further expanded school officials' abilities to use police tactics and trample on students' civil liberties. As you will remember, constitutional rights to be free from search and seizure were already undermined in the Supreme Court's decision in *New Jersey* v. *T.L.O.*

In 1991, James Acton was a twelve-year-old seventh grader in Oregon's Vernonia School District. This is a district that claimed, without any reliable data, to be in the throes of a drug and discipline crisis. When James applied for the football team he discovered that his parents were required to sign a drug-testing consent form. He and his family objected on the grounds that mandatory drug testing of football players makes the assumption that all candidates are presumed guilty until proven innocent. They claimed that this unreasonable demand was an invasion of James's privacy and a violation of his civil rights. His parents refused to sign on the grounds that there was no evidence that James had ever used illicit drugs, and James was denied membership on the football team. The parents sued.

As the case wended its way to the Supreme Court, the Oregon Court of Appeals agreed with the Actons and stated that compelled urinalysis is a substantial intrusion of privacy for schoolchildren and adults. While children are compelled to attend school by law, "nothing suggests that they lose their right to privacy in their excretory functions when they do so," and that there is no reason to believe "that the privacy interests of athletes are substantially lower than of students in general."

On June 26, 1995, the U.S. Supreme Court—in a 6–3 decision—held otherwise. The majority opinion was written by Justice Scalia, perhaps one of the least progressive of the Justices. We noted earlier his statement that "caning was done [in 1791] . . . and it would probably be constitutional now." The Court's opinion asserted that (1) schoolchildren can not expect the same level of privacy as members of the general public or as free adults, (2) peeing in a cup without exposing your genitals directly to the view of a government official was a "negligible intrusion" on privacy, and (3) there is a compelling need for athletes, who are supposed models in the school community, to demonstrate that they are drug free because of rampant drug problems in the schools.

Conservative Supreme Court Justices have always tended to ignore actual data on the extent and frequency of school crime, including student drug use. Even though surveys on drug use may seem high at any one time, they often reflect responses by casual users rather than habitual abusers. We do not justify any use—but we do advocate a rational response to survey data.

The conservative Justices seem to rely heavily on media hype about increasing crime in schools. They seem unable to make even a cursory analysis of yearly government data that do not support the rhetoric about major increases in school crime in the last twenty years. This reaction boggles our minds, especially after looking at how school officials constantly abuse every new freedom the court gives them.

Since 1995, some school districts around the country are thrilled with their newfound freedom to design newer and better assembly line procedures for collecting urine. Conservative policymakers are delighted to detail plans for increasing the number of students tested, and testing companies see big bucks in pee. For instance, in October 1997 the Dade County School Board in Florida set aside $200,000 for a pilot program of random urine testing of all high school students. Considering the questionable reliability, validity, and usefulness of urine screening, we wonder if these monies could be spent more wisely to purchase textbooks, provide drug counseling, or reduce class size.

In January 1998, Lt. Governor Gray Davis of California, during his successful campaign for governor, proposed random drug testing in all California high schools. He was willing to allocate $1 million to a private firm to conduct the testing in five high schools in a pilot program. Ignoring social science literature about adolescents and drugs, Davis said, "Faced with the very real prospect of getting caught, many kids will simply choose not to try drugs in the first place—or if they are using them, to quit." Fear of punishment rarely deters crime, especially among the population of adolescents most likely to use and abuse drugs. Witness the ineffectiveness of punitive measures to deter smoking among youth.

Now here is a real expansion of the *Vernonia* v. *Acton* decision. In January 1998, the United States Court of Appeals, Seventh Circuit, unanimously upheld the policy of Rushville Consolidated High School (in Indiana) requiring random drug testing of students involved in any extracurricular activities and those who wish to drive to and from school. This testing is for drugs, alcohol, and tobacco. We wonder how members of Congress would feel if we applied similar tests to them. Oops, Senator Helms, we just discovered nicotine in your blood; since you may have smoked it in restricted public places in the Capitol, you can't go home.

Is Drug Testing in Schools Worth the Cost?

It is pretty well known to school boards that urine tests are expensive. They cost at least $25 a pop, they are notoriously unreliable (especially for the cheaper tests that schools can afford), and labor intensive. School staff must spend time watching kids peeing. But, never fear, new technology is on its way, at least in testing for alcohol.

In May 1998, school officials in Sayville, Long Island, produced a plan to conduct Breathalyzer tests for alcohol at the beginning of each school day. Candidates for the test would be students whose breath or behavior raised suspicion. An obvious advantage for merchants is that mouthwash and mint sales would soar in Sayville. But we wonder how many educators are wannabe police officers. Who will volunteer to sniff the mouths of students, make them walk a line, or keep an eagle eye for any "strange behavior"? If any behavior is strange, it is that educators would be running around with Breathalyzer gear at the ready, eagerly waiting to catch potential drunks. What message about education and educators does this send to the students?

If you are a school official and are not interested in orifice-related testing, there is a solution for you. With little bother you can carry around, maybe in a holster, a pair of scissors. With them you can cut a lock of any student's hair. If they object, perhaps you can make a contract with the local barbers. Psychemedics Corporation in Massachusetts, for a fee, will conduct a hair analysis that will reveal the student's use of various drugs.

The point of all this is that educators should do what they know best, which is to teach children. Policing should be left to law enforcement officials, who should return to their traditional hands-off policy in schools. Policymakers should openly admit that the criminalization of some addictive substances such as marijuana and cocaine and the legality of others such as nicotine and Xanax has mired us in a punishment-oriented and destructive war on drugs. Schools have become a major battleground in this unwinnable war.

In the name of school discipline we push all types of problematic, mind-altering medications on schoolchildren. In the name of school discipline and because of moralistic fallacies about the evils of drugs, we severely sanction youth who experiment with or become addicted to them. We sorely need politicians and policy shapers who will admit to the public that we are losing this paradoxical war on drugs. They should admit that the cost to the Constitution is too high and that we need to seek a better way to solve the problem, which is further illustrated in the next section.

From Marijuana to Midol

By now you may think we are getting too ridiculous and sarcastic in our comments about how far we have come from the *T.L.O.* decision. Let me assure you, after working for forty years in schools as both a teacher and psychologist, I see no end in sight in terms of how ridiculous bureaucracies can become. Single incidents of violence, exaggerated stories of substance abuse, media hype about chaos in schools, and right-wing political rhetoric seem to cause many school policymakers to punish students in unreasoning frenzy.

It is not that we do not understand the problems that schools face when students misbehave and break the law. We have great sympathy for policymakers, administrators, and teachers who must daily face the myriad problems of society as they are reflected in the lives and behaviors of students. After so many years of working with hard-pressed schools and addicted, delinquent, and runaway students, I know something about the extent and nature of school violence and drug problems. But I also know that the power to punish is too easily abused. The lure of punishment as a weapon to make schools drug free offers us examples of how schools can go too far. Consider the following.

On October 8, 1996, the Riverwood Middle School in Houston suspended Brooke Olsen, who inadvertently brought a bottle of Advil into school in her backpack. Her apprehension was aided by a drug-sniffing dog that must have been trained in the local drug store's nonprescription painkiller aisle. Although Brooke was aware of the school's policy that all drugs must be kept in the hands of the school nurse, she forgot the bottle was in her bag. School trustee Al Moore was quoted as saying, "Nothing is more important than keeping drugs off campus." However, school board president Ann Willott agreed to reexamine their "zero tolerance" drug policy.

We recognize that Riverwood's policy about bringing any medications into school is not unusual. Most school policies require that all drugs must be kept and dispensed by the school nurse after being approved by each child's physician. However, where do we draw the line in a pill-popping society between over-the-counter pain relievers and controlled substances? Do we need police tactics to catch kids who take aspirin with the permission of their parents?

Another incident occurred when Erica Taylor, a thirteen-year-old student in Baker Junior High School in Dayton, Ohio, was suspended initially for nine days (later reduced to three days when she agreed to go to drug counseling). Erica's offense was the ingestion of a contraband Midol pill to relieve her menstrual cramps. The "pusher" was her friend, thirteen-year-old Kimberly Smartt. Kimberly was given a ten-day suspension after which she was expelled for four and a half months for absconding with two Midol pills from the nurse's office. She had gone to the office with severe menstrual pain. However, perhaps embarrassed, she told the nurse only that she had a headache and a sore right arm. She took the two Midol tablets when the nurse briefly left the office, taking one for herself and sharing the other with Erica.

Kimberly and her family sued the school in federal court, claiming violation of various constitutional rights and infliction of emotional pain and distress because of the unreasonable punishment. The suit received extensive media coverage as the "Midol Case" and many citizens thought the school's actions were ridiculous. However, Federal Judge Walter Rice disagreed with much of the public. He dismissed Kimberly's claims, stating, "Although this court is aware of many possible transgressions by public school students, which are more dangerous to both the student and the community than the unauthorized possession and distribution of Midol, it is neither arbitrary nor capricious to outlaw and punish such actions."

This is an example of the kind of conservative judicial opinion that tends to undermine students' constitutional rights in schools. It is based on legalistic arguments and assumptions about school discipline that ignore the developmental and emotional realities of students. Words such as *outlaw* and *punish* rather than *ban* or *discipline* suggest the judge's biases. This type of language and his final opinion reflect a law-and-order, policing orientation to school discipline as opposed to traditional developmental and educational approaches to dealing with the minor indiscretions of youth. It further erodes students' belief in the democratic principles of justice and equity they are taught in class.

However, the school district was delighted with the opinion, which they felt safeguarded their interest in protecting each and every student from adverse reactions to any drugs. They proved their point and reasserted their power over the lives of students.

But, to us and many Americans who read about the case, they only proved that they were unable to be guided by higher principles of morality and justice that mandate the consideration of mitigating circumstances. These include issues such as an adolescent's severe menstrual pain and the fact that Midol is not a dangerous drug worthy of suspensions and expulsions. The school's actions and the judge's opinions are true examples of toxic and dangerous thinking about school discipline.

Beyond Tinker: Dangerous New Precedents

In the 1960s and 1970s, the Supreme Court of the United States rendered some startling opinions that forced schools to reconsider the relation between democracy, the Constitution, and the way schools treated students. Probably one of the most famous was their opinion in *Tinker* v. *Des Moines Independent Community School District,* which we discuss in more detail in the next chapter. In 1969 the Court ruled that students had the right to wear armbands to protest the Vietnam War. In affirming that "students do not shed their Constitutional rights at the schoolhouse gate" the Court stated that in a democracy, "State-invented schools may not be enclaves of totalitarianism. School officials do not possess absolute authority over children."

These radical statements were interpreted by conservatives as meddling judicial activism by a liberal-dominated Court. However, far from being radical, this opinion reflected the radical, humanistic thinking enshrined by our founders in the Declaration of Independence and our Constitution. It encouraged and embraced the concept that schools should be the torchbearers of democracy. Should not schools be exemplars of protections such as freedom of speech, due process, and freedom from undue search and seizure that reflect the freedoms that citizens should enjoy under the Constitution?

The Supreme Court heralded a new era in which schools were instructed to inoculate children against simple-minded, punitively oriented pedagogues and officials whose solutions to the problems of youth dissent and questioning of authority are reflexive obedience and authoritarianism. Unfortunately, the Supreme Court has changed. Jurists such as Scalia, Rehnquist, and Thomas are doing all they can to undo the damage done to schools by their predecessors' "disease." This disease is characterized by delusional thinking involving a belief in premature democracy for students. But they are causing the real disease by allowing the poison of authoritarian thinking to enter the school body.

. . .

As this chapter illustrates, our courts are permitting the schools in the 1990s to attack the very foundations of students' belief in the right of every citizen to be free from unreasonable intrusion of person and property. In the war on drugs, schools have gone to the extreme of treating Midol as if it were illicit. Yet they are forcing mind- and mood-altering drugs into the bodies of noncompliant students and punishing parents who resist. This seems crazy to us.

But you judge whether we are making a federal case out of a few exaggerated reactions to drug use in the schools. Or are we just trying to warn citizens of the attack on our freedom? By now you should be getting a pretty good idea why we believe some schools are already dangerous and toxic and the rest are susceptible to weapons of mass intellectual poisoning.

Chapter 5

Morality, Sex, and Censorship

Censorship appears to be a difficult concept for many Americans. Most believe—in the abstract—that censorship is bad. But many abhor specific ideas, speech, and imagery that they would prefer to ban outright or conceal from children, especially in regard to their own standards concerning morality and sex. But our founders did not waffle on censorship when they wrote in the First Amendment that there should be no abridging of the freedom of speech, press, or peaceable assembly and cautioned against government involvement in religion. They did not want ideological or real wars among citizens fought over religious ideology and perceptions of morality.

The Supreme Court, in interpreting the Constitution, has historically supported a wall of separation between church and state. The Justices have generally attempted to protect schools from being a battleground on which differing religions attempt to impose their particular beliefs, versions of morality, and interpretations of blasphemy. They should be credited as defenders of the freedoms guaranteed adults in the First Amendment. However, their zeal has been lacking when these rights are exercised behind the schoolhouse gate.

In recent years the Court has had a poor record regarding the protection of students' First Amendment rights. This appears to be due in part to attempts to safeguard children from the alleged harm that can be caused by speaking, reading, or seeing sexually oriented, morally objectionable, or politically suspect material. This trend reflects pressure from a contemporary breed of theologically motivated conservatives (theo-conservatives) who constantly push their brand of religion and morality into the public arena and the schools. Their ideology endangers belief and faith in the First Amendment by attempting to breach the wall of separation between church and state and pushing schools onto the slippery slope of censorship.

Defining Censorship

Censorship is the process in which officials or others are empowered to suppress materials, speech, and ideas that are objectionable because of moral, political, military, religious, or other criteria. It is unhealthy for individuals in any society, especially in democracies. It has the potential to stunt the emotional and intellectual growth of students, making them dependent and subservient, especially when they are developmentally capable of making independent judgments.

Abuse of democratic precepts occurs when students are denied opportunities to explore ideas that are not conventional or approved by the teacher, principal, or school board. However, school censorship was hardly questioned until the 1960s, when challenges to the Vietnam War and the developing sexual revolution and Civil Rights movement resulted in many citizens' questioning the wisdom and authority of public officials. The watershed event that questioned censorship in schools was the case of *Tinker* v. *Des Moines Independent Community School District.*

Censorship in Schools: *Tinker* v. *Des Moines Schools*

In 1969, the Supreme Court delivered a major blow against censorship in schools. Fifteen-year-old John Tinker and his thirteen-year-old sister Mary Beth were part of a group of students and adults who decided to wear black armbands to protest the Vietnam War. The students who wore armbands were suspended from school until they would agree to return without their symbols of protest against the war. They refused to return until the end of the agreed-upon period of protest, at which time they filed a complaint with the U.S. District Court. The court upheld the defendant school board and agreed that the petitioners' actions posed a threat to school discipline.

The case was eventually appealed to the Supreme Court, which ruled that the school was wrong in denying students the right to express personal views on the school premises. Whether "in the cafeteria or on the playing field or on the campus during authorized hours . . . [unless school authorities have reason to believe that such expression will] substantially interfere with the work of the school or impinge on the rights of the students." This ruling is famous, as we mentioned previously, because it indicated that students have constitutional rights.

The Court's thinking about First Amendment rights of students was reinforced in the 1982 opinion in *Board of Education* v. *Pico.* In this case, the Board of Education of Island Trees School District in Long Island rejected the recommendations of its own appointed committee of parents and school staff regarding removal or restricted use of books in the high school and junior high school libraries. The board characterized some of the committee-approved books that it removed as "anti-American, anti-Christian, anti-Semitic, and just plain filthy."

The Court, while recognizing the board's broad discretion for managing school affairs, reminded the board that the First Amendment imposes limitations on that discretion regarding removal of books from school libraries. A board may not, by so doing, "prescribe what shall be orthodox in politics, nationalism, religion, or other matters of opinion." The Court also agreed with a lower court that the board had acted "on its conservative educational philosophy, and on its belief that the nine books removed from the school library and curriculum were irrelevant, vulgar, immoral, and in bad taste." The minority, more conservative members of the Court dissented with parts of the decision, since they were inclined to allow school officials more leeway in deciding on appropriate curricula. They felt that courts should not make local decisions that undermine the authority of school officials and should not second-guess parents who do not want their children exposed to certain ideas or language they consider obscene.

The minority began the devolution of the Court to the pre-Tinker era in another censorship case that was heard not too much later. This one, because sex and morality were directly involved, made it easier for the Court to support censorship.

Sex and the Supreme Court

During the 1982–83 school year, Cathy Kuhlmeier and two other students of Hazelwood East High School, St. Louis, Missouri, were staff members of *Spectrum,* the school newspaper. They contended that school officials violated their First Amendment rights by deleting two pages from the May 13, 1983, issue. Written and edited by the Journalism II class, *Spectrum* was published every three weeks or so during the school year and was distributed to students, school personnel, and members of the community. The Board of Education allocated funds for the publication, which were supplemented by sales income.

In a true exemplar of free speech, the faculty adviser to the newspaper, Howard Emerson, submitted page proofs to the principal, Robert Reynolds, for approval prior to publication. Reynolds objected to two articles: one describing three anonymous Hazelwood students' experiences with pregnancy, and the other discussing the impact of divorce on students at the school. These two pages also included articles on teenage pregnancy (in general), teenage marriage, runaways, and juvenile delinquents, to which the principal had no objections.

The Missouri District Court ruled that the students' rights had not been violated. The Court of Appeals reversed, holding that the newspaper was a "public forum," intended as a conduit for student viewpoints, and thus school officials could not censor its contents except when necessary to avoid "material and substantial" interference with schoolwork or discipline and that such a necessity did not exist in this situation.

The Supreme Court reversed the Court of Appeals. Incredibly, the opinion claimed that *Spectrum* was not a forum for public expression but a part of the curriculum of the journalism course. It was taught during school hours by a faculty member, the students received grades and academic credit, the faculty adviser exercised control over the publication, and the principal had to review it. The school's policies did not reflect an intent to expand the students' rights by converting a curricular newspaper into a public forum. That finding was a true blow by the Supreme Court to the whole concept of this book, which is that schools must model the process of democracy in order to teach the concepts.

Dissenting opinions from Justices Brennan, Marshall, and Blackmun stated that when the students registered for the journalism class they expected a civics lesson. They said that the "administrators violated the First Amendment rights of the student staff by deleting two pages of one edition merely because the administrators objected to the contents of two articles. . . . In addition, the principal went too far; he could have simply deleted the objectionable articles instead of the two pages in their entirety. There was no evidence that the readers would consider the articles an endorsement of the sexual norms of the students interviewed. Nor could the school officials justify the deletion on the basis that the articles were an invasion of privacy—since the students consented to the publication of their information, there was no potential tort liability." The dissenting Justices added that *Spectrum* is a public forum for the expression of student opinion, "students determined content and wrote the stories, it was distributed to the public as well as to the school population, there was a policy statement which defined it as a 'student newspaper,' and the school board policy supported the students' right to freedom of expression. In this case, the censorship served no legitimate pedagogical purpose." Way to go, dissenting Justices.

As shown, the emerging conservative majority of the Court has not been sympathetic to the First Amendment rights of students regarding sexuality, obscenity, or scatological humor. More recent cases show how the Court has undermined the spirit of the Tinker findings. For instance, the case of *Bethel School District* v. *Fraser* was easy for the Court, since the actions of the student could easily be found offensive by parents and students who are uncomfortable with sexual humor. You decide how bad the student's behavior was.

On April 26, 1983, Matthew Fraser, a high school student in Bethel, Washington, delivered a speech nominating a fellow student for a student elective office. Before the speech, Matthew discussed it with several teachers and two told him they thought it was not appropriate. The speech was made during school hours as a part of a school-sponsored educational program in self-government. About six hundred students, many of whom were fourteen-year-olds, attended the voluntary assembly. Throughout the speech, Matthew deliberately referred to his candidate in terms of elaborate sexual metaphors. For example:

> I know a man who is firm—he is firm in his pants, he is firm in his shirt, his character is firm—but most . . . of all, his belief in you, the students of Bethel, is firm. . . . Jeff Kuhlman is a man who takes his point and pounds it in. If necessary he will take an issue and nail it to the wall. He doesn't attack things in spurts—he drives hard, pushing and pushing until finally—he succeeds. Jeff is a man who will go to the very end—even the climax, for each and every one of you. So, vote for Jeff for ASP-Vice President—he'll never come between you and the best our high school can be.

The reactions of the students varied from enthusiastic hooting and yelling to embarrassment and bewilderment. But apparently Matthew's message was firmly inserted in their psyches. The culmination was that a solid majority voted for his candidate, who was thrust into vice presidency.

Matthew was suspended for three days for having violated the school's "disruptive conduct" rule, which prohibited conduct that substantially interfered with the educational process, including the use of obscene, profane language or gestures.

In *Bethel School District* v. *Fraser,* the Supreme Court said on July 7, 1986, that the school board acted entirely within its permissible authority in punishing Matthew for "his offensively lewd and indecent speech." Matthew's speech did not actually use obscene words, the assembly was voluntary, and the speech really did not interrupt the education of the students. In fact, the assembly was part of a school-sponsored program in self-government. So what did the students learn about how democracy works? They learned it does not work if you are a kid in school. This is a perfect example of how schools can poison the spirit of democracy.

We can not help but digress to point out the total hypocrisy that pervades this whole area of censorship, sexuality, and free speech. In the name of patriotism, conservatives have fought to censor school texts that refer to the sexual imbroglios or negative policy positions of past presidents. Yet what are schoolchildren to think when for almost an entire year the media are saturated with explicit discussions of the president's sexual behavior? We are referring to the investigation of President Clinton's affair with Monica Lewinsky and its impact on students. This event is momentous in the history of our country and the presidency. Yet the very people who want to censor sexual speech in the schoolhouse appeared to revel in the daily attack on the morality of a sitting president.

A year after a conservative Congress struggled to censor the Internet in order to protect children from pornography, it flooded the Internet with thousands of pages of sexually explicit testimony. The contradiction is that these very people created the climate in which many teachers did not allow their students to discuss and process this critical event in their lives. Many students have reported that their teachers in current events classes refused to talk about the situation because they considered it too undignified. While speech and class discussion are censored, one would expect that high school students involved in journalism would be taught the process of free speech. If you think so, you are wrong. Even teachers have been victims of the censorship juggernaut.

Censuring and Censoring Teachers

Students are not the only ones subject to censorship in schools. Take the case of Rochelle Cassie, an English teacher at Brick Township High School in New Jersey. In 1970, she was teaching one of the early courses on minorities in the literature. One of the school board members, who was also the manager of a local food store, was selling a pornographic Victorian novel entitled *The Pearl*. This confused manager assumed that this was the same book as *The Pearl* by John Steinbeck, which was taught in freshman English. This triggered a witch hunt to expunge any objectionable books from the high school curriculum.

The school board targeted Mrs. Cassie's reading list to remove award-winning books that included words they considered obscene (such as penis) and political rhetoric by minority writers who were anathema at the time.

This event attracted the attention of members of the state teachers' association, who invited Mrs. Cassie to participate in a panel on book censorship. In her presentation she quoted, without initially identifying the source, a political speech railing against students' rights to read materials that were not approved by authorities. She asked the audience to identify the source of the speech, which most attributed to Adolf Hitler. She then correctly identified the source as the vice president of the United States, Spiro Agnew. She went on to describe what had occurred in her school district.

Upon hearing about Mrs. Cassie's presentation and her description of it to her class, the school suspended her for daring to exercise her First Amendment rights to free speech. In an unprecedented action, the district's teachers called for a walkout, which effectively forced the school board to the bargaining table. After probably the only day in American education in which teachers struck on behalf of the First Amendment, Mrs. Cassie returned to her job. However, she agreed to write a letter to the board of education in which she stated that she "may have used poor judgment in reading her speech to her class."

We doubt that teachers in the 1990s would go on strike on behalf of a constitutional principle. This reflects a dangerous erosion of belief in the Bill of Rights as it applies to education. However, many teachers understand that allowing censorship based on material that is considered by some to be obscene or too explicitly sexual opens the door to other types of censorship. The following is another example of how teachers' behavior, often quite innocent, can land them in trouble.

In 1970 I was on a statewide committee of the New Jersey Education Association. We were planning to sponsor a panel on censorship in the schools, and one of the teachers, I will call her Mrs. Good, told us how she was censured and almost lost her job for her sexual behavior. What was this sweet, gentle kindergarten teacher's illicit behavior? Here is the story.

Mrs. Good was several months pregnant when she began the school year. As the baby grew, she described to the curious children what was happening in her womb. When the baby began to regularly move and kick, she recounted how she could feel it. Some of the curious five-year-olds asked if they could feel the baby. She allowed them to put their hands on her stomach to feel the baby's movements. Horrors! One of the students' parents was mightily offended by this unauthorized sex education. No teacher in the school had ever done that before.

Several other prudish parents who found out about this complained to the principal. Most parents of Mrs. Good's students defended her. Rather than deal with the media and a few angry puritans, Mrs. Good was convinced to take her maternity leave early. She said this incident scared many of her female colleagues. The message was that schools were not comfortable with the pregnant bodies of teachers, let alone discussion of pregnancy and wombs. Some may have put off their own pregnancies because of this. This is how censorship can be dangerous in schools.

Come on, you say, this incident occurred many years ago, why bring it up in the age of Title IX, which protects women from such harassment. There are many who still believe that Mrs. Good should not have been in that classroom while pregnant. After having the baby, she should not return to teaching, but should stay at home as an obedient homemaker and wife.

Using Sexual Censorship to Gain a Foothold in Schools

The modern censors have learned that attacks on books that are allegedly obscene are the levers that can pry open the schoolhouse door. At the school level, censorship of sexual topics is often followed by attacks on the teaching of such issues as evolution, women's rights, or any economic system that smacks of socialism. It isn't even necessary for would-be censors to work at the school or even the state level—if they can persuade one or two big textbook purchasers to go along, they can influence the whole country. For example, Texas and California order textbooks for statewide curricula. Since they order such large numbers of books, publishers are willing to censor certain material in order to induce these large purchases.

These adulterated, watered-down books become the standard for the rest of the country. It is too expensive to print two editions of a text when there are guaranteed sales for large numbers in two or three states. The best book on the topic is *What Johnny Shouldn't Read: Textbook Censorship in America* by Joan Delfattore. If you really want to learn about the toxin of censorship, read Delfattore's fascinating book. She begins her book with a quote from Thomas Jefferson: "Is uniformity attainable? Millions of innocent men, women and children, since the introduction of Christianity, have been burnt, tortured, fined, imprisoned; yet we have not advanced one inch towards uniformity. What has been the effect of coercion? To make one half of the world fools and the other half hypocrites."

In her book, Delfattore gives examples of how conservatives have eliminated major sections of text from many of the classics. Using censorship of sex as their entry, right-wing censors have managed to expunge or water down facts and interpretations of historical events such as slavery, the New Deal, and the advent and impact of Marxism. Let me share with you a personal example.

In the late 1950s I was teaching fifth grade. The text series I was using had a chapter on the Civil War and I slavishly clung to the prescribed material. The text, the teacher's manual, and suggested test questions all stressed that the war was fought over states' rights. Slavery was of course mentioned, but there was no emphasis on the social, economic, political, and moral impact of this institution on the South and as a factor in the war. So that is what my students learned about the Civil War.

Like many elementary school teachers of that era, I was ignorant about history and depended on the textbooks to tell me the truth. It wasn't until I did some reading on my own that I began to believe that the text must have been edited by some high functionary of the Ku Klux Klan. This type of censorship is still happening today, but it is so subtle and sophisticated that many teachers and students do not know it.

In all fairness to conservatives, Delfattore attacks textbook censorship from both the far left and the far right. Politically correct extremists on the left, "like their fundamentalist counterparts, operate on the assumption that education has two functions: to describe what should be rather than what is, and to reverse the injustices of yesterday's society by shaping the attitudes of tomorrow's." For instance, these extremists want textbooks to portray women only as having careers, whereas right-wing extremists want women portrayed only as homemakers.

Do we really want teachers who dare to teach about sex-role identity and the biological, medical, and social realities of sex and science to be subjected to a twentieth-century version of the Salem Witch Trials? We think not, but we are also concerned about the contradictions of our attitudes toward sex that are played out in schools.

Beyond Sexual Censorship

Censorship can easily be expanded from concerns about obscenity and sex to a host of locally unpopular ideas, expressions, and beliefs. Take for instance the "Coke" war in an Evans, Georgia, high school.

Mike Cameron, a high school senior, was suspended for wearing a Pepsi T-shirt on "Coke (Coca Cola) Day." The school "thought police" caught him revealing that underneath his shirt he was wearing a T-shirt bearing a Pepsi logo. This prank was done during the taking of a picture in which the student body was spelling out "Coke." The principal considered this to be disruptive and rude because it insulted visiting Coke executives. This example of censorship illustrates the insidious influence of businesses and other powerful groups that can reach through the schoolhouse gate.

However, victims of censorship may even offend people less powerful than corporate executives, as is illustrated in the infamous "Chihuahua Case." In the fall of 1997, thirteen-year-old Aaron Smith of McKinley, Texas, created a Web page on his home computer, which he used to express his unique sense of humor. The Web site was the alleged home for "Chihuahua Haters of the World" (CHOW). He reported, "Today in the California region, a seven foot boa constrictor was caught devouring a Chihuahua. I have repeatedly called the snake's home to tell him what a great job our operatives are doing out there, but he won't answer the phone."

Aaron's crime was that he mentioned the name of his school on the Web site. A Chihuahua breeder, apparently unaware of the intended humor, complained to the school principal—who suspended Aaron, removed him from his computer class, demanded that he disband CHOW and its Web page and make an online apology to all Chihuahua lovers. The ACLU defended Aaron, who was allowed back into his computer class.

While the "Chihuahua Case" probably raises a chuckle, you may not find examples of First Amendment violations of religious freedom amusing. We have heard of more than a few examples of the establishment of particular church values, prayer, and ideology in public schools, especially in the Bible Belt.

Church and State in Alabama

Pike County, Alabama, schools may teach the content of the Constitution, but some would be hard-pressed to distinguish their pedagogy from the schools of a theocracy. In 1998, the three children of Sue and Wayne Willis, grades five through eight, were the only Jews in the county schools. In a clear violation of the First Amendment clause forbidding the establishment of religion, the schools are alleged to have promoted their version of Christianity.

On behalf of the Willis children, the ACLU filed suit in the U.S. District Court contending that the children were victims of religious bigotry, verbal assaults, and anti-Semitic hate crimes. The children allege that they were forced by teachers to bow their heads during Christian prayers (we thought school prayer was against the law) and required by a vice principal to write an essay titled, "Why Jesus Loves Me." They were forced to watch events like a play titled "The Birth of Jesus" and to attend "Happy Birthday Jesus" parties. One of the children sought help from a teacher when a Gideon Bible representative (what was he doing in an American public school classroom?) tried to force her to take a bible and hold a cross in front of her face.

The children were not allowed to wear Star of David lapel pins while their classmates wore crosses, nor were they allowed to wear skullcaps, which were ripped from their heads by classmates. Further, the children reported physical assaults by classmates and swastikas drawn on their lockers.

In response to complaints to all levels of the system over several years, Superintendent of Schools John Key is alleged to have suggested what he must have considered a reasonable solution—convert to Christianity! Excuse us, is this America or are we living during the Spanish Inquisition? Does this case exemplify the traditional values that our schools should teach, or is it an aberration from the Dark Ages?

Sexual Harassment in Schools

Students represent a wide range of physical, emotional, and developmental stages. Therefore, factors that constitute sexual harassment may be quite subtle and clearly different from those that define the problem for adults in the workplace and other settings. Let us give you some examples.

At least once in the course of a career, almost every teacher catches a student passing a sexually explicit note, picture, or limerick to a classmate. Consider the following case from our research on worst school experiences:

> When I was eleven years old and in the fifth grade, I liked a particular girl. I passed her a love note which was taken by the teacher. She read the note in front of the entire class. I was very embarrassed. As I result, I withdrew, started to stutter, felt like I had to watch everybody, wanted to fight all the time, and had nightmares.

This innocuous behavior by an eleven-year-old boy did not deserve public humiliation. Another example of the censoring and censuring of innocent sexual behavior is reported by a college student who recalls an experience when he was fourteen:

> In eighth grade a girl and I were playing "footsie" under a desk during a film. The teacher stopped the film, turned on the lights and yelled at both of us. He asked if I was the one who started the behavior. I was so embarrassed I couldn't even speak. For a while I was very nervous, thought I was not as good of a kid as I used to be, felt like I had to watch everybody and thought about what happened even though I didn't want to. I felt that I had done something evil, so I didn't talk about it and tried to stay away from the teacher.

These two examples were just innocent expressions of normal adolescent feelings. Many educators are quick to mete out punishment for such behavior, without bothering to study or understand normal expressions of sexuality in adolescence. Unfortunately, because of the moralistic marauders of the right, we do not have a lot of information on this topic. For example, Senator Jesse Helms, chief of the sex police in America, led a successful attempt to quash a proposal for a major national study of teenage sexual activity. Like the Kinsey Report of the 1950s, the results were meant to provide a clear picture of adolescent sexual activity and offer guidelines that would provide us with policies to prevent the spread of sexually transmitted diseases.

One of the great paradoxes of American education, and some would say an ultimate expression of the hypocrisy inherent in our attitudes about sex and schools, has been our historical indifference to sexual abuse and sexual harassment of students. For instance, ask any high school teacher in America to be honest with you. If they are, they will most likely admit that they know or have known of at least one case in their school where a teacher or a coach had an affair with a student. They will also admit that, despite suspicion or common knowledge about the affair, staff and administrators closed ranks and looked the other way. Frequently, when the victims told their friends, who then told teachers, little was done. It generally takes the involvement of a furious parent to stir the waters.

When seduction of students becomes known to the public, schools finally act. The media jumps on these cases and has a field day. Depictions of famous cases have been made into movies that are well known to the public. But do we really care? You may be surprised by the extent of unwanted sexual activity that occurs in schools.

Defining Sexual Harassment

The seduction of students by school staff falls into the larger rubric of sexual harassment. Sexual harassment in the educational environment is any unwanted sexual attention from peers, administrators, teachers, or other school staff. The range of behaviors includes leering, pinching, grabbing, suggestive verbal comments, pressure for sexual activity, spreading sexual rumors, making sexual or sexist jokes, pulling at another student's clothing, cornering or brushing up against a student in a sexual way, using epithets referring to students' sexual orientation, date rape, writing sexual graffiti about a student, or engaging in any other actions of a sexual manner that might create a hostile learning environment. The seduction of students by staff is sexual harassment because of the power differential between the educator and the student.

In 1993, the American Association of University Women (AAUW) conducted a study that demonstrated how widespread sexual harassment is in public schools. Student-to-student harassment was the most common, accounting for 80 percent of the reported total, while teachers, custodians, and coaches were responsible for 20 percent.

The AAUW study indicated that boys and girls were almost equally harassed. The following is a summary of the seven categories of harassment with the percentage of girls and boys who responded that they had been targets:

- Received unwanted sexual comments, jokes, gestures, or looks (76 percent of the girls, 56 percent of the boys)
- Were touched, grabbed, or pinched in a sexual way (65 percent of the girls, 42 percent of the boys)
- Were intentionally brushed up against in a sexual way (57 percent of the girls, 36 percent of the boys)
- Had sexual rumors spread about them (42 percent of the girls, 34 percent of the boys)
- Had clothing pulled in a sexual way (38 percent of the girls, 28 percent of the boys)
- Were shown, given, or left sexual material (31 percent of the girls, 34 percent of the boys)
- Had sexual messages written about them in public areas (20 percent of the girls, 18 percent of the boys)

The study indicated that girls reported more symptoms as a result of sexual harassment than did boys. The symptoms included difficulties in the following areas: going to school, talking in class, paying attention, and studying. Some students reported lower grades on tests and in classes and thoughts of changing schools. These are the exact same symptoms we have found in our research on worst school experiences, suggesting that large numbers of children in American schools suffer some traumatic symptoms as a result of sexual harassment. What percentage actually develop PTSD, we do not know.

Even though student-to-student harassment is the most common as reported in the AAUW study, others have found that at least 30 percent of students reported having been harassed by teachers. One study suggested that American schoolchildren consider sexual aggression to be an expected part of school life. In this study of 1,700 sixth graders, 65 percent of the boys and 47 percent of the girls agreed with statements indicating that it was acceptable for a man to force a woman to have sex after they had been dating for six months.

The poisonous sexual climate created by schools was widely publicized in the 1993 media accounts of California's "Spur Posse." An elite clique, with many top high school athletes, had created a "Spur Posse" (named after the San Antonio basketball team) in Lakewood High School in California. The teenage boys in this case, referred to as the "Rapewood" incident, competed by attempting to have sex with as many girls as possible. They sometimes took turns having sex with the same girls, whom some referred to as "sluts." In one case, an eleven-year-old girl who was sleeping over at a girlfriend's house was ordered by a member of the posse to submit. She had sex with him because of rumors that the "Spurs" would hurt unwilling participants.

The poison of male chauvinism in schools is well illustrated in the story of the Spur Posse, but it is not unique. Adhering to the old double standard, many boys get subtle and sometimes overt approval from fathers, male coaches, and peers that "sowing their wild oats" is a perfectly normal, macho behavior. Boys may interpret this as approval for behaviors ranging from unwanted touching to date rapes and gang bangs. In much of rural America, where high school sports become the focal point for whole communities, athletes' sexual behaviors are indulged and even admired. Sexual harassment is too often considered a trivial matter, explained away by the belief that "boys will be boys." This kind of thinking is frequently institutionalized when coaches with this orientation, despite limited intelligence or academic ability, are promoted to principalships and superintendencies.

Should Students Have the Same Protections from Sexual Harassment as Adults?

The kind of cultural attitude that encourages trivialization of certain types of sexual harassment in schools but not in business is well illustrated in three 1998 opinions by the Supreme Court. In *Gebser* v. *Lago Vista Independent School District,* the Court ruled that school districts can not be held responsible whenever a teacher sexually harasses a student. Their reasoning was that when students are sexually harassed or seduced, they must report the event to a school authority. Then, if the school does not take appropriate action, it can be held liable. This ruling places much of the responsibility on students since the school is not mandated to prevent sexual harassment through training, education, and other measures. This opinion, like those concerning search and seizure, fails to encourage school authorities to actively recognize the rights of children. The Court apparently ignored the research showing that students are almost invariably damaged by sexual misconduct by educators. This is again an example of denying constitutional rights to citizens because they are in school.

By contrast, consider two opinions rendered by the Supreme Court in 1998 regarding the responsibilities of businesses to prevent sexual harassment. In these milestone cases—*Faragher* v. *City of Boca Raton* and *Burlington Industries* v. *Ellerth*—the Court ruled that businesses are responsible for any sexual conduct of supervisors, even if they did not know anything about it. Here the restraint on unlimited suit is that claims by employees can only be made if the abuse results in tangible job injury to the victim, such as firing, demotion, or transfer to an undesirable job.

In the cases involving employers, the Court ruled that if the employee does not suffer harmful job consequences then the employer can escape liability by instituting effective policies and prevention and can show that the complaining employee failed to use them. In other words, it is incumbent on the corporation to have an active program of training, prevention, and employee assistance to deal with any type of sexual harassment, whereas there is no such judicially mandated pressure on school boards. These cases say it all.

However, the Supreme Court has the opportunity to redeem itself. In January 1999, the Court heard the case of *Davis* v. *Monroe County Board of Education*. The opinion will probably be rendered after this book is published. However, despite the outcome, this case should be considered here.

In 1992, ten-year-old LaShonda Davis, a Georgia elementary school student, alleged that a male classmate repeatedly fondled her, simulated sex, and made sexually suggestive comments in a threatening manner over a six-month period. Despite multiple complaints by her mother, the school failed to promptly address the problem. The boy's behavior ceased after he was charged with sexual battery, pleaded guilty, and moved out of the state. As a result of the experience, LaShonda suffered emotional trauma illustrated by lowered grades and a suicide note.

This case will result in the first Supreme Court ruling regarding the responsibility of school officials to protect students from sexual harassment by their peers. Of course, no one can predict the Court's opinion. However, based on their previous record, we would guess that the Court will agree with the National School Board Association. Their brief supports the well established notion by conservatives that the courts should not become involved in school disciplinary decisions. Therefore, they propose that the Court rule against LaShonda Davis since schools should not be liable for sexual harassment by peers. We hope that the Court will consider the kinds of data we present here and therefore hold schools responsible for teaching about and protecting from sexual harassment by peers.

Sexual harassment is dangerous and toxic to students because it creates a hostile learning environment in which they may become fearful, anxious, withdrawn, and angry, and suffer severe loss of self-esteem. It causes a disciplinary and morale problem because students lose faith in school authorities' ability to protect them. This results in situations where victims often blame themselves or excuse the behavior of the perpetrators, as exemplified in the case of Lauren.

Lauren was a beautiful fifteen-year-old girl. Looking at her, one would never guess she had poor self-esteem, suicidal ideation, depression, and drug problems. One day her therapy group was discussing how they felt when male students and teachers "groped" them. Lauren described how Jim, a big jock, always patted her behind and asked, "When am I going to get a piece of this?" as they left English class. She stated, "Teachers and other students can do things like that and students don't want to say anything. If I complain to my classmates they will think that I'm full of myself. If I tell a teacher, they will just make some excuse for Jim. If Jim finds out I told on him, he would tell everybody that I am a prude and a dork and he and his friends would diss me. There's no point. Even though it upsets me sometimes, nobody will do anything about it anyway."

Lauren illustrates the point that a hostile school setting can discourage girls from fully participating in their own education. They learn to devalue themselves and their academic potential. Further, boys often receive mixed messages about sexual harassment.

Now we do not want to imply that schools around the country are not taking sexual harassment seriously. Title IX, the law that defines sexual harassment in all settings, has been used as a basis for guidelines in many school districts. This is good, right? Well, it probably is, but remember now we are setting up a new set of dos and don'ts with concomitant punishments for the don'ts. And—as might be expected in the land of punishment—we can count on school authorities to go too far. Let us illustrate by two cases.

In 1996, six-year-old Jonathan Prevette, a student in Lexington, North Carolina, innocently kissed the cheek of one of his classmates. This crime suddenly transformed him from an innocent unknown to an "infamous" primary school pervert. He felt the full wrath of the school authorities, who summarily suspended him from school and humiliated him for his act of affection. Jane Martin, a school district spokesperson, on being questioned about the incident, said, "An unwanted kiss is offensive at any age." Well said, oh guardian of the morals of schoolchildren in North Carolina.

Ten days after the Prevette fiasco, second grader De'Andre Dearinge, a seven-year-old at P.S. 104 in Far Rockaway, Queens, was suspended for five days for kissing a classmate and pulling a button off her skirt. He "confessed" to his mother that he kissed the girl because he liked her and he had taken the button because his favorite book was about a teddy bear with a missing button. In this case, the school district's superintendent, Kenneth Grover, rescinded the suspension after one day and admitted that accusing a seven-year-old of sexual harassment was perhaps inappropriate.

In neither of these cases were the sex police able to use "judgment and common sense" and take account of the student's age and maturity in determining if the perpetrator had committed an act of sexual harassment. Guidelines, published in 1997 by the Department of Education's Office of Civil Rights, explain how to deal with sexual harassment. These were the same guidelines that were undermined by the Supreme Court in the *Gebser* v. *Lago Vista* decision.

In dealing with issues of discipline, morality, sexuality, and censorship, it seems clear that the current Supreme Court is intent on undoing the few constitutional rights that were recognized for students in the 1970s. This Court is attempting to increase the power of school officials at the same time as legislatures continue to take away decision making of school administrators by mandating fixed penalties for misbehavior, such as automatic suspensions and expulsions for certain crimes. What is most troubling is how the influence of conservatives has increased school authorities' prerogatives to shape, through censorship and teaching of "approved" values, how students should live their lives. This can be very dangerous for those with sexual orientations not approved by local communities.

Harassment Based on Sexual Identity

During the late 1990s, the theo-conservatives have increasingly attacked homosexuals and their lifestyles. This attack, which has been carried to the schools, is based on religious conviction that homosexuality is a sickness that is anti-Christian, against most orthodox religious beliefs, and a menace to the stability of families and society. Unfortunately, such moral jihads invariably end in the type of violence many call gay bashing. Among the many examples was the brutal, fatal beating of University of Wyoming student Matthew Shepard in 1998, which received national attention.

Problems of gender identity are not mentioned in our founding documents. We assume that the assurance in the Declaration of Independence that all men are entitled to the pursuit of happiness should apply to all people, regardless of sexual orientation. Yet it is hard to be happy and homosexual in many contemporary American schools. Educators and mental health professionals recognize the many emotional difficulties of youth who suspect or believe that they are homosexuals. A study conducted in 1995 by the Massachusetts Department of Education revealed that gay males and lesbians were five times more likely than straight students to skip school out of fear for their safety. More alarming was the finding that 36.5 percent try to kill themselves each year. This makes them over three times more likely to attempt suicide than all adolescents combined.

Schools have a particular role in protecting the rights of gay and lesbian students and must be sensitive to their needs and provide mental health services when necessary. The First Amendment right to assembly and free speech should also apply to the rights of homosexuals to meet and discuss issues of mutual concern. This right should not stop at the schoolhouse gate, even in conservative states such as Utah. But it does—as illustrated in the case of the Gay/Straight Student Alliance of East High School in Salt Lake City School District.

In 1995, several students from East High School asked the school for permission to form a gay/straight alliance. The school board was against the idea but knew that it was illegal to ban only one extracurricular organization. They therefore banned all non-curricular clubs and within weeks state lawmakers passed a bill outlawing school clubs that promote illegal activity or sexual activity of any kind. Banned clubs were told they would have to meet after school, rent the space, and purchase a large insurance policy. These burdens were in addition to not being able to post notices of meetings, meet at lunch, or be included in the school's yearbook.

Publicity about this case resulted in an outpouring of anti-gay rhetoric and support for the school board from powerful policymakers, politicians, religious leaders, and conservative action groups. At one point the Utah legislature discussed giving up all federal aid to schools in the belief that this action would allow them to bar the Alliance. The Mormon Church reportedly is so strongly against homosexuals that its influence is credited by many for a state censorship law. This law forbids teachers from saying anything in the classroom that would imply acceptance or advocacy of homosexuality.

Two of the Gay/Straight Alliance students enlisted the aid of the ACLU and several gay advocacy groups and sued the school. James and Keysha Barns, father and daughter plaintiffs, brought complaint in federal court to assure the civil liberties of everyone, regardless of sexual orientation. As we write, the case is not yet settled, but the whole situation offers a tragic footnote.

In September 1997, seventeen-year-old Jacob Orosco, the president-elect of the Alliance, killed himself. During the preceding year he was heavily involved in establishing his identity and self-esteem and working for the Alliance. Before his suicide he was struggling with the task of finding $400 to pay for the insurance policy demanded by the school board as a condition for permitting the Alliance to be part of the school.

The problem of the harassment of gay and lesbian students has not yet been resolved by the courts. However, the ruling in May

1998 in *Nabozny* v. *Podlesny* by a panel of the U.S. Court of Appeals, Seventh Circuit, may set precedent. In this case, Jamie Nabozny alleges that during his four years in middle and high school in Ashland, Wisconsin, he was taunted, beaten, and subjected to a mock rape by classmates. Repeated appeals to school administrators for help and protection by Jamie and his parents fell on deaf ears. They were told that Jamie must learn to expect such treatment because he is gay. These assurances did not help much when he was beaten so badly by a group of ten students that he required surgery. As a result of all this, he attempted suicide several times and even ran away from home to escape the school abuse.

The court ruled that Nabozny could pursue his gender and sexual orientation claims under the equal protection clause of the Constitution. As we write this book, other similar suits are wending their way through the courts. It will be interesting to see how the Supreme Court deals with the constitutional protections of gay and lesbian students in schools. In this case, denial of relief clearly is associated with physical and verbal assaults by educators and peers and the creation of such a hostile atmosphere that murders and suicides result. How much more damaging and toxic can schools become?

• • •

In summary, toxicity in schools is not always the result of outright acts involving police tactics or overtly obvious punitive school policies. An agenda of censorship in the schools, which undermines students' faith in the First Amendment, often begins with an attack on alleged obscenity and sexually oriented materials. These attacks have set the schools at or over the edge of the slippery slope of censorship across all areas. This agenda is forwarded through various types of political activities from both political extremes. The dangers inherent in these attacks are not generally recognized by the public or our Supreme Court. They are not sufficiently acknowledged as toxic to the minds and spirits of students in a democracy. They represent a type of insidious psychological and antidemocratic maltreatment that threatens the very liberties we want future generations to preserve.

Chapter 6

Toxic Punishments, Laws, and Litigation

Toxic school discipline practices such as paddling, psychological maltreatment, and wide-scale urine screening reflect regional and national beliefs and assumptions about school misbehavior. But there are other punishments such as suspensions, retentions, and lowering of grades because of misbehavior that take unique forms based on local school norms. The legality and effectiveness of many of these practices have been challenged since they fit within the broader pedagogical and constitutional frameworks of the other toxic disciplinary practices we have discussed.

Challenges to these practices may be made in the courts if a student is clearly denied procedures and programs spelled out in current law. It is possible to claim denial of constitutional rights or to file tort claims.

Disciplinary Practices That Deny Services Mandated by Law

The 1997 Individuals with Disabilities Education Act (IDEA) provides a good example of procedures and programs spelled out in current law that provide for sound disciplinary planning. Certain provisions of this law are meant to protect students with disabilities from toxic punishments. Under IDEA, children with suspected disabilities must be evaluated by schools and provided adequate remedial services. Students who are classified as having emotional, intellectual, neurological, or physical disabilities may not be inappropriately punished for misbehavior related to their disability.

Since the law already exists to protect children with disabilities, one would assume that school authorities would eagerly comply. Wrong. We can't tell you how many districts disobey the law and—without the expert advice of school psychologists and other specialists—simply decide what services they should provide to children with disabilities. Aggressive children are often the most frequent victims of illegal, toxic punishments by schools that ignore the requirements of IDEA.

For instance, physically abused children who are classified as emotionally disturbed as a result of the abuse are often aggressive in school. It is clear that they learned to be aggressive as part of the abuse they endured. Therefore, it would not make sense to paddle them or suspend them for expressing their anger and frustration through verbal or physical aggression. This does not mean that these behaviors are approved or should be accepted, but that punishment is unlikely to change that behavior.

Schools are required to develop an individual educational plan (IEP) for each classified student and these plans must spell out proper remediation programs. For abused students and other classified students, these plans must focus on positive and effective remediation and treatment techniques. While appropriate punishments for aggressive behavior should be included in IEPs, the major goal is to teach acceptable methods of dealing with anger and frustration.

The provision of appropriate services under IDEA is time-consuming, expensive, and difficult. In too many situations parents are just not informed of their rights or children do not receive the services spelled out in the IEP. As a result, schools too often succumb to the lure of punishments such as suspensions, expulsions, or excessively long and frequent time outs. The major solution for students who are victimized in these cases is for their parents to know their rights under IDEA. Also, if you have such a problem, you may turn to the growing numbers of citizens who advocate for parents in these situations. These advocates, some of whom may have been victimized by schools themselves, may be professionals, interested laypeople, or parents who understand how the system works.

Torts Versus Constitutional Claims

Tort law involves cases in which some kind of injury has occurred. The injury can be physical or emotional and has to last an appreciable amount of time. You can sue for *compensatory damages,* which means that you expect to recover any monies lost as a result of the injury. This includes medical expenses, costs for psychotherapy, and even tutors or private school costs incurred to continue the education of a child who is recovering from the maltreatment and unable or unwilling to return to the school where the abuse occurred. You can also sue for *punitive damages.* The purpose here is to punish the claimants for acting inappropriately, in a negligent manner, or with reckless disregard for the health and safety of the victims.

If you can demonstrate that the maltreatment was committed with malice, the act may rise from a tort action to the level of a criminal offense. *Malice* is defined in law as an intent to cause harm, knowing that there is a strong likelihood that some harm will result from the act.

Another purpose of punitive damages in all the cases with which we are familiar is to make the schools pay for their horrific treatment of the victims. The plaintiffs invariably want to protect other children from being damaged. Therefore, a purpose of punitive damages is to force the district to stop the toxic discipline.

In the case of physical and emotional abuse of students, tort claims will not be successful unless you can demonstrate long-term physical or emotional harm to the child. Normally paddling on the buttocks results in bruises that last no longer than two or three weeks, so it is important to document the long-term emotional damage caused by the assault. We will tell you how to do this in the next chapter. Of course, in the cases where broken bones and internal injuries have occurred, parents have had stronger claims.

Are Severe Punishments in Schools Cruel and Unusual?

Constitutional claims against schools are very difficult to establish in cases of physical and emotional maltreatment. Winning cases usually involve issues such as racial or gender bias. Claims against individual liberties are much less successful, but can be won. Unfortunately, many jurists—including the current majority of our Supreme Court—do not consider students to be citizens protected by the usual civil liberties afforded adults. They are reluctant to interfere with the power of schools to discipline students. You should at least have a basic understanding of the major constitutional cases that have shaped judicial opinions regarding both corporal punishment and psychological maltreatment.

On October 6, 1970, in Dade County, Florida, James Ingraham was a fourteen-year-old eighth grader in Drew Junior High School. James and other students were requested by a teacher to leave the stage of the school auditorium. They moved too slowly. The school principal, Willie Wright Jr., took James and the other students to his office to be paddled. James protested that he had not disobeyed the teacher and did not deserve a paddling. Because of his resistance, Wright called in Lemmi Deliford, the assistant principal, and Solomon Barnes, an assistant to the principal.

James Ingraham alleged that he was severely paddled more than twenty times. He went home despite threats from the principal that he would bust him on the side of the head if he left the school. His mother took him to the hospital where hematomas were observed. He was prescribed ice packs, painkillers, a laxative, and a sedative to help him sleep.

The blows were not considered assault and battery. At the time, it is doubtful that any prosecutor in Florida would have pressed charges. The administrators maintained that the paddlings were a protected disciplinary procedure under Florida law. The students claimed that the beatings were cruel and unusual and did not allow proper due process under the Constitution. Other students at Drew Junior High who had also been severely beaten (one coughed up blood after several beatings) banded together with a suit that eventually reached the Supreme Court.

On April 17, 1977, the Supreme Court denied the students constitutional protection under the cruel and unusual punishment clause of the Eighth Amendment and the procedural due process clause of the Fourteenth Amendment. Since then, this particular ruling has invariably been invoked by defendant educators who have beaten, punched, kicked, and bruised students. Ironically, in every other setting but the schoolhouse, damage similar to that inflicted by Willie Wright would require prosecution by the state.

The Supreme Court decision was based on a number of erroneous assumptions that are embedded in popular folklore and have no basis in fact. For instance, Justice Powell, who wrote the majority decision, implied that mistreatment of students was an "aberration." He assumed that the mistaken use of paddling was minimal and that corporal punishment is necessary to maintain discipline. He stated that there was no discernible trend toward the elimination of corporal punishment and that elimination of corporal punishment would have a negative effect on the "decorum" of the learning environment in the school. Social science research shows that none of these assumptions are true. Further, one particular legal assumption defies logic and reflects the lengths to which courts are willing to go to avoid becoming entangled in school disciplinary procedures.

The majority of the Supreme Court stated that the cruel and unusual punishment clause of the Eighth Amendment does not apply to schoolchildren since it is intended to protect criminals. So, based on the Court's decision, a child must go to jail to be protected from a beating. For instance, assume that two fifteen-year-old brothers, call them Don and Ron, are caught in a delinquent act. Don is classified as emotionally disturbed and is placed in a special education class in the public school. Ron is considered a delinquent and sentenced to incarceration. Does it make sense that Don can legally be beaten by his teacher whereas Ron is theoretically protected from his jailers? If this bothers you, you should know that despite the severe beating, the Court refused to rule on whether it violated Ingraham's right to due process. Since due process is integral to all types of school discipline cases, let us briefly consider some legal precedents in this area.

Due Process

The Fourteenth Amendment guarantees due process to all citizens. There are two types of due process that have been defined by the courts. *Procedural due process* assures citizens of such rights as proper notice and the right to be heard. *Substantive due process* means that the state can not arbitrarily deprive you of rights such as life, liberty, or property. There must be a reason for the government action and the basis of this action can not be arbitrary or capricious. The Fourteenth Amendment protects citizens against unwarranted state interventions (which includes state laws as well as school personnel's actions), while the Fifth Amendment, based on federal law, protects citizens against federal government officials.

Guarantees of substantive due process safeguard citizens against the deprivation of personal liberty, which in the case of corporal punishment should prevent educators from invading the physical integrity of students. There should be a reasonable relationship between the nature of the crime and the societal purpose and extent of the punishment. The Supreme Court, however, has allowed contradictory federal circuit court decisions regarding substantive due process to stand in the cases of *Cunningham* v. *Beavers* and *Garcia* v. *Miera.*

On May 6, 1987, Principal Mary Sue Bruno observed the horrific misbehavior of five-year-old Crystal Cunningham and six-year-old Ashley Johnson. These two miscreants dared to snicker in the hall, a crime deserving two swats with a wooden paddle on each of their behinds delivered by Principal Bruno. These recidivists were again paddled by their teacher, Rosa Cook, when they repeated the snickering sin. Realizing the enormity of these repeated crimes, Ms. Cook gave each an additional three swats across their buttocks.

Needless to say, neither child wanted to return to school, especially after an examining physician and child abuse workers determined that abuse had occurred. Despite these events, Harry Beavers, superintendent of schools, decided that abuse had not taken place and therefore there was no reason to discipline the punitive paddlers. When the case was heard by the Texas Court of Appeals for the Fifth Circuit, the plaintiffs got a good taste of Lone Star justice. The court denied the appeal, reasoning that state law allows corporal punishment up to the point "of deadly force."

When the Supreme Court refused to review *Cunningham* v. *Beavers,* it sent a definite message to educators in a pretty violent state. Texas has consistently ranked as one of the higher states in number of homicides (sixteenth in 1996), and in the last civil rights data it made the number one spot in number of school corporal punishments and number six in proportion of students hit. In that atmosphere, what is "deadly force"? Does that mean teachers can whip students senseless as long as it does not kill them?

The Tenth Circuit Court of Appeals in New Mexico viewed severe spankings differently than the neighboring Southwesterners did. On February 10, 1982, nine-year-old Teresa Garcia was paddled by Principal Theresa Miera for hitting a boy who had kicked her. Since Teresa would not willingly bend over for the paddling, teacher J. D. Sanchez was called for assistance. Sanchez held Teresa upside down by her ankles while Ms. Miera struck her so hard that the paddle was split into two pieces as a result of five whacks on the front of the legs between the knees and the waist. The beating left a two-inch cut on her leg, which made a permanent scar.

Three months later Teresa was accused of tattling that she saw a school staff member kiss a parent on a school bus during a field trip. Teresa was punished by two paddlings on the buttocks. When she refused to be hit again, Ms. Miera enlisted another accomplice, Edward Lebya. Mr. Lebya, in a wrestling match with Teresa, attempted to bend her over a chair so she could get three more licks. During the struggle, Teresa injured her back.

Finally the adults triumphed and swatted Teresa three more times with such force that her buttocks were bright red. Needless to say, professionals other than those in the schools considered the damage to be child abuse. The court in considering this case said that "at some point, excessive corporal punishment violates the pupil's substantive due process rights." Unlike the Texas jurists, this court said that "when a school official's conduct is shocking to the conscience, brutal, or offensive to human dignity, it offends the due process clause."

In summary, if a child is brutally corporally punished it is difficult to obtain constitutional relief. Even though the Supreme Court left open the definition of unacceptable injuries as defined by substantive due process, we are somewhat pessimistic that the current conservative-leaning Court is likely to be protective of schoolchildren's rights.

Popular School Punishments and Discipline Strategies That Rarely Work

Promoters of punishment are well acquainted with what makes it work. It is well known that a combination of increasing psychological and physical pain can make almost anyone do almost anything. The rule for effective use of punishment is that the more you increase the discomfort and pain, the more likely the misbehavior will stop in the short term. However, the more severe the punishment, the more serious the eventual consequences for the punishee, the punisher, and others who get in the way.

For instance, long-term incarceration keeps felons from repeating offenses while they are in jail. But most of us know that the longer the punishment the more likely that the offenders will do it again when they are free. These same principles apply to the punishment of students.

We admit that in general, progressively more severe punishments are increasingly more effective in immediately stopping misbehavior. For example, increased frequency and duration of school suspensions will tend to limit the student's time in school and therefore reduce the student's opportunity to misbehave in school. Yet the long-term consequences of denying a student an education for most of the school year are obvious. But schools continue to depend heavily on such punishments. Let us examine suspensions and other counterproductive punishments.

Suspensions and Expulsions

As we mentioned before, behavioral scientists define punishment as a procedure for reducing misbehavior. It includes giving students a consequence for misbehavior such as engaging in a task they do not like or staying out of a favored activity. Nonphysical punishments in schools include time out from positive situations, suspensions, detentions, and requirements to complete service to the school or community. Of all these, probably the most popular attempted punishment—and the one that is most frequently not technically a punishment at all—is suspension. Why isn't it a punishment? Let us take the example of Steve, a fifteen-year-old who was in group therapy. Steve was not particularly fond of school, and he hated his science teacher.

On a beautiful Friday in the spring, Steve decided to cut the last period of school when he had science class so he could go to the beach with some buddies. When he returned Monday, he was given in-school suspension. He walked out on that and when he returned the next day he was suspended for one week. When he returned, he confronted his science teacher, who gave him an "F" for a test that was given while Steve was on suspension. An argument ensued during which he called his teacher an asshole. Guess what—automatic suspension of three more days for obscene language. Needless to say, Steve's parents, both of whom worked, were not overjoyed by the news that he would again be home unsupervised.

When we discussed this in group, Steve's response was, "Hell, I hate school anyway. If those fools don't want me in their school, I don't care. I have plenty of better things to do with my life than sucking up to a bunch of teachers." By definition, suspension was not a punishment for Steve.

Students like Steve enjoy suspension because it gets them out of classes they find to be more punishing than the conditions of suspension. Even when their parents hassle them and administer additional punishment at home, it does not matter. It is patently absurd to use suspension as a punishment for truancy or class cutting, as it simply forces such children to do what they want to do anyway. It is far better to give kids like this weekend detentions. They really hate that.

You should know that federal laws limit the maximum period of suspension for all but extreme misbehaviors to ten school days. Also, your kid has the right to an informal hearing, with you present, if suspension is mandated by the school. You have a right to know why the suspension is given and to question the events surrounding the misbehavior. If the suspension is for more than ten days, in most states you have the right to a formal hearing with your attorney present. We know of many cases where the schools have gotten around this by giving repeated one-week suspensions. When the student returns to school, teachers know what buttons to push to encourage the student's existing propensity to misbehave. The button is pushed, the student loses it and is sent home for another week. I once worked with an eleven-year-old who had been suspended over fifty times the previous year.

In-school suspension (ISS) is an improvement over out-of-school suspensions. However, when used frequently with a student, it is ineffective. Here is a situation where we support an obnoxious punishment. Theoretically it will work if students are removed from reinforcing settings (classes or activities they like) and sent to a place they do not want to be. In many ISS sessions students must remain in the room all day. They must complete all classwork under conditions that are more demanding and stringent than those in the regular classroom. They are not usually able to go to the lunchroom, or to any class they may enjoy. It removes the student from social interaction with peers and the mainstream of student life. Unfortunately, ISS does not bother students who hate their classes or have few friends in school. While it tends to be overused with these types of kids and is therefore often useless, we are not familiar with any legal actions against it.

Detention is probably the most effective but least used punishment. The student must come into school early, stay after school, or return to school on the weekend. It is least used because of the monetary and time demands of teacher or staff supervision of the students. Again, we do not know of any legal challenges to this punishment.

Expulsion from school is the most severe punishment and is often challenged. Beginning in the early 1990s, states began to pass laws requiring automatic one-year expulsions for some offenses. Most frequent is the possession of a gun or other weapon in school. These are based on the so-called "zero tolerance" principle. By law, expelled students must be given due process, parents and students must receive written notice of the charges, and a hearing date must be scheduled to give the student time to prepare a defense, which is usually within two weeks of the offense. In most states, at the hearing the student has a right to be represented by legal counsel, face the accusers, cross-examine witnesses, and present a defense. The student has a right to an impartial tribunal whose decision must be based solely on the facts presented at the hearing.

Schools are legally vulnerable for expulsions if you can show that they have not assured equal protection under law by treating all students the same way. They must prove that all groups of students are included in all activities and can only exclude students from activities if there is adequate, documented justification and the students have been afforded due process prior to exclusion.

Zero Tolerance Policies

In a very informative article in *The Nation,* Annette Fuentes describes the new mood of meanness toward children. She claims that the last two decades have witnessed a dramatic change in our attitudes toward children and youth. She describes the "zero tolerance" mantra of public schools and juvenile courts as an expression of the belief that the young are automatically suspect. And the most suspect are minority youth.

In the zero tolerance zone of some fourth dimension, one should never confuse policymakers with the facts. As we mentioned in the introduction, youth crime has not changed dramatically in recent years. Today's violent youth commit about the same number of crimes as were committed fifteen years ago. Further, there has been no statistically significant shift in the age of offenders. So what is going on?

If you are a politician and you really want to get elected in America, get tough on crime. It doesn't matter that crime is actually decreasing, conservative candidates for office believe that if you scare the hell out of voters, you will get their votes. Slogans associated with this strategy include "zero tolerance," "just say no," and "three strikes and you're out." Of course, few politicians consider how these slogans may affect innocent students, such as eleven-year-old Myles Kuly.

During lunch in November 1996, Myles, a student in Monroe, North Carolina, distributed some juice made from homegrown peppers. One of his buddies burned his eye on the juice and Myles, charged with "possession and distribution of a habanero pepper" was suspended for one day. His mother, Barbara, was quoted as saying, "there is something wrong with this picture," when a straight-A student who skipped a grade is suspended for this offense. We are sure the elders of Monroe revel in their consistency in zero tolerance for drugs.

Students have been suspended for carrying "weapons" such as penknives, paring knives, and nail clippers. How many angry, alienated, impulsive, or just plain rebellious adolescents really think about the consequences of their misbehavior. We believe the only solution to zero tolerance policies is to zero them out.

State lawmakers in Pennsylvania, as in other states, have passed zero tolerance bills that include automatic expulsion for any weapons brought to school. Now, don't get us wrong, we are not supporting students' bringing guns and knives to school. However, this kind of knee-jerk reactionary legislation takes decision making out the hands of those educators who understand developmental, maturational, and environmental factors that may prompt children to bring anything to school that can be conceptualized as a weapon. The job of education is to diagnose the reasons why kids might bring weapons to school and identify the students most likely to do it.

For instance, extensive research shows that most weapons are brought to school by students who are afraid of being attacked by others. Wouldn't it make more sense for schools and police to discover and deal with the children who extort and bully others, rather than applying zero tolerance policies to their victims?

In the summer of 1998 I was on a two-hour news show on school violence. The Pennsylvania state commissioner of education and the state attorney general spouted the usual rhetoric about increasing violence in schools and how their get-tough, zero tolerance policies would deter youth violence. They ignored the data that was right in their faces. I, and other experts in the field, including a principal and a sampling of high school students, gave them the facts that youth violence has not increased appreciably and that most kids, even in the inner city, feel safe in school.

They also ignored the fact that in a rural state such as Pennsylvania, where many children work on farms and outdoors, youth often carry penknives and other tools to school. They may bring them to school either by accident or stupidity, but zero tolerance treats them as potential killers.

Retentions

The debate over school retention versus social promotion has polarized citizens for many years. For some, it seems to be a moral issue. They appear to believe that it is immoral to allow students to pass to the next grade if they have not passed the work required.

They believe that the threat of retention is a punishment that will motivate children to do better in school. Yet all the data show that this simplistic solution to a complex pedagogical problem does not work. Let us give you an example.

A number of years ago, a dynamic superintendent took over the Philadelphia School District. Dr. Constance Clayton developed ambitious plans to compensate for the enormous problems faced by the district. This was a district defined by demoralized staff, large numbers of minority children from horribly economically stressed environments, lack of adequate school buildings, insufficient books and supplies, and all the other deprivations faced by inner-city schools. To help compensate for these ills, she decided that all students should be taught at the same pace so they would move in unison through the curriculum. Students who could or would not complete the prescribed curriculum by the end of the year were punished by retention.

This would force every student to learn at the same rate and complete the same material. Of course, this pedagogical strategy completely ignores everything that psychologists and educational researchers know about children's individual differences in maturity, learning, and emotional development. It also ignores the great range of ability of teachers to adapt to these individual differences.

In March 1998, the National Association of School Psychologists (NASP) stated in a press release that "retaining a child in third grade is child neglect on the part of the school . . . retention punishes the victim of poor instruction . . . and . . . the school's failure." The overwhelming research shows that children who are retained fare no better academically after being retained. Further, retention, especially if it occurs more than once, creates students with very low self-esteem who are likely to exhibit a wide range of undesirable behaviors, including dropping out of school, bullying younger classmates, and other antisocial behaviors.

Deborah Crockett, then president of NASP, also said that social promotion is child neglect because it reflects a failure on the part of the school to teach children appropriate skills. From these conflicting views, we can see that school failure is a complex problem that requires multiple solutions. The literature shows that effective diagnostic assessments, individualized teaching, and appropriate resources can go a long way in ameliorating school failure.

When Dr. Clayton's policy was announced, I quickly called a few senior Philadelphia school psychologists and inquired whether or not they had informed the superintendent of the data that contraindicated her retention policy. Unfortunately, few administrators consider the extensive data that school psychologists could willingly provide to inform them about the problems associated with retention.

Three years later, when teachers began to complain that some students were repeating the same grade for the second time without gaining academically, policymakers started to listen. While a few students in the earlier grades may have benefited from retention, all the predictable disadvantages of a rigid retention policy accrued. Dr. Clayton is no longer superintendent, but you can bet your bippy that some new superintendent will come up with a brilliant idea called retention. More toxic education for the masses.

Lowering School Grades as a Punishment

The Family Educational Rights and Privacy Act gives parents the right to challenge grades and other information in students' records. The courts have allowed school authorities the right to use academic sanctions for poor academic performance. But there is less agreement in allowing school authorities to reduce a student's grade as a punishment for absences or misbehavior. Grades should be objective, measurable indicators of students' mastery of material and not instruments of punishment.

Legal challenges may be successful when teachers lower grades because of poor attendance or other nonacademic reasons, or as a malicious or arbitrary response to student misbehavior. For example, students might politely but strongly argue in class for the legalization of marijuana. No matter how much the teacher might disagree with the students, an academic penalty for their position is not appropriate. However, the teacher may give separate grades for academic and behavioral progress. For instance, if students arguing for the legalization of marijuana become obscene and disruptive, they may receive a lower grade in the area of behavior if this category is included in the grading system. If grade reduction is used throughout the school or in the classroom, then these rules should be published in the school's student handbook as well as in the teacher's course syllabus.

. . .

In conclusion, there are many violence-prevention procedures that sound great but are ineffective. Most are punitive in intent and nature and in the long run not cost-effective. We do not have room in this book to consider every punitive punishment invented by educators and policymakers. But let us conclude with some that have become popular in recent years.

The public appears to believe that metal detectors, mandatory school uniforms, dress codes, and other authoritarian approaches stem youth disruption and violence. Many assume that militaristic procedures such as boot camps will make obedient citizens out of rebellious youth and delinquents. However, research shows that sending delinquent students to boot camps is not effective in changing their behavior after they return home. Yet legislatures continue to support them with scarce resources.

Metal detectors are hailed as a way to keep weapons out of schools. Yet students with weapons have been able to bypass these devices, demonstrating that the peace of mind they offer is illusory. Unfortunately, security techniques such as metal detectors and lockdowns during drug searches have limited success even in correctional institutions. Given that prisoners are able to obtain drugs and weapons during incarceration, how can schools hope to be successful using these techniques in their far more open institutions? How useful is it to embarrass and inconvenience everyone for the potential sake of catching a few perpetrators?

Policymakers from the president on down proclaim that school uniforms reduce school violence, despite no convincing data. Mandatory uniforms force conformity in a society that purportedly fosters freedom and individuality. In many situations they are inequitable, arbitrarily applied, and oversimplify a complex problem. Uniforms are a poor substitute in inner cities for remedies for the overcrowded classes, underfunding of academic programs, decaying buildings, and poverty that are the real causes of violence. But they continue to be promoted despite the fact that there is no valid evidence that uniforms prevent school violence.

Now that we have presented an overview of the meaning of dangerous and toxic education, we will turn in the last three chapters to issues of amelioration.

Chapter 7

Taking a Stand

What to Do If Your Child Is Maltreated in School

By now, through the eyes of victims, advocates, researchers, scholars, educators, policymakers, and the judiciary you have a pretty good idea about the nature and extent of toxic discipline in schools. This material is presented in broad overview, with as many examples as space permits. However, as mentioned previously, everything we have said here is backed by research and clinical experience. There is a bibliography in the resource section at the end of the book for those inclined to seek original sources. So now it is time to give you practical advice if you believe your child has been maltreated. Also, we wrote this book in the hopes that even if your own child is not a victim, you can become an advocate for others.

Has Your Child Been Victimized?

How do you know if your child has been victimized? You probably believe that your child will tell you. Unfortunately, this is not always the case since your child may be fearful of retribution by the teacher, being punished again at home, or because of general lack of child-parent communication. Lacking a direct report of abuse, the next best indicator is any unusual and sudden change in your child's behavior. The usual behavior of young children who have been maltreated in school is withdrawal and crying; older children are more likely to react with anger and plans for escape or revenge. In most of the cases with which we are familiar, changes in behavior were apparent even when the child did not directly complain to the parents.

Specific types of abuse can be associated with certain types of injuries. Excessive drills have resulted in deaths, tying children to chairs has left rope burns, excessive time outs in closed spaces have triggered phobias and seizures, and grabbing children by the hair has resulted in hair loss. Also, blows can cause bruises and internal damage. For example, a student in Texas suffered a strangulated hernia, and one in Michigan suffered partial deafness as a result of paddlings. Name-calling and denigration can cause children to withdraw, become depressed, and even have suicidal ideation. Humiliation about poor academic performance can cause older students to drop out of school.

Once you suspect abuse, you need to determine if it really occurred or if the child's change in behavior is related to something else. This is important—a child's tears about what a teacher did might be more related to the child's own feelings or interpretation of the event. For example, say eight-year-old Sharon comes home crying because her teacher told her she did poorly on a test. Her tears might be more related to her own sense of failure and the pressure she feels to achieve than to the objective feedback from her teacher. Obviously, Sharon's tears were not caused by maltreatment by the teacher, but rather by her interpretation of the meaning of the event.

In some cases it may not initially appear that a change in behavior is related to something that happened in school. One of the most telling symptoms of maltreatment is avoidance of school. For instance, ten-year-old Jimmy began to sulk, refused to go to school, and talked about hating his teachers. A discussion with Jimmy revealed that after doing poorly on a test, his teacher publicly stated, "You got a 'D' on your test but I guess I can't expect anything better from someone like you." That was clearly psychological maltreatment.

Sometimes parents do not communicate daily with their children and miss important cues. For instance, Julie—a first grader with a generally cheerful disposition—began to cry easily, complain about going to school, and appear depressed. Her parents ignored her symptoms, assuming that she was just avoiding new, more difficult schoolwork. It wasn't until several months later that they discovered Julie was terrified of an unusually stern, punitive, and demanding teacher. She had been severely scolded several times for innocuous misbehaviors such as whispering to a classmate. On one particular occasion Julie hadn't heard or understood the teacher's instructions for an assignment and was afraid to ask her. Also, she had heard other children being paddled. Julie was usually well behaved and compliant and was either ashamed or afraid to tell her parents that she felt terrified of her teacher, whom her parents had praised.

You can discover school abuse by daily discussions about school with your child. Ideally these should begin as early as preschool. If this practice becomes a daily ritual, for example at the dinner table, children will be eager and comfortable about sharing all their school experiences. If it only occurs following a crisis or about tests, grades, or school misbehavior, many children will think you are only interested in them when they have problems in school. They may feel that you are overintrusive and just checking up on them so you can punish them. Therefore, it is important for parents to establish that they are interested in all aspects of their children's school experiences. It is especially important that children feel they won't receive double punishments for admitting their misbehaviors in school.

In general, depending on location and socioeconomic level of your school, there is a better than 50 percent chance that you will uncover some type of maltreatment. If it is low-level, random, and lacking a pattern, you may not feel advocacy efforts are needed. In any case, by now you understand that the ultimate consequences of all types and levels of maltreatment are psychological. So, you need to make a judgment call about what to do.

The nature of the maltreatment will definitely determine what you will be able to do about it. For instance, if you expose sexual abuse of your child, you are much more likely to get swift reaction from authorities than if the teacher was sarcastic and demeaning. Further, discovering abuse is a lot different from doing something about it. The nature and extent of the maltreatment, whether it is continuing, whether other children are victimized, who witnessed it, your clout in the community, your support network, family backing, and persistence and determination will all determine what you will be able to accomplish if you decide to act.

A mother in Georgia, whose twelve-year-old son was severely paddled, summed it up. She said, "We always paid our taxes, respected authority, went to church, and thought the people in power would protect us. It just ain't so. When you are a little person, they try to tell you that you ain't got no rights. But I'm not giving in, no matter what they do." She went on to get a lawyer from many miles away.

Four Steps to Decisive Action

If you determine that maltreatment has occurred, you should consider the following four steps before you decide what action you will take.

1. Identify the injury.
2. Document the injury.
3. Document the event.
4. Determine culpability.

These steps are meant to be general guidelines, since the details will depend on the type of maltreatment you suspect. For instance, in pure psychological abuse, there would be no bruises to photograph.

Identify the Injury

While physical injuries such as welts and bruises are usually visible, it is difficult to generalize about how to identify less overt damage. This is not only because of children's individual physiological and emotional responses to maltreatment, but also because of the different symptoms typical of varying age groups. Since some children do not complain about abuse even when there are obvious bruises from physical assaults, you need to be alert to the cues that suggest maltreatment has occurred.

In our experience, older children are more likely to complain about unfair, unjust, or abusive disciplinary practices at their schools. Younger children, on the other hand, generally don't understand the nuances between strict and unjust discipline. Primary grade children still hold the teacher in awe and don't yet fully comprehend the limits of the teacher's or principal's power to punish. Until middle school years, children tend to see misbehavior and punishment in concrete terms. Younger children often feel that severe punishment is justified by certain types of misbehavior, whether or not there are mitigating circumstances. For example, if five-year-old Bill falls and screams, "Shit, that hurts," he may accept a severe paddling for swearing. The fact that he was in pain and that the curse was blurted impulsively is not considered by a young child to mitigate the offense.

In numerous cases of severely paddled primary schoolchildren, parents told me that they first discovered the abuse when the children were bathing or changing clothes. In some cases the children had gone several days without complaining. Therefore, if your child's teacher has a reputation for paddling, daily checks for bruises may not be a bad idea.

Teachers with a reputation for being tough disciplinarians may also use excessive amounts of verbal abuse. Good disciplinarians can be strict. But strictness does not imply the enforcement of rules with sarcasm and ridicule. Nor does it reflect biased attitudes, favoritism, or use of unreasonable punishments. If your child's teacher seems overly punitive, document what goes on in the classroom through your daily discussions with your child. Always ask about the good and bad events of the day. Do not focus on the negative, since you do not want your child to feel like a spy who is out to get the teacher.

Also, remember that teachers are hardworking people. Like the rest of the population, many are either single breadwinners or in families where both parents work. Therefore, they are subjected to daily stresses concomitant with these lifestyles. They may occasionally lapse and lose their tempers. While personal stresses do not excuse professional lapses, teachers with these problems need compassion and help. At the same time, their problems should not be allowed to serve as an excuse for abuse of students, which is too often the case.

In summary, the best way to identify possible abuse is to develop daily dialogues with children about school. If you can establish a relationship in which your child feels free to talk about school, you will easily identify abusing teachers and traumatic events. However, never administer punishment as a result of these discussions if children report their own misbehavior. If children are punished in school, which is a likely outcome of their misbehavior, why punish them again at home? Our Constitution doesn't allow a citizen to be punished twice for the same crime, so why do it to schoolchildren?

Document the Injury

Just because you observe teacher-inflicted bruises on your child, that doesn't mean that anyone will believe you. Just because your child develops stress symptoms from being publicly ridiculed and humiliated by a teacher doesn't mean anyone will take it seriously. Therefore, before you do anything else, you must obtain some official record of the abuse. The following anecdote provides an exceptional example of effective documentation.

Ten-year-old Brian was in gym class with a substitute teacher, Mr. Savage. The students were on the playground, adjacent to a road. They were in two lines parallel to the road and were kicking a soccer ball back and forth. The boy across from Brian kicked it over his head and into the road. Brian laughed and was immediately accosted by Mr. Savage, who grabbed him by the neck, shaking him and screaming. Brian was shocked but knew that his crime did not warrant a lightning strike to his neck. But, fearful that his parents would not believe that a teacher would do such a thing, Brian decided to document the event himself.

When Brian returned to class, he wrote a description of what had happened. His peers who had observed the event indicated its accuracy by short signed statements attached to the document. When he arrived home he reported the event to his mother, who was an experienced teacher. She was furious. She telephoned the witnesses and talked with them to verify the account. She then called the principal to alert him and requested that Mr. Savage call her and apologize.

When Mr. Savage called Brian's mother and apologized for losing his temper, he probably regretted that he had not victimized a different child. He was quickly apprised of her extensive credentials in education. This was followed by his own punishment, which was a long harangue about the nature of children, the disciplinary infractions to be expected, and effective strategies on how to deal with them. The lecture ended with the comment, "Mr. Savage, if you can't learn to control your temper with students, you should consider another profession."

This kind of effective response could occur more frequently if children were aware of toxic teaching. In most cases, you will have to document the event after the child tells you about it. Depending on the type of assault, you must immediately obtain physical evidence and documentation from witnesses.

Documenting Physical Abuse

If your child has bruises, you should immediately take clear, color pictures. Don't wait until the next day. Try to have a witness when taking the pictures to document the day they were taken. I received one picture where the parent held up the daily newspaper next to the child to indicate the day of the event. If you are not an experienced photographer, get help from a friend. It is extremely important that these first pictures show the colorations of the bruises, since they may someday be used in court. Therefore, you should immediately get the pictures developed in a one-hour photo processing lab—and take new ones if the first set doesn't come out clearly.

Polaroid pictures have not been very reliable in the past, but they may have improved in recent years. In several cases we have found that Polaroids did not show sharp contrasts in color. We have no experience with photos taken with digital cameras. However, we have been assured by a professional photographer that this technology should produce good pictures, especially if exposure and lighting are optimal, as is the case for all photos. The advantage with digital cameras is that the pictures can be produced immediately. If any pictures do not accurately represent the bruises, then throw them away and keep only good quality photos. Poor photographs could be used against you in court.

For example, in the case of *Jeremy Ward* v. *Muldrow Public Schools* in Oklahoma, the parents relied on Polaroid pictures that did not accurately depict severe welts. These red welts were left by a leather paddle shaped like the sole of a size 12½ cowboy boot. Even though the parents had a physician's written description of the welts, this did not match what was portrayed in the pictures the jury observed.

Once welts and hematomas begin to heal they turn into various shades of blue, brown, and black. If possible, you should take dated pictures of these bruises. Bruises normally heal in two to three weeks. After you have taken your own pictures, you need to go to a physician or child abuse official to document the bruises. If you don't have a trusted family physician, we highly recommend that you go to a hospital. Since you may be filing child abuse charges, ask for a physician with experience in identifying child abuse, usually a pediatrician. The American Academy of Pediatrics was one of the first national organizations to pass a resolution against corporal punishment in the schools.

It is important that you have a clear account of what happened before you take your child to the doctor. Younger children may be scared and confused, especially if they are taken to a hospital emergency room. When questioning your child, be sure not to suggest answers or ask leading questions such as "That teacher really hurt you, didn't she?" Instead ask, "How did it feel after the teacher hit you?" or "What exactly did the teacher say that made you feel so bad?" Obtain a clear picture of what happened, how the child felt, and who else saw it happen. Even though you may be very angry, it will not help to put words in your child's mouth.

If the doctor takes Polaroid pictures, ask for several copies immediately for your own records. Ask for his signature to attest to their validity since there are cases where photos have been lost by officials or emergency room physicians have waffled when testifying in court.

Try to obtain a copy of the physician's diagnosis as soon as possible. This is written on the patient's chart. You may have trouble getting this official chart, but you can ask the examining physician to write the diagnosis for you. Be persistent about obtaining a written record before you leave the office. We have become extra cautious about records, because in a few cases pictures disappeared and physicians denied that they had told the parents that child abuse had occurred. If you litigate, the absence of this type of evidence can be devastating.

You may want to take your child to your own physician. Make sure this is a person you know and trust. We have seen too many cases where local physicians have professional and personal ties to the schools and are reluctant to engage in anything "political." What can be more political than testifying as an expert witness against your own community school board? Be sure that the physician knows that you may litigate the case. If he or she waffles about helping you, or expresses doubts about testifying, go to someone else immediately. Do not be timid in exploring your physician's willingness to help you in court.

Most states that permit school corporal punishment protect educators from child abuse charges resulting from their attempts to discipline children. This protection occurs because the mandatory reporting laws and the processes for investigation generally do not encompass public schools. However, you can file assault charges with law enforcement authorities, a measure we will discuss later in this chapter.

Documenting Psychological Abuse

It is relatively easy to document cases of psychological maltreatment, especially when they happen in the classroom or on the playing field, since students and other school staff are often present. Unlike paddling, which usually occurs behind closed doors, teachers' sarcasm, ridicule, name-calling, and put-downs often happen in front of the whole class. Confrontations between teachers and students in hallways, lunchrooms, and at assemblies offer fertile grounds for observing maltreatment.

Too many coaches feel that abusive verbiage is necessary to motivate athletes. They have no compunction about verbally assaulting players during daily practices and sometimes even during public competitions. Ironically, while this type of maltreatment occurs far more often than physical abuse, it is often expected or tolerated by players, parents, and the public. Whether committed by coaches or other educators, it is even less likely than physical abuse to be taken seriously by prosecutors.

In the case of psychological traumatization by the teacher, our experience has been that the onset of symptoms is usually not as dramatic as in the case of physical abuse. Also, the symptoms may develop after a series of events rather than from a single episode. Your best initial step is to seek an evaluation by an experienced psychologist who is knowledgeable about trauma. Seek a psychologist experienced in evaluating abuse and maltreatment of children.

Professionals who specialize in this area may be members of the International Society for Traumatic Stress Studies. If possible, find a doctoral-level school psychologist who is also licensed for private practice or works in a recognized hospital or mental health clinic.

If you use a local professional, it is inadvisable to select one who receives referrals from the local school district. His or her relationship with the school might create a conflict of interest to the detriment of your child. Finally, it will also be helpful if the professional is familiar with the material presented in this book.

Getting Charges Filed

In many states, child abuse statutes do not cover schools. Even so, you should insist that the physician or psychologist who examines your child and determines suspected maltreatment file child abuse charges with the appropriate state authorities. This may help your case if you go to trial. Even if it does not, it is important for the long run to accrue as many charges of school abuse as possible to support eventual state legislation against school maltreatment.

Unfortunately, in several cases in which I have been involved (for example, *Gaspersohn* v. *Harnett County* and *Cipsic* v. *Pinellis County Christian School*), the judges did not allow the physicians or state child abuse authorities to testify. The judges, I assume, reasoned that since their state child abuse statutes didn't cover teachers, the testimony would be irrelevant. However, as the public has become increasingly aware of the nature and extent of child abuse and violence against children in society, the situation seems to be improving.

Document the Event

It is extremely important to obtain facts about what happened. In many cases educators will deny that the events took place as described by the child or student witnesses. Once they hear the child's version, they may try to obtain support from other educators or students that the victim's story was false. Once the school's economic and political juggernaut begins to roll, you will definitely recognize the intimidation attempts.

When you discover the abuse, immediately record your child's account of the event. Obtain the following information and try to make the account as detailed as possible: (1) date of the event, (2) time, (3) physical setting, (4) what the teacher and class were doing before the abuse, (5) what your child did or said that resulted in the abusive response, (6) what classmates or other witnesses did, if anything, (7) what your child felt when the event happened, (8) what your child did while it was happening, (9) exactly what the abuser did, (10) what the abuser did afterward, (11) how your child felt afterward, and (12) what your child did afterward.

Determine who witnessed the event and if possible get written statements as soon as you can—before intimidation by school authorities begins. Seeking help from your child's classmates may place you and them in harm's way. It may not be easy to get other parents to cooperate. On the other hand, if victims and witnesses band together, they can form a potent network of opposition to toxic schools.

In the ideal situation, you should meet with these parents and their children and get written statements of what happened if you do not already have them. These statements should be notarized if possible. In some cases, children who witnessed the incident later change their stories because of covert and overt threats by the school. It is much more difficult to get witnesses to change stories after they have provided notarized accounts of the events. After obtaining as much documented information as possible you will need to confront the offender to help determine culpability.

Determine Culpability

An important point to remember when severe punitiveness occurs is that besides documenting the event, you need to be familiar with the disciplinary procedures of the school as an early step in determining culpability. Most schools have written guidelines for the administration of discipline. They generally have prescribed punishments for specific misbehaviors and list a hierarchy of punishments based on the nature and number of misbehaviors a student has committed. For instance, if eight-year-old Kirk will not stay in his seat, the hierarchy may start with talking to him to explain why he must stay in his seat and warn him of the punishment if he does it again. The next time he is out of his seat he could get a time out. The third offense might trigger sending him the principal, followed by a call to his parents.

Also, in many school districts, especially at the secondary level, staff are required to document each misbehavior that results in punishment. Usually, when all other disciplines have failed, paddling and suspensions are listed as last resorts in the hierarchy. Therefore, it is important to understand whether the teacher, in paddling or otherwise disciplining your child, followed the guidelines required by the school district.

Research and case litigation reveals that a high percentage of abusive discipline resulted because the offender did not follow school discipline guidelines. This increases the culpability of offending teachers and may make their supervisors and other administrators liable. In almost every case in which we have been involved, the teachers did not follow the prescribed guidelines. Even when the guidelines have not listed specific hierarchies of steps to be taken before any punishment is used, it is often clear that teachers have tried little else before applying more severe punishments.

Guidelines that spell out what teachers should not do in the area of verbal maltreatment are rare, and tend to be vague at best. Even when schools have something called a "Manual of Student's and Teacher's Rights," the question is often addressed by saying that teachers should show respect for children's dignity. By this statement, the guidelines imply that teachers should not denigrate, humiliate, or put down students. But we have never seen a manual that spells out the kinds of verbal maltreatments that teachers should not use.

In cases where teachers have done something that clearly and grossly violates the school's norms for disciplining children, you may be able to get support from other families and school authorities. In Florida, one of the most punitive states in the country, a teacher was summarily suspended and eventually fired for chaining several kids to his motorcycle and dragging them across a playground. This obviously offended the sensibilities of educators—who apparently approve of bruises from paddlings but not from pavements.

Here is what an eleven-year-old Ohio student said about his experience in a fourth-grade art class.

We had to do a project with rope. The project was to make a bag out of a pants leg and use the rope for a drawstring. My teacher started to tease me and put the white clothesline I had around my neck. I felt silly and everyone was laughing. It started to hurt as he tightened it. It was burning and I was trying to take it off. I wanted to cry but I didn't. Then during lunch I wanted to see the principal but the lunchroom teacher wouldn't let me go. When I went to class my teacher kidded me about the red thing around my neck. He let me go to the nurse and she put some cream on my neck.

The teacher claimed he was only kidding around and at the suggestion of the principal he apologized. The school superintendent stonewalled when the parents complained, and invited them to sue if they wanted to. He said they just didn't have enough evidence of harm. Several board of education members agreed with the parents that the teacher used very poor judgment. Since the teacher was nontenured, they did not renew his contract the following year. They acknowledged that mock strangulation was not an approved pedagogical technique.

You will probably be furious when you discover your child has been maltreated. However, we suggest that you be calm and well prepared before confronting the offending educator. Present the facts as you know them. If the person admits to the offense, apologizes, and asks what can be done to make up for the damage, you may want to begin a constructive dialogue so that you can collaborate to help your child heal from the trauma.

Unfortunately, in many cases we have examined, the offending teacher, coach, or principal has denied, lied, stonewalled, and trivialized the event. You will then have to take your complaint up the bureaucratic hierarchy to determine how many officials you want to hold liable. You will probably be required to put your complaint in writing. Be sure to document each personal communication. If you are tough enough to take on a secondary argument on top of your complaint, demand that you be allowed to record meetings, although they will think of many reasons why they can not allow it.

If you follow these suggestions, you will eventually have a clear idea of who is culpable. But you also need to determine the extent of long-term emotional problems your child could develop from the school trauma.

Determining Educator-Induced Posttraumatic Stress Disorder: Using the MWSES

Since the war in Vietnam, many Americans have become aware of how the trauma of battle can cause soldiers to develop severe stress symptoms called posttraumatic stress disorder (PTSD). You may know veterans who have had familiar symptoms such as flashbacks of combat scenes or severe anxiety reactions to and avoidance of anything related to the war. These reactions to intense trauma have been documented throughout history. Yet it is only recently that researchers have studied the syndrome we now call PTSD.

Historically, most of the research has been on adults. It is relatively recent that research has focused on children. Most of the studies have concentrated on physical and sexual abuse, terrorism, and the effects of horrendous natural disasters. Even though there has been more emphasis on children's PTSD in recent years, there are still major problems in defining the nature and extent of this syndrome.

Diagnosis of PTSD in children has been problematic if the traumatic event was not beyond the realm of normal experience. For instance, professionals have not easily recognized that children are subjected to many common and apparently normal disciplinary procedures that can cause psychic harm. Historically, the publication of Helfer and Kempe's *The Battered Child* in 1968 heralded medical and legal recognition that parents are limited in how severely they can discipline their children. It took several decades before the medical and psychological community recognized the relation of these abuses to PTSD in children.

Diagnostic reforms in recent years recognize the differences in developmental stages and life experiences between children and adults in terms of symptoms related to trauma. However, the nature and horrendousness of the trauma for diagnosis of PTSD are still pretty much based on adult criteria.

For both children and adults, the concept that diagnosis is dependent on specific types of events makes PTSD unique. Most mental illnesses do not require a specific type or intensity of triggering event as a prerequisite for diagnosis. For example, twenty-five-year-old John can be diagnosed as severely depressed because of continuing denigration by his boss. Also, twenty-five-year-old Steve can become just as depressed from the death of a loved one. But, unlike depression, PTSD is not regarded as arising from events of normal life. Thus there is a real problem in diagnosing the syndrome in someone who has suffered only from common disciplinary practices rather than from the kinds of horrific experiences that normally cause it. Historically, courts, educators, legislators, and many professionals have refused to recognize that students abused in the name of discipline could have PTSD. This is because most people in authority have judged that being swatted, smacked, verbally assaulted, and continuously denigrated was part of growing up.

I thought differently in 1983 after an all-day comprehensive evaluation of Shelly Gaspersohn. I identified all the symptoms needed to diagnose PTSD. My testimony was either discredited or ignored because the judge and jury believed the testimony of a psychiatrist hired by the school board. He spent less than an hour with Shelly and decided that being beaten on the butt by an administrator in North Carolina was not "beyond the range of normal experience" for adolescent girls in that state.

Following defeat in the Gaspersohn case, I began a program of research to prove that children can develop PTSD from experiencing or witnessing abusive discipline in schools. Meanwhile, others were relating PTSD to severe parental discipline, which was finally recognized as child abuse. We have found that children are more vulnerable and have less control over a wider range of stressors than do adults. For instance, young children repeatedly traumatized by baby-sitters have no control over the offenders' daily visits and may be too fearful or incoherent to communicate these experiences directly to their parents. An adult abused by a supervisor at work has many options available, including not returning to work, but a child has no way out.

In the past, most professionals failed to recognize that children's and adolescents' reactions to stress are mediated by their ages. For instance, traumatized six-year-olds might have recurrences of bed-wetting, clinging to parents, and being fearful about leaving home. Adolescents may become severely depressed and anxious or angry, hostile, and aggressive.

We studied childhood PTSD within the framework of developmental factors, regional differences in school discipline, and a complete range of symptoms. We ignored the criterion of horrific trauma, since we believe that horror, especially with children, is in the eyes of the beholder. Our research and clinical studies have led to the identification of a subcategory of PTSD we call educator-induced posttraumatic stress disorder (EIPTSD). Currently, diagnostic criteria do not allow for subcategories of PTSD. However, we believe this will change. Pressure to recognize subcategories has evolved from professionals who have studied such areas as rape, terrorism, and wife battering. Each group can point to unique factors related to the nature of the trauma and concomitant symptoms.

Recognition of EIPTSD is important because diagnosis involves specific assessment techniques, understanding of child development and psychopathology, and experience with schoolchildren. Also, as the only instrument available for this purpose, the *My Worst School Experience Scale* (MWSES), which we have mentioned before, should be part of a comprehensive clinical evaluation. Therefore, if you decide to have your child evaluated, you should know something about this instrument.

First, let us consider the type of school traumas that can cause EIPTSD. These include acts by educators that result in peer humiliation, discrimination, isolation, rejection, or sexual corruption. Teachers' physical and verbal assaults, overly punitive sanctions, and ridicule can traumatize children.

We have found at least 105 symptoms that can result from educator maltreatment. We have taken related symptoms and grouped them into seven clusters based on statistical analysis: (1) depression and avoidance of school and the offender, (2) oppositional, angry, and defiant behavior at home and in school, (3) avoidance of things or people reminiscent of the trauma and general hypervigilance resulting in constantly looking out for people or places that will cause more pain, (4) somatic complaints such as stomachaches and headaches, (5) reexperiencing or having intrusive thoughts about the trauma, (6) depression, hopelessness, and suicidal ideation, and (7) nightmares and unpleasant memories related to the trauma.

Because the MWSES is a clinical instrument and should be included as part of a total evaluation, we have not included it in this book. It designed to be used by professionals. However, you can use the checklist given here to screen your child for signs of events that have resulted in changes in behavior. If your child shows symptoms in any or all of the checklist categories, you might want to consider seeking help from a mental health professional.

EIPTSD Checklist

1. Child has difficulty paying attention, thinking clearly, focusing on schoolwork, or completing tasks.
2. Child has developed sleep disturbances such as nightmares, fear of going to sleep, or renewed bed-wetting.
3. Child has developed aggressive or oppositional behavior, hostile thoughts, or threats.
4. Child avoids the person who inflicted the trauma, the school where it happened, and anyone or anything related to the event.
5. Child has repeated unwanted thoughts about the event.
6. Child has developed illnesses such as stomachaches and headaches that do not appear to have any organic basis.
7. Child appears depressed, has lost interest in previously enjoyed activities, or spends more time alone than before the incident.

Even though your child may have disturbing symptoms as indicated in the checklist, a clinical evaluation may not reveal a full-blown case of EIPTSD. In fact, most children tend to survive maltreatment with minimal or no symptoms. I spent a year of my childhood with a mean-spirited teacher I'd have sworn was emulating Genghis Kahn and Hitler combined. You can probably say the same. Like me, you survived, in part because society expects children to survive that sort of thing, which is a major problem in studying and understanding PTSD related to abuses in school.

Probably about 1 percent to 2 percent of all students actually develop EIPTSD and are forever victims from these experiences unless they get help. Most of these children are never diagnosed with PTSD. They may drop out of school early, foster lifelong hostility to school and other authorities, develop debilitatingly low self-esteem, or become delinquent.

The point is that we are all built differently. Heredity, brain chemistry, early experiences, and a host of other factors determine how we react to stressful events. We can not yet predict who will get PTSD.

For example, I once encountered a first-grade class of seventeen children whose teacher tied some to their seats, taped their mouths, continuously put them down, denigrated them, and generally psychologically assaulted them. I gathered a team to evaluate the children. The range of symptoms that were directly related to the abuse included vomiting, nausea, headaches, stomachaches, and earaches reported before or after going to school each day. Some children had nightmares, fear of the dark, thumb sucking, crying, bed-wetting, underwear soiling, insomnia, excessive dependency, difficulty concentrating, excessive shyness, depression, hyperactive and anxious behavior, fear of strangers, withdrawal, and school avoidance. One child began pulling out her eyelashes and another pulled out some of her hair. Of this group, five had sufficient intensity, frequency, and duration of symptoms to be diagnosed with PTSD. Almost all the others had enough symptoms to disrupt their lives.

You are now reasonably informed about the nature of EIPTSD and what you need to do if you suspect your child may have a problem. There are compelling reasons to determine the longevity of symptoms and underlying emotional trauma in children who have EIPTSD. First, of course, you need to know what your child is suffering so as to determine the kind of treatment to seek. Over and above the clinical reasons, however, there are legal reasons; it takes a clear account of symptoms and trauma to persuade a court to award damages. You may well need a compensatory damage award to provide the resources for treatment. And if you win an award of punitive damages you may help persuade educators, school boards, and insurance companies of the penalties for maltreating children in the name of discipline.

Determining Your Goals

Before you decide whether or not to litigate, you must consider your goals. Most of the parents of victimized children with whom we have worked are little different from others in their communities on almost all dimensions that define families. Most expected school personnel to act as trusted caregivers and surrogate parents. Most did not have experience with recalcitrant bureaucracies and officials who lie, deny, and conceal. These types of parents tend to be less punitive than their peers and perhaps more protective of their children's rights. They have little preparation to deal with the cascading events that typically occur when they seek redress of their grievances against the school.

It is very difficult to be objective when your school, after victimizing your child, begins to victimize your family. The most challenging task, after you discover that the school will not offer a simple apology and assurances about your child's health and safety, is to determine your goals in carrying your case forward. This section offers a guideline for assessing your goals and your chances of success in reaching them.

Safeguarding Your Child's Mental Health

Anyone who has been traumatized knows that a victim's greatest fear is retraumatization. Even thinking about the trauma can cause intense feelings of anxiety. After the trauma, the memory of it can trigger the same physical responses of fear and anxiety that were felt when it occurred. Typically, victims develop uncontrolled physiological reactions such as sweating, heart palpitations, and knots in the stomach. The more traumatic the event is perceived to be by the victim, the stronger the physiological and psychological reaction to being placed in any area associated with the traumatization. In situations of interpersonal traumatization the victim tends to avoid the place where the trauma occurred or being near the victimizer or anyone similar. This information and what you have learned about EIPTSD should be of primary and immediate concern in terms of your child's mental health.

In school abuse cases, depending on the severity of symptoms and the offender's refusal to apologize, the victim may be too traumatized to return to the school building or to the class where it occurred.

Much of the damage can be undone if the abusive educator is willing to apologize and assure that the maltreatment will never happen again. Without an apology, it may be necessary for the child to remain home for a few days to get treatment. In some cases the child may have to go to another school if the victimizer refuses to initiate the healing process.

Obtaining a Positive Response from the School

Given the importance of corrective action on the part of the abuser, we believe that the first goal should be to obtain an apology and assurances that the abuse will not recur. This will help your child to feel safe about returning to school. But the timing of your contact with the school in pursuit of this goal may conflict with the schedule needed to complete the four steps that we outlined as important in verifying that maltreatment occurred. The sequencing of your initial communication with the school will depend on many factors. For instance, if you discover signs of physical abuse late in the day after the regular school session, it is unlikely that you will be able to reach the alleged abuser until the next school day.

If the alleged offender was a teacher, and you discover the abuse before school closes, you might be able to reach the principal, who may know nothing about the event. Unfortunately, your accusations may give an unsympathetic principal time to contact the teacher and agree on a mutual defense strategy. Or if the alleged abuse is severe, the principal may contact higher school officials and the school board attorney who may advise the principal to take no action until a full investigation is completed. At the first meeting, if the alleged offender is a teacher, he or she may feel defensive or threatened and may ask the principal or a union representative to be present. Therefore, it might be best not to tell the principal any details until you meet. Besides, if the abuse is severe, your afternoon and evening may be tied up with a medical exam.

Avoid school appointments that start right before school unless the teacher or principal assures you that the teacher's class can be covered for a longer meeting. Otherwise, you will just get into the issue and the teacher will have to leave for class, feeling that you had your opportunity to present your case.

We can not tell you the proper sequence for your first contact with the school, since conditions and people vary. But, whether you go immediately to the school or contact the teacher or principal on the phone, even though you may be feeling homicidal, try to stay calm. Ideally, this first communication will occur after you have documented the abuse. The purpose of the first communication should be to clarify your understanding of the event, obtain verification of the encounter as your child described it, and obtain an adequate explanation and apology. To enhance these goals you must not speak in an angry, accusatory, or threatening manner. If you leap to the attack, you will only make the school officials more defensive and resistant to admitting that they did wrong.

To keep yourself rational, it will help to have a calmer spouse or some objective third party participate in the communication. While your rage is understandable, if it is unleashed it can destroy your chances of achieving your primary goal of helping your traumatized child. Some angry parents have threatened retaliation or physically attacked the offender. A number of parents who have succumbed to the temptation to launch direct attacks have been successfully prosecuted by unsympathetic law enforcement officials. In all these instances, the parents' case against the school was lost at the beginning.

You should state that you just want to clarify what happened between the teacher and your child. To enhance the opportunity for the educator to apologize, you should express your understanding of the difficulties teachers may have with misbehavior. You can empathize that teachers, like parents, sometimes have bad days and "lose it." You should also describe your child's feelings of shock, hurt, fear, and sudden mistrust of the offender. Try to convince the offender that only he or she can undo the traumatization.

Any of these approaches may make the offender and other school authorities very defensive. But let them be the first to become belligerent. Don't give them the ammunition to portray you as an angry, unreasonable parent who is out to get the teacher or the school. Above all, do not make threats.

You may have a problem obtaining an apology if the educator or higher-level administrators have contacted the school attorney. Even if the school authorities sympathize with your child, their lawyer may inform them that an admission of abuse will make them liable in litigation. Therefore, even if you feel that the person you complain to is sympathetic but unable to act, you must be guided by your child's best interests. You can not wait until the school decides what to do. You must decide whether you will demand an apology by a certain date, whether you are committed to possible litigation, or if you are willing to drop the matter.

Make sure that any promises the school makes are given in writing. For instance, the school might agree to provide counseling for the child. However, if you accept this without clarifying the qualifications of the mental health professional, you could be stuck with an unqualified or incompetent therapist or one who works for the district and is placed in a position of conflict of interest. For example, the school might suggest the school counselor as a therapist. This could be a conflict of interest because the school may pressure the counselor to break confidentiality regarding your possible plans for litigation. Also, the counselor might be friends with the abusing educator.

In addition, PTSD can sometimes require long-term therapy involving a variety of treatment modalities, and you might be stuck with a therapist governed by the short-term treatment policies of an HMO. In any case the immediate treatment of your child should govern your thinking. So don't let school authorities bully you into signing on the dotted line before you have thought it out carefully. If possible, have an attorney go over your agreement before you sign it.

Seeking Redress Within the System

There are no data to determine how many cases of abuse are resolved in the first stages by apologies, assurances, or overwhelming intimidation that prevents the parents from going further. In most of the cases we have studied, the parents carried their complaints through the system to the school board. By this time the cases have generally received media attention and the victimizers have developed their offensive strategy.

Sometimes empathetic administrators will take nonpunitive actions to change an abusive teacher's attitudes or behavior. This may include recommending or insisting that the teacher engage in psychotherapy, work with a teacher mentor, or consult regularly about classroom management and discipline problems with the school psychologist. In some instances, the abusive teacher may be someone with an exemplary history. This scenario occurred in a school where I was working. The principal was aware of the stresses in the offending teacher's personal life, but he did not connect this with the problems in her classroom.

Mrs. Jones was an experienced fifth-grade teacher in an inner-city school. She was well respected by staff and parents and generally considered to be a good disciplinarian. She had requested that I conduct a psychological evaluation of Sammy, a student she felt was so emotionally disturbed that he belonged in a special education class.

I observed Sammy, who was quite active in class. He spoke out of turn, left his seat without permission, and became aggressive when he did not get his way. What Mrs. Jones hadn't told me was how she handled these problems. Whenever Sammy did something wrong she would call him names such as "baby," "brat," and "Mr. Sour Puss." She constantly rejected his requests for help and never called on him when he raised his hand to answer questions. Her interactions with him were negative, critical, and sarcastic. She never once praised him but rather focused on reminding him of past indiscretions and expected future misbehavior.

After about three consultation sessions with Mrs. Jones, during which she continuously focused on Sammy's evil ways and how she could not take it anymore, I summarized what was going on between her and Sammy. I also summarized our interactions during the sessions. I told her I was puzzled because of her successes in previous years with difficult children like Sammy. I suggested that maybe something else was wrong and that she seemed tense and somewhat depressed. She immediately broke into tears. It was then that I discovered that her marriage was breaking up and that her own son, about Sammy's age, had become a behavior problem at home and school.

It didn't take much for Mrs. Jones, basically an excellent teacher, to realize that her abuse of Sammy was a result of other personal frustrations. She was able to recognize her need for help. We collaborated on a plan that included therapy for her and her son as well as extra support in school. This was a success story because the teacher was willing to do something about her abusive behavior. Also, I helped her to seek support from the principal in terms of some relief in the classroom while she was in the process of therapy.

While we do need to be sensitive to teachers' needs, children should not become victims of stresses in teachers' lives if the school will not act. If you do not get satisfaction within the school, you may decide to file charges. This will most likely be triggered if your child is bruised, bleeding, or in any other way physically damaged.

Filing Assault Charges with the Police

While parents can charge educators for assault and battery, it is difficult to obtain cooperation from prosecutors. Prosecutors are guided by a generally conservative judicial tradition that suggests that the courts should avoid becoming embroiled in school disciplinary problems. However, knowing this, you can not prejudge the situation. Individual prosecutors have been outraged by abuses and have charged teachers with assault and battery. However, in most cases with which we are familiar, parents have had to obtain attorneys to assist in convincing law enforcement authorities to file criminal charges against the abuser. When this is not successful the attorney may have to file civil charges.

Theoretically, anyone can file assault charges. Whether the police or prosecutors will do anything about the charges is another story. It is especially difficult for charges to be taken seriously if your child has been psychologically assaulted, since you have no physical evidence of abuse. However, you may be able to successfully file harassment charges against the teacher if you can demonstrate a pattern of verbal assaults. Your case will be strengthened if you can show that the assaults continued after you made ongoing efforts to make the teacher and authorities aware of the situation.

In many rural areas and small towns, parents have reported to me that the police have discouraged them or refused to allow them to file charges. It is important that you show officials the evidence of the bruises—you may find a sympathetic officer. In the *Garcia* v. *Miera* case in New Mexico, the investigating officer was so outraged when he observed the actual bruises on Teresa Garcia's legs and buttocks that he took the paddle away from the offending educator.

In Talladega, Alabama, law enforcement officers not only accepted charges, but the District Attorney vowed to prosecute a teacher for brutally paddling little seven-year-old Jason Morris. The case was quickly brought to trial and Judge John Coleman found the teacher guilty of third-degree assault and fined her $250 and court costs. So even in rural Alabama, at least one mother who took pictures of her bruised child to the sheriff's office found that the system did work for the victim.

Filing Child Abuse Charges

Every state has a child abuse agency. It is usually in a department with a title such as Human Services, Youth and Family Services, or Child Welfare. Most states have child abuse hot lines listed in the phone directory or easily found through information operators.

Child abuse authorities have a peculiar difficulty in dealing with school abuse in regard to reporting procedures. In every state it is mandatory that suspected child abuse be reported. That is, if you suspect child abuse and don't report it, you are liable for prosecution. To encourage reporting there are strict rules protecting the confidentiality of the person reporting the suspected abuse.

Mandatory reporting laws were developed to deal mostly with abuse in the home. Neighbors, friends, and relatives would be most reluctant to report suspected abuse if they feared retribution. Yet in the case of school abuse, the parents or physician are almost always the persons reporting. This is soon known to the alleged abuser and to the school community. Therefore, the potential investigation of the case presents additional problems of confidentiality for the workers and the reporters.

All states have quite elaborate laws to protect teachers from arbitrary suspension or firing. These are related to the tenure process and require that any punitive action against a teacher must follow a series of due process procedures. While these personnel procedures are usually carried out behind closed doors, teachers are allowed rights such as being faced by their accusers, presentation of written charges, and the right to counsel. However, in any significant action against a teacher, the media eventually become involved as teachers, unions, administrators, school board members, parents, and sometimes students get drawn into the morass of charges and countercharges. This is not an arena familiar to most child abuse workers, and is certainly one that taxes their ability to function within their own guidelines of confidentiality.

When you call to report abuse, you will be assigned a case worker who will investigate. Workers will respond most rapidly if they believe a child is in imminent, life-threatening peril. Most school abuse cases do not fit that profile and will probably receive low priority. Typically, child abuse case workers are overworked and poorly trained; they have a high burnout rate. When you inform them that the abuse occurred in a school, you are immediately creating problems. You are asking that one state agency investigate problems in an institution governed by another state agency. Therefore, in many states, child abuse workers will be reluctant to investigate cases in schools. They may be unclear about what to do and will probably seek help from a supervisor. If the problem is shifted to higher levels of supervisors, it may reach a level where the employees' political concerns make them quite reluctant to cross agency lines.

Another problem is related to the level of the agency to which you report the abuse. If the case is kept at the local or county level, the higher-level authorities may be closely politically connected to educational officials. This is especially true in less populated areas where all the governmental agency personnel know each other. It is very difficult for an outsider to influence these local oligarchies. In this type of situation your only hope is to get help from agencies outside the local oligarchy. For instance, you might get support from a state child abuse association associated with the National Committee for the Prevention of Child Abuse. They can pressure government agencies much more effectively than you can. Another possible source of help is a county child advocate.

If the agency is organized at the state level, political implications may still operate. But whichever agency you deal with, if the state laws protect teachers, you probably won't get much help. However, we think it is important that all school abuse cases be reported by physicians and parents. Physicians have specific guidelines for diagnosing and reporting. Eventually, the record of these cases will make an impact on lawmakers if both parents and physicians keep reporting and following up to determine what happened. And at a personal level, your official record of the actions you have taken is important if you decide to sue the school.

Instituting Litigation

About two-thirds of the distressed parents who call us have been unable to find a lawyer to help them or were dissatisfied with the first lawyer they employed. On the other hand, most of the attorneys with whom we have worked on these cases have been exceptional in terms of dedication, desire to achieve justice, and lack of concern for how much money they will make. In our experience, there are four major issues to consider up front if you are going to sue. These are time, money, selecting an attorney, and understanding teachers' due process rights.

Time and money are usually on the side of the school. School personnel often wear parents down with bureaucratic procedures and constant delays. They know that the more they delay and communicate with your attorney (if you get one), the more it costs you. They also know that if you have taken your child out of school, you don't want to interrupt his or her education too long. Also, if they wish to make things really difficult, they may try to force your child back to school through truancy laws. You may counter this by placing your child in a private school, applying to pay tuition in a neighboring public school, or setting up home schooling. In the latter situation, check with your state department of education for guidelines.

You may be morally outraged at the injustice and inequality in power between you and the school when you receive short shrift from the school authorities after your child has been abused. While some lawyers may feel the same and be willing to offer immediate help, most will first weigh the probable cost against the possibility of successful litigation. There are two ways in which they can consider their fees.

A lawyer who takes the case strictly on a fee-per-hour basis will make money whether or not you win the case. A lot of hours can be generated in dealing with the school board and their attorneys, who are usually on retainer. For the school, the initial financial drain from your case is negligible. They will be much more concerned with the bad publicity than the initial costs of the case and will therefore attempt to keep the early maneuvering between lawyers out of the public spotlight. Meanwhile, the meter in your lawyer's office keeps ticking away.

If you do hire an attorney on an hourly basis, it is crucial that you make sure that the person has no social, political, or religious

ties to the educational establishment. We know that lawyers are ethically bound not to take cases if they have a conflict of interest or
dual relationships. Unfortunately, we know of too many cases where
attorneys were not straightforward with the distressed parents about
past and present relationships with school authorities. The parents
eventually either gave up, thinking they had gotten good legal advice, or ended up poorer but wiser after firing the attorney.

If you do hire a lawyer on a fee basis, try to find one with some
experience in dealing with schools and with a good track record
in liability (tort) litigation. Perhaps even more important is a background in advocacy law. Attorneys who have worked as public defenders, in poverty law centers, and in consumer rights movements
are knowledgeable about fighting for the rights of individuals
against government agencies or corporations.

Unless you have a really strong case, a lawyer whom you know
and trust, and adequate financial resources, we would suggest trying
to avoid hiring an attorney on a per-hour basis. You may be better
off finding a lawyer with experience in malpractice, liability, or
worker's compensation who will take the case on a contingency basis.
This means that the lawyer will not charge you or will just charge you
for certain expenses, with the anticipation of winning the case and
receiving a percentage of the award or settlement as the fee.

Depending on your financial status and the attorney's confi-
dence in winning the case, you can negotiate how much of the secondary expenses you will pay up front. These include fixed costs
such as secretarial services, postage, and so on, which someone
must cover. There is a major advantage and disadvantage in this
type of relationship.

To accept the case on a contingency basis, the attorney needs
to be convinced that there is a good chance of either settling out
of court (which is usually preferable) or winning in court. Therefore, if an experienced lawyer accepts your case on a contingency
basis, you have a pretty good chance of some settlement. You can
be sure that the lawyer, who has invested his or her own time and
money, will work very hard on your behalf.

The problem with the contingency approach is that, in general, the financial settlements in school abuse cases are not very
high compared to other types of awards in damage cases. Cases I
am familiar with range from settlements of a low of $13,000 in the
rural South to a high of $80,000 in the Southwest.

Because of state laws and professional ethics, attorneys' fees usually top out between 30 percent and 40 percent of the settlement. This usually occurs after fixed expenses such as typing, travel, and fees for expert testimony are deducted. Because of the limited fees, very successful and experienced lawyers may not wish to take on cases of this type.

Most of the lawyers with whom we have worked have tended to be young, or at most at the mid-career level. Despite this, most have done excellent jobs. With any lawyer you should feel free to negotiate fees. Generally there are state limits on what percentage of settlement or awards they may accept—but you don't have to agree to the maximum.

A third alternative is to obtain help through the American Civil Liberties Union (ACLU), a poverty law center, law school legal clinic, or other advocacy group. However, these approaches are difficult for most parents to take. The ACLU will generally not take cases unless constitutional issues are involved, and conservative politicians—with increasing power in Congress and state legislatures—have severely limited the resources and types of cases that poverty law centers and other publicly funded advocacy legal groups can take on.

In any charges against a teacher, school authorities are bound by state laws covering personnel actions. These well-established laws and regulations are ingrained in the minds of all school constituents. Therefore, to deal with the school, it is important to understand the thinking of the teachers, administrators, and school boards. The first thing to understand is that in most states a teacher can not be summarily dismissed, suspended, or penalized without following proper procedures. Therefore, if you go into the school demanding that the teacher be punished, you are probably asking for an impossible solution.

You must understand that the most immediate action an administrator can take, even if he or she believes that the teacher has abused your child and wants to take strong action, is to suspend the teacher, usually with pay. This means that a substitute teacher will have to be hired and that the school board attorney will have to begin dealing with both the teacher's attorney and quite often the attorney from the teacher's union.

In general, local teachers' unions, administrators, and teachers will deny that abuse is even a possibility in their schools. They will assure you that if abuse were occurring, they would of course take immediate action. However, it is very difficult for school administrators to discipline a teacher without proper documentation, which is rarely available. Further, in too many cases abusers have been popular, macho coaches, who revel in their toughness. Often, their rough-and-tough treatment of athletes carries over into their classrooms or administrative positions. While parents may accept a coach kicking a football player in the butt to get him to move faster, they may not accept the same behavior in their daughter's math class. Unfortunately, coaches—especially if they have winning records—are often revered in the community and are nearly immune from disciplinary actions by higher-level administrators. (Of course, it may be another story if their teams consistently lose.)

It is administratively easier to support an abusing teacher than it is to fire one. Therefore, rather than be defensive, the school authorities typically go on the offensive. When this happens, the battle of the lawyers begins. This is where you will quickly find out if you have an attorney who is willing to give you the dedication, time, energy, persistence, availability, support, and enthusiasm needed to persevere over the powers of officialdom.

· · ·

This chapter gives you a cookbook for what to do if you decide to take a stand against toxic teachers or dangerous schools. Much of what we recommend is based on the assumption, grounded in our case experiences, that schools' responses will probably be to deny, lie, stonewall, and bully. There are probably many situations where schools do not respond this way, but we never hear about them— parents whose complaints are addressed and redressed in a civilized manner have no need to call in the heavy artillery.

We remind you again, we are not teacher or school bashers, but rather advocates for the rights of educators, students, and parents. If our schools are to be exemplars of justice and equity, parents have the right and responsibility to resist maltreatment and seek redress. And when schools deny redress, you need to know what they are likely to do. This is presented in the next chapter.

Chapter 8

Taking Action
Understanding the Playing Field and How to Make It Even

In Chapter Seven we introduced the steps you must take when you suspect school maltreatment. In this chapter we will consider some of the consequences of various strategies and discuss what you and your family can anticipate if you decide to take legal or political action.

Taking Action: What You Should Know and Do

If you are going to do something about the maltreatment of your child or other students, you need political savvy. This chapter will give you an overview of what you need to know to develop a strategy. We will begin with what happens if your child has been abused and you have decided to litigate. This picks up from the end of the preceding chapter, where we discussed selecting an attorney.

Know Your Local Politics

There is no question that regional differences and local politics have a profound effect on shaping the initial stages of a school abuse case. Many attorneys have business, social, political, or even religious affiliation with school officials, especially members of the school board—and in a small community, it may be hard to avoid such connections. In a case of a severe paddling of a primary grade student in Florida, the attorney for the child spent over a year making no progress. It turned out that he was a deacon in the church that sponsored the Christian school where the child was paddled. Most of his efforts seemed to have been aimed at keeping the case from the media and discouraging the parents from actually going to court.

Your potential attorney may have local political aspirations. If you are in a rural or conservative area, your attorney's political goals will not be enhanced by appearing to be so liberal as to defy traditional beliefs about discipline. Yet by taking the case and getting you to be "reasonable" with the school authorities, he can be viewed as an ally of the local political establishment and still collect his fee from you. Be very wary of that pattern, especially if the attorney keeps you out of the process so that you don't know what is happening.

Of course, politics could work to your advantage if the potential attorney sees winning against a school board as a stepping stone to career growth or political power. The attorney may be very interested in child abuse and want to be identified as a politician who opposes any abuses of children.

Whether politics refers to your attorney's desires to make good connections and further his or her career or actually maneuver in the real world of politics, try to determine what will help you most. This is perhaps a cynical view of the workings of our legal system, but it is a view tempered by reality.

If you live in the Bible Belt or any generally conservative rural area, it will be difficult to find an objective judge or jury if you decide to go to trial. One problem is that jury members may be concerned that successful litigation will raise insurance rates and eventually their own taxes. Also, in a culture where corporal punishment is considered a God-given mandate, they may not believe that students can develop EIPTSD from school paddlings. Our research shows that the best jury for the victim would be made up primarily of upper-middle-class citizens with degrees beyond the bachelor's level, who are professionals, who reside in or come from the Northeast, are either Jewish or Catholic, and grew up in homes where there was little or no spanking, psychological maltreatment, or harsh punishment. It is best if they have read books on parenting and education.

You will have the worst chance if your jury is made up primarily of citizens with high school or less education who come from or live in the rural South or other predominantly rural areas, are either Baptists or Fundamentalist Protestants of other denominations, and were spanked often as children. You are in real trouble if they believe the advice of James Dobson or the other self-proclaimed Christian parenting experts who base their suggestions on Biblical injunctions.

The best remedy to local biases is to get your trial into a federal court. This means that at least part of your claim must be based on violations of federal laws or constitutional freedoms. These may include claims such as violation of equal protection or due process rights. You need to discuss this with your lawyer. Even though you may get a conservative judge, your chances of getting a fair hearing and a decent jury will be enhanced in a federal court, where local political issues are less likely to affect the outcome. Make sure to discuss this with your attorney. Also, understand that before you go to court you will probably have to wend your way through the school's system of grievances and appeals, which are in part controlled by law.

How Your School May Try to Intimidate Your Family

Parents know that teachers have tremendous power to get back at kids. When I was an idealistic beginning teacher in a small rural school I was shocked that one particular teacher scapegoated every child from a family he disliked. He even instigated his students to abuse one of the children of this family, who was in my class. Several of his students were ridiculing the particular child in the lunch room when three of my students told them to stop. Name-calling and threats emerged from both sides. The abusive teacher sent my students to the principal. When I found out what had happened, I was furious—but relatively powerless to stop the abuse, despite my complaints to the principal. That teacher carried on a vendetta against the children of that family for years.

You must recognize a teacher's potential for getting back at your child or a sibling. A common technique is for educators to make snide remarks to the victim or siblings, alluding to the parents' willingness to sue about anything. Unfair disciplinary procedures may be used. Other kids may be encouraged to scapegoat, ridicule, or isolate the victim. Sometimes the intimidation is generated outside the school.

For example, Troy Ashment, a fourth grader in Wyoming, was paddled by his entire class at the behest of his teacher. His mother alleged that the Elders of the Mormon Church implied that the parents should drop the suit because all parties were Mormons and it would be an embarrassment to the church. The parents dropped out of the church, and eventually won a settlement and moved out of the area.

If your child is intimidated, keep written records of all events. Seek documentation of witnesses if possible. If intimidation continues, you might demand your child's immediate removal from the offending teacher's class or school building. It is preferable to do this in a written letter from your lawyer. This also helps your attorney keep abreast of all events. If you have not worked with an attorney before, do not be shocked or angry if you don't get an immediate response to your requests. Our experience has been that busy lawyers are not always instantly accessible. However, if their slow responses are frequently too late to be helpful, you might reconsider your choice of attorney.

The Age-Old Ploy of Blaming the Victim

Frequently, those in power manipulate the situation by actually blaming those they have victimized. For example, we blamed the Indians for being heathens and for attacking settlers after we took the Indians' land, denigrated their religion, killed their game, and slaughtered their women and children. Slaves were blamed for being ignorant and intellectually inferior when we denied them education. Some judges still blame raped women for wearing provocative clothes. So this concept should not be new to you.

Invariably, defendant school boards will try to show that the victim deserved the punishment. They may fabricate stories of prior misbehavior by the abused student. They may explain the victim's symptoms as resulting from abuse at home! They will try to find anything in your family that shows that you caused the child's emotional problems. They will dredge up divorce, parental squabbles, previous spankings or harsh discipline, alcoholism in the family, disciplinary or academic problems of siblings. They will even claim that your litigation is the cause of the child's ills. How many times have I heard the statement, "If only the parents would drop the matter the child would be OK." This is almost invariably absolutely wrong, as in the following case.

In 1998 Robert Griffin, a psychologist in rural northeastern Pennsylvania, called about an interesting case in which a coach openly assaulted a student. Even though the student was injured, witnesses were present, and the outraged parents threatened litigation, the system beat them because of their lack of persistence. This sad illustration of blaming the victim is told by Mr. Griffin, since the agreement with the school board prevents the parents from talking about the case.

In the fall of 1997, a sixteen-year-old junior named Shane Acrenese was at football practice in Pittson Area High School. Because of a sprained ankle, he was not able to run laps as quickly as required. Assistant coach John Garibaldi called him over, ordered him to take off his helmet and in a rage threw him against a metal fence. Mr. Garibaldi then punched him in the face and refused his request to use the phone to call his father. Meanwhile, his brother, also a member of the football team, called their father who came immediately to the practice field.

Mr. Acrenese was greeted by a smiling Mr. Garibaldi who was sitting with his arms folded. An argument ensued in which Mr. Acrenese apparently made some threats. The police, who had been called by the father, arrived and referred Shane to the hospital where he was treated for a back injury, concussion, and facial contusions.

While the family waited for the police to complete their investigation, the media publicized the incident. This infuriated the school board, which supported Mr. Garibaldi's claim that Shane had attacked him and that he had acted in self-defense. As punishment for alleged assault, for which Shane needed medical treatment, Shane was suspended for five days. In addition, Mr. Garibaldi filed harassment charges against both Shane and his father.

The school's investigation did not include an interview with Shane's brother who witnessed the assault. As publicity increased, the school board decided that Shane's "attack" was grievous enough to recommend expulsion for this young man who had no previous disciplinary record. The threat of expulsion apparently dampened the family's desire to sue the school since Shane would be denied an education for the rest of his junior year and senior year. They agreed to a one-month expulsion, after which Shane would be permitted to return to school under the condition that no one in the family communicate with the media. This ploy resulted in the community's impression that Shane had been the aggressor. Meanwhile, the harassment charges against Shane and his father went forward.

A year later, the local magistrate upheld the harassment charges against Shane and his father and exonerated Mr. Garibaldi. Meanwhile, school officials had checked into the background of Mr. Garibaldi and discovered that he had been involved in similar incidents. Mr. Garibaldi was forced out of the school district but apparently retained the loyalty of the head football coach. Fellow players requested that Shane return to the team, but the coach threatened to resign if Shane was allowed to play again. Shane, a religious, well-behaved student who attended church twice a week and had no history of school misbehavior, was emotionally affected. He was deprived of playing football his last two years in high school and felt that his dreams of playing college football would not be fulfilled.

This case illustrates how school officials can completely distort the truth and blame the victim. If Shane's parents had the resources and persistence, they might have prevailed, especially in light of Mr. Garibaldi's alleged history of abuse. Although he was never evaluated, we suspect that Shane suffered from EIPTSD, even though the condition can be minimized by a very supportive family such as his.

Children who have developed EIPTSD need reassurance and support. They need to know that you will protect them and be there for them. Despite the fact that they may have to give repeated, painful accounts of the traumatic event, this will help them in the long run. Not talking about it can cause more harm. When they are able to talk about the event without becoming emotionally upset, they will have mastered the trauma. This means that memories and verbal recounting of the event no longer cause emotional reactions such as crying or anxiety responses. They are then able to go on with their lives. So do not let anyone tell you that victims are better off forgetting about what happened to them.

The Child Already Had Problems, So Why Blame Us?

It may be true in some cases that a maltreated student already had problems. But does this justify adding to them? Many of the children we have evaluated had histories of learning disabilities or emotional difficulties prior to the school abuse. Some had been physically or sexually abused. From a legal point of view, prior injury does not free the perpetrator from responsibility. Nonetheless, if the student victim does not have any identifiable existing trauma, the school may fabricate some. This does not affect the validity of the case itself—according to tort law, you take victims where you find them—but it can make the suit more difficult for the family.

The analogy often used by lawyers is based on the "eggshell" theory. If a driver hits a person who receives serious long-term head injuries because his skull was abnormally thin (like an eggshell), the driver is not free from liability because of the abnormally thin skull of the victim. If abused schoolchildren already have emotional problems from abuse at home, all the more reason not to abuse them in school.

By now, you probably know more about school abuses and EIPTSD than most school authorities. Most school personnel are not only unfamiliar with the literature on school maltreatment, but they are also generally ignorant of the literature on school discipline. Because maltreatments are invariably based on improper or excessive disciplinary procedures, you will be way ahead of school personnel if you are familiar with their own disciplinary codes. You may also have an advantage by reading some of the books on school discipline listed in the resource section at the end of the book.

Wearing You Down

You can predict that the school will try to wear you down. Schools are relatively stable institutions and generally have the time and resources to drag out the litigation longer than you are able to afford. They know that you fear for your child, and that you will become impatient with due process procedures and multiple levels of administrative meetings.

School personnel may discover if there is dissension in your nuclear or extended family, with some members urging you to drop the action against the school. This will encourage them to stall. They may also stall until the school year is over and everyone is taking vacations. This will put you on hold over the summer and help weaken your resolve. Therefore you need to maintain your anger, indignation, and sense of purpose if you want to achieve your goals.

Your lawyer can counterattack the stalling procedures by actively calling for fact-finding under court-ordered deadlines. Attorneys can institute many depositions of school personnel. They can tie up busy administrators with paperwork and bring in expert witnesses who will cost money for the board to depose. (This is where it's helpful to have a contingency fee arrangement rather than pay-as-you-go—if you're paying by the hour, these measures quickly become very costly for you as well as for your opponents.)

Time can also help you publicize your case and to build a coalition of allies. It can help you learn to deal effectively with the media. Also, time can help you enlist the aid of experts and professional groups.

Other Accusations

Since schools are so much a part of the political fabric of communities, it is likely that a defendant school will attempt to generate sympathy for itself by painting you as a selfish, money-grubbing parent. The school officials will probably point out that you are in essence suing the community rather than them. Since school officials generally will not have to pay out of their pockets, this should not be an issue. However, they will publicize their interpretation that you are going for the deep pockets lined with citizens' tax money. They will garner public sympathy with the claim that money used for litigation should be used for educating students rather than paying lawyers to defend the school. They may allege that your interest in monetary gain overshadows your judgment as good parents since continuing the case is causing pain and embarrassment for your child, family, friends, and the community.

Although most school boards have attorneys on retainer, the time they spend on abuse cases is not free, since they could be doing other work. Often, the teachers' union will also retain a lawyer to defend the abuser. Sometimes accused abusers will hire their own attorneys. Cost to the school board will include time away from the job for the accused abuser and staff witnesses and other school personnel. The attorney's clock keeps ticking while deposing all of these parties in addition to student witnesses, plaintiff victims, and their families.

Additional expenses accrue from expert witnesses who charge for their time preparing for and testifying in depositions. These expenses can mount up rapidly. When teachers are required to be present during legal proceedings, substitute teachers must be paid to cover their classes. School officials are aware that most of these expenses eventually come out of the taxpayers' pockets, if only in higher fees for school liability insurance.

This latter point is very important to understand in convincing school boards to settle cases. Whether schools have their own liability funds, pool their funds with other schools, or use commercial insurance companies, they will not be popular with their insurers if expensive trials are required. This is a point made in several articles I have read in professional education journals cautioning schools to apply discipline fairly and appropriately.

Defendant schools frequently allege that the victim's parents have a grudge against the teacher or that they are out to get the school for some perceived past injustice. In other words, they will think of some way to show that your primary motive is revenge.

Publicity: How You Can Use It

Schools are essentially political entities that, above all, fear bad public relations. Most administrators struggle to maintain the status quo and avoid the media, except to publicize accomplishments or to announce school functions to the public. But in the long run, even bad publicity does little harm to tenured educators.

Because school superintendents are not entitled to tenure and school board members are elected officials, they are more vulnerable than teachers. Because they are vulnerable, they are likely to attempt to make you look bad in the media. They can protect themselves from public exposure by hiding behind state laws requiring that all school personnel deliberations and decisions be confidential. Therefore, they may feel free to attack you publicly.

But the media love nothing more than the classic American struggle between the little guy and city hall. Add a touch of child abuse and you have the ingredients that increase newspaper circulation and TV viewing time. This is the worst nightmare of educators. This fear of confrontation, litigation, and public ridicule can be one of your best allies in moving a case toward settlement. But be careful—local media coverage may be sympathetic to the school. This is especially true in conservative rural areas where the newspaper editors are part of the local oligarchy. That is why it is important to seek coverage in the nearest metropolitan area and at the state and national levels.

Some lawyers thrive on publicity as it provides free advertising. In at least three cases with which I am familiar, the parents' prospective lawyers were very tentative about taking the cases. I spoke with the attorneys about media coverage and opportunities to present their cases at the national level. I reviewed strategies to increase their probability of getting positive local and regional coverage. Immediately afterward they agreed to take the cases and intelligently used the media.

A negative factor in responding to the media is that it can be very painful for your child and family. Your child may be asked repeatedly to recount the traumatic events in public settings that are not necessarily therapeutic. For instance, a severely paddled adolescent from Ohio appeared with me on the *Oprah Winfrey Show* and cried in front of the audience and millions of viewers. This was a humiliating experience for an adolescent.

The more national media coverage your case receives, the more hostile will be the response from local authorities. It may also mean hostile reactions from friends or sympathizers of the offending teacher or school. When popular coaches are the abusers, complaining parents may even receive threatening phone calls, as in the Kunz case (described later in this chapter).

It is clear that the media, if sympathetic to your cause, can be valuable agents in forcing the schools to settle cases quickly. But even if some school officials want to settle the case quickly, their hands may be tied by their own internal political pressures. We have seen cases where a long-entrenched, recalcitrant majority of board members are so used to getting their way that they will fight to the bitter end, even though all evidence suggests that they will lose the case. The presence of dissenters on the school board who favor settlement calls for media accounts that point out the clear differences of opinion among school board members.

Family Stress

If you decide to take on the school system, you should know that you will pay a price. Hostile attacks by school authorities can trigger various reactions in your family. The nature and severity of these reactions will depend on many factors. These include your family's previous experiences with the school and your family's mental health. Your reactions will be affected by family cohesiveness, marital stability, and the extent of your support network. Perseverance will depend on how fervently you believe in your cause and your ability to withstand becoming a victim.

No single pattern of stress symptoms applies to all families, but most experience some initial combination of feelings of anger, rage, and disbelief. Common initial reactions when school authorities trivialize the event or lie, deny, denigrate, or ignore parents are, "This could not really have happened to my kid," "It was all a mistake," and "I will beat the crap out of that teacher."

If no apology or restitution is quickly forthcoming, your anger and incredulity may turn to anxiety, depression, and fear for the mental health and physical safety of your child. We have noted differences between the reactions of mothers and fathers of victimized students. When initially confronting schools, mothers tend to be angry, fearful, and protective of their children. Fathers frequently experience intense rage, and in some cases they have physically attacked school authorities.

As the counterattack from the school increases, both parents may become fearful, depressed, and somewhat paranoid about what is being said about them in the community. They may fear—sometimes realistically—anonymous threats and worry about the educational future of their child. Financial concerns and negative reactions from friends, relatives, and neighbors may increase feelings of depression and paranoia. In some cases parents develop PTSD as a result of the continued barrage from the school board.

When maltreated children return to school, some students may harass them, not infrequently with encouragement from some school staff. Staff and peers may ridicule your victimized child with statements asserting that he or she couldn't take the punishment like other kids. Verbal assaults on the child may include false allegations about your motives for suing a popular educator, especially if the perpetrator is a coach.

Family stress may be intensified regarding whether to send children back to the classroom or the school where the maltreatment occurred. If the victim is experiencing intense stress symptoms, the decision should be made in consultation with a mental health professional with experience in childhood trauma. If one is not readily available, even a phone consultation with an expert will be helpful. One way to find someone is to call the county or state professional association of psychologists, psychiatrists, or social workers. Remember to stay away from any professionals who might have a conflict of interest because of previous or current employment in the school district or personal relations with school officials or staff.

If no professional help is immediately available, use your judgment based on what you have read in this book. Do not force the child back into a situation that will cause more stress for your family. The ultimate goal is to help the child return to school and not be afraid of the abuser, other educators, and the whole educational enterprise. The return to school may have to be done in stages.

Victims who return to school in stages will need to discuss their apprehensions each day. Parents must reassure them regarding irrational fears and take steps to intervene if any harassment occurs. Children's statements, behaviors, symptoms, recollections of what happened in school, and validation by witnesses need to be documented. This will require constant talking, reassurances, and support from family members, friends, clergy, and others.

A major treatment strategy for PTSD is to desensitize the victim to fears associated with the place or person associated with the trauma. This is one reason therapists help the victim through slow steps, using specialized techniques, to repeatedly tell about the event until this can be done without experiencing the stress symptoms associated with it. Therefore, even if you can not obtain immediate therapy for the child, you can help your child through your understanding that victims must master trauma in order to become survivors.

Now that we have told you the worst you can expect, we will give you the good news. All the families with whom we have worked, even those who have lost their cases in court, have come out stronger. Refusing to be victims, they became survivors. Let us tell you what we mean by this.

In the field of trauma studies we distinguish between victims and survivors of interpersonal trauma. A victim is someone who has not mastered the psychological effects of a trauma. A victim continues to suffer PTSD symptoms such as avoidance, anxiety, and unwanted recurring thoughts of the event. However, a survivor psychologically masters the trauma and is able to confront and deal with the perpetrator. Part of doing this is refusing to see yourself as a victim and realizing that almost all offenders are emotionally and morally deficient. Their credibility is entirely dependent on some type of force. The use of force, like punishment, is only effective in the short run.

One way to become a survivor in school maltreatment cases is to remember that the school is wrong, no matter how its personnel try to distort the issues. After reading this book, you now know that you are not alone. You know about the pedagogical inadequacies of educators who must rely on force and fear to motivate students. You know that as an American citizen, taxpayer, and concerned parent, you have a right to be treated with dignity and respect. You and your child are entitled to due process under school regulations and law.

There are many positive aspects to seeking redress for a student who has been maltreated. These include the pride of fighting for right and justice and becoming a positive model of whistle-blowing. This offers a good example for children in these days of going along to get along in order to avoid offending those who are in control of your life. Contesting the school, even if you lose the battle, will often reinforce your bond with your child and the rest of your family. And you may, as in many cases, force your school to eliminate abusive disciplinary practices and become more humane.

If you follow the recommendations we offer you will become aware of techniques of effective education and discipline. You may force your school to significantly change its discipline policies and put teeth in the rules that govern what teachers can not do in the name of control. Many survivors' families have taken their combat experiences with local boards to the state and national levels. In most states that have banned corporal punishment in schools, survivors have been leaders in the battle.

You can turn bad into good if you apply an ancient principle of Asian martial arts. Let your enemies' strength and force be used against them. Even though a local oligarchy may seem all-powerful, their worst enemy is their arrogance and belief that they are the omnipotent fish in a small, easily controlled pond. Based on their belief in their own power, they will often say and do stupid things. For instance, in almost all the cases with which we are familiar, the offending educator had a history of abuse. When the parents complained to a principal or higher-level administrator, the official would say something like, "Gee, I can't understand this. Nobody ever complained about Mr. Jones before. I am sure that this is a mistake. Your child must be exaggerating."

Now this is just plain ill-advised, especially if you get it on tape. As soon as the story of your child's abuse gets around, particularly if it hits the media, former victims will emerge. If they are able, they will contact you. Just document everything. But documentation should be done within a framework of understanding how schools and the law may affect the outcome of your litigation.

Educators' Rights and Other Legal Issues

To deal with the school, it is important to understand the thinking of teachers, administrators, and school boards. The first thing you should know is that most school principals will do anything to avoid rocking the boat. They want to keep everybody happy. This means a balancing act between reassuring parents that they are important, keeping teachers content so they do not rebel, and running a school with no problems for their bosses. Principals know that if they antagonize any one of these constituencies their careers are either on hold or in jeopardy. The exception may occur if they have extremely strong support from one group that can protect them.

When most principals are confronted by an angry parent, it is likely that they will shift gears in an effort to keep the waters calm. However, if the complaining parents do not get satisfaction and the principal is encouraged to stonewall, parents can anticipate a difficult time. For instance, let's assume you complain to a principal and he or she sides with you from the beginning. The principal decides to reprimand or take other disciplinary action against the abusing teacher. The principal's hands may turn out to be tied.

As previously mentioned, a teacher cannot be summarily dismissed, suspended, or penalized without following specific legal procedures. If you march into the school demanding immediate punishment for the teacher, you are probably asking for an impossible solution. Before principals take any disciplinary action against teachers, they will consult a higher-level administrator and probably the school board's attorney. The superintendent will generally not act without the approval of the personnel committee of the school board, the president of the school board, and the school attorney. After clearing these hurdles, if the teacher is to be suspended, all parties understand that there will a series of lengthy and private due process hearings.

Depending on the charges, the school board may suspend the teacher with or without pay. In either case, a substitute teacher will have to be hired. Also, the school board attorney will have to begin dealing with both the teacher's attorney and quite often the attorney from the teacher's union. Invariably, either some or all of the people working in your child's school building will become hostile to the principal, you, and possibly your child.

Unless the assault on your child is particularly horrific it is highly unlikely that any immediate action will be taken. It is more likely that your charges will be followed by separate investigations by the principal, the superintendent, the school board, and perhaps the school attorney. It has been our experience that school board attorneys advise school personnel not to admit to anything. They are generally not concerned about the mental health of your family, since their job is to protect the school treasury. This is a shame, because they do not seem to understand that often a simple admission of guilt followed by an apology and a promise to discontinue maltreatment can avert litigation.

In general, the school community collectively will deny that abuse is even a possibility, while swearing up and down that of course they would take immediate action if abuse were really occurring. Unfortunately, as noted earlier, the reality is that it is administratively easier to support an abusing teacher than it is to fire one. This predisposes school authorities to go on the offensive at once, without looking at the possibly troubling facts of the matter. If you decide to persist in pressing your allegations, you will probably face a long battle. Before you proceed, you need to be familiar with two concepts that will help in determining strategy. These are qualified immunity and educational malpractice.

Qualified Immunity

Legislatures are supposed to protect the public treasury from ill-advised use of taxpayers' funds. Now, do not laugh, we said "supposed to." A way to do that would be to set very high standards for all public employees, including elected officials, and to provide constant ethical oversight and supervision. But there is an easier way to protect public funds from incompetence and negligence. Legislatures can pass laws giving public officials and employees certain types of immunity from being sued. This is called *qualified* (or sometimes *sovereign*) *immunity.*

Qualified immunity laws protect government officials who act in good faith within their authority in all but the most exceptional cases. These laws are meant to protect them from the burdens of civil trials and from liability for money damages arising from the performance of their duties. They are not protected when their violations of laws or constitutional rights are clearly recognized as violations by any reasonable person. This makes your attempt to sue difficult since you must prove that no reasonable school official could have believed that his or her maltreatment of your child was lawful and within the guidelines of established law. The problem is that reasonableness, especially in the arena of education, is a vague concept that is defined by where you live. For instance, take the case of *Jenkins* v. *Talladega City Board of Education.*

In 1992, Cassandra Jenkins, Onieka McKenzie, and Anthony Jemison, second graders at Graham Elementary in Talladega,

Alabama, were strip-searched for $7 that was missing from a classmate's purse. Under the supervision of Susannah Herring, music teacher, with the assistance of Melbal Sirmon, guidance counselor, the two girls were stripped twice. First, they were sent into bathroom stalls, told to remove all of their clothes except for their panties, which they were required to pull down to their ankles. They were then told to exit the stalls for inspection. When no money was found and after consulting with the principal, the girls were ordered to return to the restroom at which time they were told to remove their dresses in front of the two women and to shake their dresses to assure the money was not hidden. Again nothing was found. During all of this, it was decided that Anthony, who had also been accused of the theft and claimed to know where the money was, should not be strip-searched. He was removed from the investigation.

After investigation, the school board concluded that the two educators had committed errors in judgment by not immediately notifying the principal and by not calling the children's parents. Despite these findings and the superintendent's recommendation that Herring be fired, the board declined to impose any serious penalties.

The parents of the two girls sued the school district claiming violation of civil rights. Only the girls were stripped and they claimed that in other searches in the Talladega schools, race seemed to determine who would be searched. A three-judge panel of the U.S. Court of Appeals, Eleventh Circuit, agreed with the defendant school board that the plaintiffs failed to prove discrimination claims based on either gender or race. The court also dismissed any violation of any Alabama tort law, thereby denying the possibility that the strip searches could cause any emotional damage. The court then decided on its own to examine whether the two educators were entitled to qualified immunity from the alleged unconstitutional searches.

While the court recognized the responsibility to strike a balance between individuals' constitutional guarantees and the rights of public officials to carry out their duties in a reasonable way, two of the three judges concluded that Herring and Sirmon acted in "blatant disregard of the Fourth Amendment" and they were therefore not entitled to qualified immunity.

The dissenting judge's opinion was heavily weighted in favor of the two educators. His rationale was that the courts should not attempt to second-guess school personnel. Since the school district did not have guidelines for strip-searching and there was no established law in either Alabama or the Eleventh Circuit to determine the nature of violations, the educators had no basis to believe that they had done anything wrong.

We must assume that the dissenting judge's reasoning resonated with the rest of the court, which decided to reexamine the panel's finding. On June 2, 1997, the full court granted the two educators qualified immunity. They stated that "in the absence of any detailed [legal] . . . guidance, no reasonable school official" would be able to determine whether age, sex, or grade level should be considered when deciding to strip-search students.

The court justified this strip search on the grounds that the female students were searched by female teachers, the girls were prepubescent, and supposedly teachers frequently assist eight-year-old students in the bathroom in such instances as when they accidentally wet themselves. These conclusions are so preposterous that they almost do not deserve a response—but we will offer one anyway.

While it is laudable that male teachers did not examine the children, children are taught not to take their clothes off in front of adults other than close relatives or medical personnel. Candidacy for nudity should not be measured by the yardstick of prepubescence. For example, a twelve-year-old girl may not yet be pubescent but in terms of emotional development, would be extremely embarrassed by a strip search. Finally, it is not true that teachers "frequently" assist second graders in the bathroom. Accidental wetting is extremely rare at this age and even when it occurs in school, teachers do not change the children's panties or observe their genitals.

The court's opinion suggests that educators are not expected to have common sense, knowledge about child development, understanding about effective discipline, or sensitivity to children's embarrassment about public nudity. We do not know if psychological or pediatric experts testified in this case. If they did, they surely presented mountains of evidence about the potential emotional impact of being forced to strip before adults other than family members. They could have pointed out the sexual abuse prevention curricula that are taught in almost all kindergartens in the country, which stress children's right to privacy about their bodies. How can educators justify the paradox between what they teach children about privacy and an act in which an official requires children to expose themselves?

Not all federal circuits or states extend the protections of qualified immunity with such a loose interpretation of facts as did the Eleventh Circuit. For example, in 1996 the Ninth Circuit ruled in favor of the students in *P.B.* v. *Koch* and did not grant qualified immunity to the school principal. Alfred Koch, principal of Preston High School in Idaho, used excessive force in disciplining three students. In one incident, he squeezed a student's neck after he mistakenly thought the student had referred to him as Hitler. He punched another student in the chest after the student made noises during a ceremony at a basketball game, and he slammed still another into a set of lockers for refusing to remove his hat.

The material presented in this book, backed by research and scholarship, should inform educators and the courts about the problems with strip searches. But if you are considering litigation, you need to know what immunities your schools have. This varies so much from state to state that you will need good legal advice to determine how the laws will affect you and how you can frame your litigation so as to avoid pitfalls.

As is illustrated in the case of *Jenkins* v. *Talladega City Board of Education* and other cases we have presented throughout this book, many contemporary courts are reluctant to interfere in the schools, especially in the arena of discipline. This is in part due to the influence of Supreme Court decisions in the last two decades that have favored the authority of school officials over the rights of students. However, the thinking of the judiciary is unquestionably affected to some degree by the failure of American education to develop consensus for clear standards of practice.

Malpractice in Education

Now, since educators are professionals, would you not assume that they have a set of ethical and practice standards that governs their profession? For instance, should not every primary grade teacher know all about the research and contemporary standards for teaching reading, be required by law to periodically take a specified number of continuing education credits, and be able to practice within the boundaries of mutually agreed-upon standards of the teaching profession? Wrong.

There is no consensus among educators about the best methods for teaching. Therefore, since there is no professionally acceptable standard for practice that can be used in court, the law does not recognize malpractice in education. This is different from almost all other professions—psychologists, lawyers, physicians, and engineers all can be held to specific standards, but not teachers.

The one exception is that there are certain minimal legal standards in special education law. The IDEA and ADA govern certain procedures and practices. But even with kids with learning, emotional, behavioral, or developmental difficulties, the law only requires that the children be classified and given individual educational plans (IEP). In schools there is no malpractice penalty related to how educators implement the IEP or if the educational strategies do not work. Unlike other professionals, most educators, who are responsible for developing and executing IEPs, are not required to participate in ongoing professional training and education related to their employment in order to maintain their certification. These types of professional requirements help to ensure that practitioners in other professions maintain minimal levels of competence.

Finally, there are no requirements that classification be based on diagnostic criteria used in medical and clinical settings that serve children with emotional and educational difficulties. Acceptable assessment standards for diagnosis are defined for mental health professionals by their national organizations and are based on contemporary scientific knowledge.

There are general malpractice standards that you can use in tort litigation against educators. Officials have a legal duty to protect students from injury and if they breach that duty they may be liable under tort law. To prove malpractice, the physical or emotional injury must result from a breach of the official's duty. You must prove the action was intentional or negligent. Also, you must show that the educator should have known that the action would cause harm to the student. Further, the action must be the immediate cause of the victim's symptoms and potential long-term physical or emotional harm.

The final point is that you need to find a sympathetic judge and jury. To recap our advice from the beginning of the chapter, if you live in the Bible Belt or any other conservative rural area (like western Pennsylvania), always seek a trial in federal court. You are more likely to get a reasonably well informed judge who is not part of the local oligarchy and a jury that is not swayed by the local politics of punitiveness. It is unlikely that you will find a perfect jury even in federal court, but that isn't necessarily a problem as a large proportion of cases with which we are familiar have been settled out of court. Also, based on our experience, given a good lawyer and a few educated jurors matching the profile recommended earlier—or even a few compassionate jurors of any type— your chances of winning are vastly improved.

In the best of all possible worlds, of course, children would not be maltreated in schools, you would not have to go to court, and schools would be exemplars of justice, equity, and democracy. Is this possible? We think it is and we have data and cases to prove it. Consider the following tale—a somewhat unusual and inspiring story of a teacher who witnessed abuse and the victim's parents who would not allow themselves to be crushed by the onslaughts of abusive educators and stonewalling school officials.

Angry Parents and a Whistle-Blower Teacher Strike Back

I have been an expert witness against abusive teachers and principals in cases all over the country. It is sad to report that plaintiff parents rarely receive overt support and encouragement in their quests for redress from educators within the system. Often the abusive educator has a history of known or suspected maltreatment of students. In other cases the ill-treatment of students is institutionalized and therefore acceptable. I am even familiar with cases of educators who committed perjury to protect their colleagues from conviction on abuse charges.

But what happens when a teacher witnesses an outrageous assault on a student and refuses to commit perjury in legal testimony? What happens when the teacher is requested by her principal, and is under pressure from her colleagues, to change her account of what she saw? Such a case occurred in the Easton, Pennsylvania, public schools. This case involves the intersection between a teacher's assault on students, toxic school climates, child advocacy, law enforcement, litigation, and judicial decisions. Here is what happened.

Joshua Kunz's parents, Caryn and Michael, asked that I evaluate the emotional effects of an assault on him by a teacher in Easton Area Middle School. The admitted assault took place on January 24, 1997. Joshua and other students were in the lunchroom of their school. It was witnessed by other students and Mrs. Sandy O'Brien-Werner, a teacher.

Joshua reported that his math teacher, Mr. Roy Cortez, a football coach for another school with an alleged history of assaults on students, and Mr. Barry Snyder, another teacher, were on duty in the lunchroom. Joshua and his friend Randy began to "horse around" with Mr. Cortez. Randy caused a coin to fall down the back of Mr. Cortez's shirt. Mr. Cortez became enraged and grabbed Joshua and Eric Bugby (who was not really involved) and assaulted them so violently that Joshua needed medical attention for a mild concussion and nasal contusion.

We completed a comprehensive evaluation of Joshua and his family. We found Joshua to be a tall, good-looking, and highly articulate gifted thirteen-year-old. His family is nurturing, caring, highly educated, and somewhat perfectionistic. A candidate for Eagle Scout, he has developed the high level of curiosity, high academic achievement, and advanced understanding of morality common among gifted children. In our opinion, the assault caused him to develop posttraumatic stress disorder.

Joshua's father, a former engineer and currently a high school science teacher, and his mother, a chemist, are well educated and quite conservative and traditional in their values. They come from families where education is highly valued and respected. Because of their backgrounds, when they charged Mr. Cortez with assault they expected school authorities to be empathetic, compassionate, and fair.

We wondered if the Kunzes had an "axe to grind" with the school. But their conservative religious orientation, involvement in education, and dedication to providing their children with a code of values are all factors that would contraindicate any inherent dislike of the educational establishment or the offending teacher. When we questioned them about their motivation in pursuing charges over the alleged assault on their child, both parents expressed a need to seek justice for Joshua and vindication for their efforts to make the school safe for all students.

Mr. Cortez was convicted of assault by a local magistrate, given probation, and suspended for three days. The parents filed civil charges. Since the civil litigation in this case has not been not resolved as we write this book, we have asked Caryn Kunz and Sandy O'Brien-Werner (called Mrs. OBW at school), with attorney approval, to briefly tell their stories.

How a School Can Victimize a Whole Family: An Account by Caryn Kunz

To say that this experience has had a major impact on our family would be like saying being pulled from a riptide by a lifeguard is interesting. Our family has been challenged, emotionally, spiritually, intellectually, socially, morally, and ethically.

As parents, we have told our children to behave, be respectful, do well in school, and walk away from the bullies, and you'll do fine. Unfortunately, these lessons in morality do not apply in this unhealthy school, which confused rigid control with discipline and abuse with punishment.

Despite accusations, our family is not liberal, insane, money grubbing, or pathologically permissive. We are both from very conservative backgrounds with parents and relatives in the educational field. Before this experience we would have said there is nothing wrong with appropriate corporal punishment administered in love for the good of the child.

Two years ago I saw a boy run out of the Easton Middle School screaming, "I'm going to *kill* Mr. Kish!" (The principal.) At the time I was appalled at what the student said and wondered what he did. Now, I would ask, "What was done to that boy?" Was he paddled black and blue, set up and lied about, shaken and choked, screamed and sworn at, mocked and humiliated, or perhaps just thrown against a filing cabinet?

We have been a family under siege. Not only do we have to fight the very system that is supposed to educate our children, but also the local legal authorities who supposedly protect our children. If you are as naive as we were about local politics, you should know that the county district attorney has sole prosecuting jurisdiction. Even though, by definition, a simple assault by a school employee is considered aggravated assault and the employee should be suspended, in this "kangaroo court" (the prosecuting assistant district attorney's words, not mine), the district attorney refused to refile charges and also refused to suspend Mr. Cortez's license when the state requested it.

Mr. Cortez was allowed to remain in the school, daily harassing Mrs. OBW and using his classroom as a stump to get the low-level students to threaten our son with beatings. Professionals within the legal system would state that if anyone assaulted their child they would have a lot more to worry about than the legal system. Really? Just what are parents to do in a school that checks to make sure when you walk in the door you sign in or you may be arrested for trespassing? They have taken parents to court for swearing at a principal. If we had lost our tempers we would have been arrested on the spot.

As parents we were told by our son, Josh, about administrators' maltreatment of students, but found the anecdotes hard to believe. Before that fateful day when our son was assaulted, we spent more than two hours "chatting" with Mr. Kish, asking about his disciplinary policies. We were shocked to find that screaming, swearing, and bigoted, lying remarks were directed at parents as well as students. Needless to say we were very apprehensive about receiving an impartial investigation into the assault. We told a school board member about our fears the day after the assault, not knowing he was a good friend of Mr. Cortez. We are not paranoid, but we believe our fears were used against us.

Joshua had to give testimony to a police detective, the head of secondary education and head of elementary education, the assistant district attorney assigned to the case, and hospital employees and doctors. Yet all this would have been for naught and the incident made to disappear if Mrs. OBW, one of the two teachers who witnessed the incident and screamed for the assailant to stop, had not refused to recant her account of the event. At one point we received a phone call threatening her life. The superintendent of schools has said to us that "he," meaning Cortez, would be crazy to harm our son again or touch another child. Yet we allege that he did it at least two more times.

After a few months of dealing with the school system, police, county officials, and finally state officials, this resembled something out of Kafka. We went from not knowing basic legal lingo to having the pager number of the chief of police. In a lighter moment we stated that we needed a wall-size flow chart to keep track of the relationships and tentacles of this situation. One of the most frustrating aspects was that all of this could have been settled if people had done their jobs and followed the law.

Why did we pursue this instead of just removing our son from the situation? At first, we just couldn't believe that someone, anyone, wouldn't help. What we came to realize was that the playground bullies just get bigger and meaner, but don't go away. We always believed that if you have a problem you should be able to "tell a teacher." What we learned is that the teacher doesn't always care.

Our son has been labeled as "bright, white, and polite" by the establishment in the community. When we talked to a minority community leader about our experiences, he earnestly asked us what kind of treatment we thought we would have received if our son was poor and black. It has taken many people, family friends who are teachers and guidance counselors in another district, lawyers, psychologists, a neurologist, an intact extended family (grandparents, uncles, and aunts), Boy Scout leaders, and an enormous amount of family time and effort to prevent the ruining of our son's attitude, his sense of justice, emotional well-being, and life. Our son has a safety net, but how many children do?

What we are now cognizant of is the impact a toxic school has on even the bystanders. We saw the pain in our son, but also in other children who were terrified by what they witnessed. We have also learned that there can be courageous people in a sea of fear and intimidation. We owe an immense debt to the teacher who perhaps prevented our son from becoming a vegetable. We are forever grateful to those who gave our son asylum in their classrooms and refused to go along with the harassment of Mrs. OBW.

The Penalty for a Teacher Whistle-Blower and Child Advocate: A Summary by Sandy O'Brien-Werner

Many of us are familiar with corruption in the American prison system. It runs fine as long as there is a tacit understanding between the warden, the guards, and the toughest inmates. When I worked in the middle school, Principal Joe Kish ran it as if he were a warden. He punitively disciplined faculty and students alike. At faculty meetings, he swore at us (I tallied his use of "bitchin'" nine times at one meeting) and threatened that disobedience would result in our being shoe salesmen. He warned students that if they did not take care of the bathrooms, he would shut them down and "let the pee run down their legs."

From before the time the middle school opened, I had known not to cross Joe's buddy Roy Cortez. Tales of Cortez's temper were legion, including allegations that he dumped unruly students headfirst into garbage cans. Unfortunately, a few years ago I became one of Roy's targets.

As a faculty sponsor of the ski club, I joined other sponsors in requesting that no tests be given on the day after the students returned from their weeknight trip. Cortez received an unsigned letter criticizing him for not complying with our request. He incorrectly assumed I was the author and convinced most of the faculty that I was a coward for not signing the letter. I did not realize he was angry with me until I found out about the letter. I confronted him with the truth, yet he continued to question my veracity. Given this background, I should not have been surprised that he made me a scapegoat for witnessing and truthfully reporting the assault on Josh and Eric on Friday, January 24, 1997.

Following the advice of the union grievance chairperson, when the anticipated call from the Kunzes occurred, I listened to their story without offering any information. Despite this, a rumor began to circulate that I had called the Kunzes and urged them to go to the police. I tried repeatedly and unsuccessfully to reach the principal over the weekend and was not able to talk with him until Monday morning.

The principal informed me that he could not use my account of the events because it would "fry" Cortez. He edited my statement and asked me to retype it. I was later told by the district attorney that he could find no reason to bring charges against Kish for making me change my statement. Meanwhile, by lunchtime Monday, I had only one person to sit with; the others simply would not eat with me. Rumors had spread that I had advised the Kunzes to follow my lead and report the incident to the police.

At the time of the assault, I was the building representative of the Pennsylvania State Education Association (PSEA) and chairperson of the largest department in the building. I asked a colleague to call PSEA to aid Cortez in obtaining a union representative. I felt there might be a conflict of interest since my report could be used against Cortez and the union which I represent.

I maintained confidentiality about the case and therefore could not defend myself when my colleagues began to "shun" me. I was isolated, rejected, avoided, and ignored by most teachers and the secretarial staff. Terrible things started to happen. For instance, I found big gobs of tobacco-stained spit on my windshield and received hate letters in my school mailbox signed "Concerned Faculty Members." The mail suggested that I transfer to another school and that I memorize vocabulary words such as rat, fink, and paranoia. I also received two nasty letters demanding my resignation as union rep. I even found potting soil in my mailbox.

One day I walked out to my car to find someone had keyed it down the front fender. My house was pelted with eggs, candy, and paint balls. Kids drove by yelling, "I hate you!" I was falsely accused of blabbing to parents, going to the police to demand Roy's arrest, becoming best friends with the superintendent and thereby not following the chain of command, and causing a complete breakdown of the educational process in the building.

There was nothing I could say or do that was not misconstrued or twisted around to mean something sinister. I literally did not talk to anyone unless I had to. People who remained friendly to me were also alienated. On the bulletin board of the second floor faculty room was a list of six people to shun, all people who spoke to me.

At team meetings, I anxiously anticipated some sort of assault. I frequently found pictures of me on the table or on the wall with my face blackened out or with a nasty remark added. Similarly, messages were left saying things like, "A good man's reputation will be restored." The campaign against me began to appear in the local papers. For instance, an editorial stated incorrectly that Eric had attacked Mr. Cortez when in fact he had been sharing his seat with Josh. A good percentage of the letters were written by my colleagues, almost all favoring Cortez. A teacher on my team said to me, "Well, some seventh grade boys say [the assault] never happened," and that, apparently, was good enough for her.

As things escalated, I believe the staff got out of control. Principal Kish frequently told me about his efforts to make "those guys" quit harassing me, especially through my school mailbox. Then came the devastating day when Cortez's picture appeared in the paper in an article about his arraignment. At this point, the shunning and harassment went into high gear.

Someone went into my classroom and poured milk all over my desk, my chairs, and the table on which I worked. On that table were flowers my husband had brought in to cheer me up, my manuals, and—this was the worst—my students' handwritten AMVETS essay contest entries that I was to have hand-delivered that day after school. They were ruined.

I really fell apart then and called the police who investigated and removed the milk cartons for analysis. Later, a neighbor confided that Joe Kish told her the only fingerprints the police had found on the milk carton were mine, thus insinuating that I had sabotaged myself.

Throughout all of this, my local union, for whom I had worked so hard in the past, not only failed to offer support but denigrated me. They supported Cortez in the newspapers, suggested that I was a liar, and attempted to have me expelled from the PSEA for breaking the code of ethics. PSEA rejected these charges.

The only bright spot came when a community coalition brought my plight to the attention of the press, which then attacked the school. The day the attack appeared in the newspaper, Principal Kish sent out a memo, dated the previous day, warning all faculty to desist all malicious activities directed toward any individuals and/or their mailboxes.

Something good happened for the middle school. The Superintendent, Bernadette Meck, "promoted" Principal Kish to the position of Administrative Assistant for Auxiliary and Support Services, where he handles transportation. I do not know the emotional effects of this experience on Mr. Kish, but I can say that this experience has been devastating to me. I have gone through periods of depression, anxiety, and fear. But I refuse to be a victim and will survive this experience.

I would have never believed that something like this could happen to me. But the support of my family and old and newfound friends, and my understanding that I did the right thing when so many waffled, have all helped me to become a survivor. It has not been easy and I still have periods of depression and doubt. My new understanding of the potential danger in schools will be used to sensitize me to the needs of students and parents. No teacher has the right to hurt children, but everyone has an obligation to step in and stop unnecessary punishment, perhaps preventing a tragedy.

I love teaching secondary school English, but if I stay in Easton this is not in the cards. I was transferred to an elementary school where I am teaching gifted children and am considering obtaining a master's degree in the area of gifted education.

. . .

We have carefully examined the allegations and supporting materials in the Easton case. While Sandy might sound paranoid to some, after interviewing her, examining numerous documents, and checking with others, we believe that everything she reports here is true. It is sad that she, her family, and the Kunz family, have had to pay so dearly in their quest for simple justice. They feel angry and helpless, but we have encouraged them to see how their courage, belief in justice, and persistence has made them fearsome advocates for students' rights. Mr. Cortez admitted guilt to a criminal act and entered a program for first-time offenders. Mr. Kish was transferred to the central administration building to become an administrative assistant. It appears to us that he was kicked upstairs to a desk, given a ridiculous title, and squirreled away where he can do minimal harm.

Despite the disinformation campaign, both families have mobilized support networks and made thoughtful parents aware of what can happen to their children. We believe that many teachers will think twice about smacking students around. Finally, a number of actions by the school superintendent who inherited this situation (not reported here because of space limitations) moved the school a smidgen away from its dangerous and toxic culture of the past.

Sandy's report, as far as we know, is the only insider-written public account of how educators may operate to protect their own, even when they do so illegally. It does not surprise us in the least, since many victims of toxic educators with whom we have consulted have recounted similar but unsubstantiated scenarios.

So what can you personally do to detoxify schools? If you want to heed Sandy's closing words of advice, we will give you action plans in the next and final chapter, where we lay out what needs to be done to make schools democratic and models for just communities.

Chapter 9

How Can Schools Be Democratic and Stop Maltreatment?

Unsettling as this book may be, we're not out to lead the charge of the teacher bashers and public school detractors or to undermine education or educators. Nor do we oppose the police or denigrate police tactics—in their proper place. However, we do want to make you aware of the poisonous practices that have made too many schools toxic to the emotional, physical, and academic health of children. We also maintain that, except in very exceptional situations of imminent danger, police tactics such as strip searches, random urine screening, and massive drug searches have no place in schools.

We are done with our nay-saying. This chapter will help you assess the level of democracy in your community's schools—which is a matter of concern to every citizen whether or not the kids are coming home with signs of trauma—and discuss how and why schools that reflect democracy help our nation fulfill the promise of a life governed by the pursuit of liberty, happiness, and emotional health. Americans can enhance the quality of life for people of all ages by promoting democratic schools, or they can see the quality of life slowly—or not so slowly—eroded for themselves and their families as their schools settle into an authoritarian and repressive mold.

Democracy in the Schools

American schools are rooted in participatory democracy more than those in any other Western industrialized nation because of the system of local control. Citizens at the local level elect school boards to represent them in setting policies and regulations in each district. Unfortunately, democracy is extremely fragile—and at the local level, it is particularly susceptible to the dictatorship of the majority. By this we mean that in areas such as discipline and students' rights, punitive and authoritarian community impulses can rule policy-making and exercise severe sanctions against individuals who do not conform to community standards. When students are accused of misbehavior, this tendency can be magnified by punishment-oriented policymakers who ignore evidence that supports democratic prevention- and treatment-oriented approaches to the problem. As a result, individuals' rights can be easily trampled, parents without political clout or resources are often prevented from protecting their children, and students' sense of the promise of democracy is stunted before it can blossom.

Our founders attempted to correct the suppression of individual rights and freedoms by balancing the judiciary with the other two branches of government. We have shown in this book that the judiciary, especially as it has become more conservative, has generally failed to heed the maxim that the Constitution does not stop at the schoolhouse gate. As a result, the forces that might shape democratic schools are weakened. Democratic schools start with the policies designed by elected school boards. If these boards are not informed about and forced to consider the issues we discuss in this book, they may be less likely to understand the educational context that should provide for the intersection between the process and content of democracy in the schoolhouse.

The idea that American schools should be exemplars of democracy is not new. In recent history, John Dewey was perhaps the educational philosopher most associated with attempts to transform rigid, conservative schools into progressive institutions reflecting the ideals of democracy. He was an educator, philosopher, psychologist, and writer who in the 1930s and 1940s urged schools to take democracy seriously as an underpinning of education. Needless to say, he and his liberal ideas of progressive education were excoriated by conservatives, who still blame the implementation of his theory of progressive education for many of the ills they perceive in schools. His critics fail to resonate to the idea of democratic schools.

What Is a Democratic School, Anyway?

A democratic school begins with a school board that respects and empowers all members of the educational community to participate in policy development and implementation. Therefore, school governance, as a common concern, enhances participatory democracy. By this we mean that everyone feels that they have a stake in the success of the school. For instance, a national study that compared violent and safe schools demonstrated that safe schools were characterized by leadership that instilled in students a sense of fairness, belongingness, and empowerment to effect change. It was not the strict, authoritarian, rule-bound schools that were the safest.

One of the best indicators that your school district is oriented toward democratic principles is the morale of school staff. Morale will be high if the school board and administrators seek consensus by responding to the needs of teachers, students, and parents. Policymaking is characterized by committee efforts to define problems and consensus building to shape solutions. Committees may be made up of teachers, administrators, parents, and representatives of other constituencies. The hallmark of these democratic schools is that the recommendations of these committees are seriously considered and often adopted.

While disagreements among school board members are healthy and sometimes desirable, democracy is defeated when the board is politically polarized to the extent that constant ideological and economic battles paralyze the educational process. As a result, school administrators frequently attempt to survive either by aligning themselves with the most powerful factions on the school board or by avoiding decisions and actions that would anger either side. In either case, the process for enhancing democratic decision making is stymied.

When school boards and administrators are either paralyzed by conflict or entrapped in authoritarian leadership, students and parents will suffer. These situations cause poor morale among teachers. When teachers are dispirited, students will inevitably suffer. When officials denigrate, demean, or ridicule teachers, teachers will tend to denigrate, demean, and ridicule students. In addition, in situations of poor staff morale educators tend to focus on their careers and survival within the system rather than on the needs of students and parents.

Children are at serious risk of maltreatment in disciplinary situations in dysfunctional, authoritarian schools. Such schools rarely provide equitable means for redress and can usually be changed only through political efforts. This requires electing different school boards and hiring democratic administrators. This solution is complex and beyond the scope of this book.

Another approach to change is personal action based on knowledge of democratic schooling and if necessary, the threat of litigation. Ideally, when maltreatment occurs, you can identify either individual or systemic abuses and pressure or encourage school officials to ameliorate the problem. To do this at a systems level, you need some guidelines to identify problems and develop a plan of action to make the school more democratic and sensitive to children's needs. The following section sketches an approach to developing such a plan.

Assessing School Climate

We believe that the best antidote for toxic climates characterized by punitive discipline is large infusions of democracy. This is the best prescription for administering schools and enhancing the lives of children. Yet, as we have outlined throughout this book, this medicine is considered by many as a cause rather than a cure to the punitive excesses of discipline we have documented. The level of democratic practice in every school district and school building can be measured through climate assessment techniques. Every school district and building has a climate, which may range from authoritarian to democratic. Effective discipline is dependent on a healthy school climate.

School climate includes all aspects of the environment of a school that may affect learning and discipline. Communities, parents, students, teachers, and even the school buildings contribute to the climate. Almost invariably, however, the principal is the chief determinant of the climate in any school. Almost any educator who works in more than one school can tell you about the differences between them. Sitting in a teacher's room, watching the students at lunch, observing the secretaries, watching students and teachers in the halls, and attending staff meetings all offer valuable clues about the climate of a school as determined by the principal's leadership style.

The scientific way to diagnose school climate is to develop a questionnaire that is answered anonymously by students, staff, administrators, and even parents. Sounds impossible, but it isn't. Effective change to eliminate toxic practices and change the school culture may take at least three to four years of effort, beginning with school climate assessment.

There are many books on school climate, some focusing on systematic and intentional modeling of democracy in discipline policies and practices. This topic is too lengthy to discuss fully here. You can find out more about it in my book *School Discipline and School Violence*, from which some of the following is taken. This brief overview will familiarize you with the concept as it applies to our concerns.

First, for climate assessment and change to occur, school boards and administrators must be open to using social science methods to bring about democratic change. Change begins with the commitment to openly seek information from students, parents, and school staff regarding the functioning of the schools.

Democratic leaders feel free to listen to criticism, assess problems, and consider options for change. Authoritarian leaders are rarely open to public criticism or self-analysis and therefore are generally unwilling to conduct climate assessment. When authoritarian administrators are forced into the climate assessment process, they often sabotage the process, ridicule any information that is contrary to their own beliefs, and undermine change efforts.

Climate assessment begins with the process of problem identification. This is best done by a committee representing teachers, administrators, students, and parents. Through brainstorming and consultation with their constituencies, they identify areas of concern. They may need technical help to learn to write items for a climate assessment questionnaire. The list they develop will be unique for each school, but it will probably include many of these items:

Discipline codes and policies

Staff morale

Availability of professional support services such as school psychologists, social workers, and counselors

Teacher communication with parents and administers

Availability of resources such as books and other teaching materials

Use of nonteaching personnel to help in monitoring halls, playgrounds, lunchrooms, and security

Extra staff to help with discipline problems

Adequacy of libraries

Availability of texts, pencils, chalk, and paper

Problem clarification may take several sessions of brainstorming by the steering committee. After areas of concern are discussed, members of the committee meet with their constituents to confirm that all problem domains have been identified before developing a climate assessment questionnaire.

Items are then developed to measure the extent of problems in each area. This is where technical help may be necessary to develop a questionnaire that can be easily administered, scored, and interpreted. The questionnaire usually consists of statements to which the respondents can indicate their feelings about the nature, severity, and extent of the issues included.

School climate assessment related to discipline involves asking questions about organization, structure, and leadership. For instance, are clear guidelines concerning school rules made available to parents and students each year? Were the guidelines developed with input from parents, students, and teachers? Do they spell out the rights and responsibilities of both students and school staff? If so, do they indicate that teachers must show respect and concern for students and treat them with the same dignity that is demanded from students? Are penalties for misbehavior meted out in an overly legalistic manner or are they based on an understanding of individual differences and mitigating circumstances? Does the pattern of punishment reflect fairness and equity for all groups? Does the school have a positive motivational or discipline plan to encourage appropriate behavior—and are staff trained in the system? Do teachers understand individual reasons for misbehavior or do they have an attitude of "The kid is bad and it's the parents' fault"? Do school staff attempt to make school an interesting and rewarding place for students?

The effects of diversity of students on discipline policies and practices should be formally studied in climate assessment. It is important to identify if students are unfairly disciplined because of race, class, gender, sexual orientation, ability, religion, or family background. Are teachers aware of the best motivational techniques for various groups and has the school attempted to implement a variety of corrective approaches such as peer counseling, peer tutoring, or cooperative learning groups?

Diagnoses of climate factors that affect discipline should include questions about teachers. For instance, are significant numbers of teachers burned out and therefore apathetic or overly punitive toward misbehavior? Are teachers involved in developing policies and practices regarding misbehavior and are there systems of rewards or recognition for teachers who develop and carry out positive, preventive, and effective discipline programs? Are parents, students, and mental health personnel involved in planning discipline strategies? Do teachers have adequate access to consultation with support personnel such as school psychologists and counselors? Are adequate resources available to individualize programs for chronically misbehaving students, even though they may not be classified as having disabilities? To prevent misbehavior, are all students taught at appropriate grade levels?

The construction, administration, scoring, and feedback of results can take up to a year. Once the results of the assessment are obtained, the committee presents them to school staff, administrators, and other constituencies. By using an assessment instrument, it is possible to quantify the results in a way that issues and problem areas can be prioritized.

Using the results of the survey, school staff can determine which areas have the highest priority and what resources can be expended for solutions. Because of democratic participation in the process, various school constituencies including teachers and students own the process and the possible solutions to the problems. Therefore they will be likely to commit to solving the problems by developing programs to prevent misbehavior, sensitize teachers, parents, and students to each other's needs, and thereby enhance the total school climate.

The implementation of problem solving is way beyond the scope of this book. It involves a variety of activities from researching how other schools have resolved similar problems to developing local strategies, consulting experts, and employing a variety of resources to strengthen the school. While we believe it is important for you to understand how schools can become detoxified by making themselves democratic and thus sensitive to the needs of students, we understand that you may have little opportunity to effect change at the system or school level. But you may have influence at the classroom level, especially the one in which your child is a student. So it is important to have a good understanding of what democracy means at the classroom level.

Democracy in the Classroom

The success of democracy ultimately depends on educated citizens who have internalized the social contract between themselves and society. This contract is the mutually agreed-upon rules of decency, civility, respect for others and their property, and devotion to justice, fairness, and equity. Rules and laws that spell out the social contract are followed not because of fear of punishment but because their importance is understood. We voluntarily and rationally internalize the controls needed to follow these rules. We understand that we have the right to dissent and to change the rules if we believe that the rules have become unjust or are applied unfairly.

By using democratic processes in parenting and teaching, we help children develop internalized controls based on the social contract negotiated among parents, teachers, and peers. Teachers in democratic classrooms emphasize cooperation, mutual goal setting, and shared responsibility. Students behave because it is the right thing to do and because they respect the rights of others.

In comparison to internalized controls, external controls are developed as a result of authoritarian, punitive parenting and teaching. External controls depend on fear of punishment as the major deterrent to misbehavior. Authoritarian teachers emphasize competition, the assertion of power, and reflexive obedience. Since power over the students is the source of control, it is inevitable that the use of physical and verbal power is abused, thereby leading to the maltreatment of students.

Now some may say that it is unrealistic to use democracy as a basis for running a classroom. After all, students do not elect their teachers and even if they did, most are not mature enough to really practice democracy. These critics are just plain wrong and I can prove it because I was a democratic teacher. Let me share some of my experiences with you.

In the fall of 1957, for my first teaching assignment, I entered a third-grade classroom of thirty-four unruly children in a small rural New Jersey school. Between kindergarten and the time I arrived, my charges had had seven teachers—they were not about to be easily disciplined. Unlike my unsuccessful predecessors, I had not been trained in education, but like them, I had received no formal courses in theory, research, and practice in school discipline. I had little more to go on than the practical examples of my own teachers of childhood and the advice and examples offered by my colleagues.

The conventional wisdom about discipline from fellow teachers could have been reduced to a few simple maxims, which included the following: "Don't be too friendly, you're not here to win a popularity contest," "Don't smile till Christmas," and "If you have to get rough, don't leave any marks on the children." The latter bit of advice was rather confusing, since I knew that corporal punishment had been illegal in New Jersey schools since before the turn of the century.

As I began to read about discipline, I ran into the age-old conflict between opposing liberal versus conservative views of the nature of children. Even then, I read a lot about what we have talked about in this book. I decided I wanted to be a democratic teacher. When I attempted to discuss these issues with many experienced educators in the late 1950s, I was shocked by their inability to connect the concepts of democracy to school discipline and by their hostility to the ideas of John Dewey, an early promoter of progressive education.

After one year as a third-grade teacher, I taught fifth and sixth grades. In those grades I integrated democratic principles into the process of education, especially as they related to discipline. Students and I mutually developed rules for the classroom, and we had regular class meetings to discuss and solve problems. Concerns such as seating, free time, and projects were negotiated. Most important, I focused on developing a climate of trust, friendship, and respect. The students knew that I was the teacher but that all suggestions and ideas they put forth received fair and just consideration.

What I had learned about democratic discipline as a teacher led in 1964 to research I conducted for my doctoral dissertation in school psychology. I reasoned that removal of the teacher in authoritarian classes, where discipline is based on external controls, should lead to loss of control by the students. Conversely, removal of the democratic teacher should make little difference in misbehavior since the controls are internalized. I decided to test this hypotheses back in 1963.

I administered the Hyman Authoritarian-Democratic Classroom Climate Scale, which I had developed for the research. It was administered to the students in many fifth-grade classes from which we identified two authoritarian teachers, two democratic teachers, and two teachers who measured in the middle. These teachers were told by their administrators, without prior knowledge of the request, to leave their classrooms. They remained absent for forty-five minutes. The climate of the authoritarian classrooms, according to trained observers, deteriorated into complete chaos after the first thirty minutes. The students went crazy. Their model for control was punishment by an external authority—the teacher.

It was interesting to follow the descent into chaos in the authoritarian classes. As students became more confident of the teacher's absence, they became more unruly. Bullying, fighting, and threats to get the teacher and the principal occurred. In the democratic classes you wouldn't have known the teacher was missing. These children had internalized the values of their classroom. The students of the democratic classes did seat work, formed work groups, or quietly observed the playground. There was no fighting or scapegoating as there was in the authoritarian classes.

The experiment clearly demonstrated the differences between internal, democratically inspired controls and external controls imposed by an authoritarian teacher. Both types of classrooms provide structure and rules. Yet democratic classes give students a feeling that they have a stake in how the class functions. An ethos of fairness is clearly evident. Structure may be maintained without the use of punitive methods. Firm, consistent, and fair teachers do not have to be mean. Providing structure and an orderly learning environment is consistent with democratic principles, which can therefore be taught as both content and process.

Teaching the Content and Process of Democracy

We have discussed how the process of democracy can be infused within a classroom. What we have presented is based on actual research and the experience of many educators. In addition to modeling the process of democracy, we must make sure that students thoroughly understand the Constitution and Bill of Rights—not only as historical documents but as guidelines for how lives should be lived. We realize that there are many interpretations of these documents ranging from both poles of the political spectrum. We obviously believe that our interpretation best hits the mark.

Understanding Civil Liberties

In considering the best source of information about the Bill of Rights, it seems to us inevitable that we must turn to the American Civil Liberties Union. In this section, we have adapted materials from the ACLU and borrowed heavily from a presentation its executive director, Ira Glasser, made in 1997 to a group of educators in California. We use this material advisedly and with full understanding of the history and status of the ACLU.

Glasser makes the point that the ACLU is the oldest and consistently most active organization in America devoted to the protection of individual rights. Therefore it is our country's most conservative organization—it attempts to conserve the liberties expounded by our founders in the eighteenth century. Yet it is a political lightning rod, little understood by many Americans who consider it to be a liberal, radical, left-wing organization.

Judge Learned Hand, a leading twentieth-century jurist, wrote, "Liberty lives in the hearts and minds of men and women; when it dies there, no Constitution, no law, no court can save it." School is the one institution where liberty can be successfully instilled in the hearts and minds of all citizens. We believe that the hostility toward the ACLU, the public's passive response to the erosion of protections guaranteed in the Bill of Rights, and opinions expressed in the media and in surveys indicate that many Americans do not really support the liberties defined by our founders. We suggest that, in part, this is because schools have failed to teach future citizens about the importance of protecting and assuring the constitutional rights of every American to keep their own rights out of danger. To correct this and assure that schools will not be toxic to the physical and emotional health of students, here is what Americans have to do.

The Bill of Rights as a Set of Values

The Bill of Rights should be taught as a set of values and not just as a legal document. We do not have free speech just because of the First Amendment. We have the First Amendment because our founders believed that free speech is a fundamental, inalienable right that guarantees democracy. The First Amendment is just a statement that helps protect free speech. If we do not understand freedom of expression, how can we protect it? If students are not taught, within developmental limits, how to freely express their ideas, how will they ever truly learn to understand the nature and concept of free speech?

At all grade levels, students should be taught to express their feelings and ideas in appropriate ways. They should be encouraged to question what teachers say. They should challenge information they are given—both alleged facts that do not seem correct and interpretations of events with which they do not agree. Students should be better taught to analyze political propaganda, to read and critique news information, to consider different perspectives on political issues, and to understand that conflict in democracy need not be avoided. Constructive conflict leads to healthy change.

Students learn best through the presentation of case studies, mock trials, and videotapes dramatizing conflicts between police procedures and constitutional issues. They must learn much of this through guided experience rather than only from textbooks. One of the best sources of curricula in this area is the Constitutional

Rights Foundation in Los Angeles, which is described in our resource list at the end of the book.

To encourage legitimate dissent, every grade level should provide for periodic classroom meetings during which students are encouraged to question school rules and authority. They should be taught to do this respectfully, thoughtfully, and with consideration of others' rights and feelings. Teachers should reward and encourage students who legitimately dissent. Students will feel free to dissent if teachers provide a democratic climate in the classroom.

The purpose of teaching free speech is to encourage future citizens to develop habits for introducing new and sometimes unpopular ideas for debate and consideration. Students must learn to stand against censorship and the slippery slope down which it can lead to the establishment of thought police exemplified by the witch hunts of the McCarthy era. They must feel free to question authority in all forms, including police, government officials, and politicians. Otherwise, why call ourselves a democracy?

Participatory Democracy

Our founders realized that one of the greatest dangers to democracy is the complacency and apathy of the citizenry. Democracy is based on the participation of an educated and an informed public. While schools can not shoulder all of the responsibility, their failures are reflected in our abysmally low voter turnout compared to other democracies. The adult tendency toward apathy about government authorities can be averted if students have the real-life experience of influencing school policies that adversely affect their lives. This may mean actually taking student councils, school newspapers, and other student forums seriously.

One might question our judgment in suggesting the somewhat radical concept that children should be taught to freely express themselves and to dissent within the system. By teaching children from an early age to express themselves and to dissent, we are preparing them to feel that others will listen when they do this as voting citizens. Judging by low voter turnout and the relatively low level of political participation compared to previous times, many U.S. citizens do not feel they have a voice.

In addition to many other benefits to our democracy, encouraging students to express themselves will enhance students' self-esteem and sense of empowerment—when someone in authority listens to them, the underlying message is that they are worth listening to. In addition, feedback from students will sensitize teachers to their actions that students consider offensive and demeaning. This should considerably decrease maltreatment of students and make schools much less toxic.

Schools must teach that the freedoms guaranteed in the original Bill of Rights were mistakenly denied to classes of people on the basis of their race, class, gender, and sexual orientation. Most scholars understand that the Declaration of Independence and the ten sets of liberties included in the original Bill of Rights expressed humanistic ideals that were contradicted in practice by many of its signatories. Women were substantially excluded, African Americans were totally excluded, and Native Americans were not even considered human.

Correcting Flaws in the Bill of Rights

To correct the exclusionary faults of our founders, it is important to emphasize that these men were radical visionaries who called for freedoms that were beyond those available to most people of the world in their day. They were limited by the context of their culture, but they constructed a dynamic system of government that enabled forever the expansion of rights to all classes of people, even students. But students need to understand that the system only extends rights when disenfranchised groups create change through dissent, sometimes within and sometimes outside of the system.

For instance, the right to vote, which was originally limited to propertied white men, was not extended to African Americans until 1868, when Congress passed the Fourteenth Amendment following the Civil War. The Nineteenth Amendment, passed in 1920, gave women the right to vote only after a long and brutal struggle for suffrage. These changes illustrate the importance of students' understanding and appreciating the value and necessity of creative conflict between the disenfranchised and governmental authority.

We need to teach students that each generation must identify the injustices and inequities of its own times. They must expand individual liberties and rights. This message is derogated when history texts, in an attempt to preach a false message of patriotism, do not truthfully teach about history. For instance, how many texts that mention the Mexican American War accurately report the fact that defenders of the Alamo were also fighting to assure that Texas would be a slave state? Further, in the name of patriotism, textbooks have traditionally painted rosy pictures of our country's founders that have distorted or ignored their human frailties, inconsistencies, and struggles.

In recent years, revisionist historians have tried to influence the writing of historical texts used in schools and colleges. They want to teach about the realities of American life for all people. They stress the historical importance of understanding the lives of such groups as women, workers, and minorities. The picture they paint is not a pretty one and many conservatives have fought the revisionists' attempts to portray the realities of history.

For instance, Thomas Jefferson, who wrote that "all men are created equal," kept slaves. Slavery was abominable and at some level Jefferson knew it, yet he owned many slaves. Further, as did many slave owners at the time, Jefferson had sex with at least one slave with whom he fathered a child, according to recent genetic studies. This does not undo the value of his contributions to our country. It does show that even one of our most cherished patriots shared human frailties with all of us. It is important for students to understand this. At appropriate ages students should be made aware of these realities and discuss them. Teaching the facts of history does not undermine democracy. Rather, it can strengthen our beliefs when we realize that historical leaders, like ourselves, were fallible but still strove to establish a country based on worthy ideals.

The Bill of Rights and Self-Interest

Students need to learn that the Bill of Rights is rooted in self-interest. It expresses our yearning for freedom but also reminds us that we must continue to fight for the freedoms of all citizens, lest we eventually lose our own freedoms. When the government denies a right to any individual, it sets a precedent. This invites officials to abuse its power by denying that same right to others and perhaps ourselves.

Today the Bill of Rights is often seen as an act of charity we extend to minorities, the poor, and others who need it. But the early Americans refused to ratify the Constitution without it because they understood that their own interests were at stake. Today, that sense of self-interest is not strongly felt by most Americans. But sooner or later everyone needs the Bill of Rights, including students.

All students, at appropriate ages, should be taught about the important laws and legal precedents that have defined their rights. We teach them from an early age that no one, not even their parents, has a right to sexually molest them—yet we do not teach them that police and school personnel do not have the right to make them take off their clothes unless there is probable cause. We need to teach them how to resist unconstitutional police tactics and why the tactics were considered unconstitutional in the first place. These lessons can best be learned through role-playing. Students can enact scenarios featuring innocent victims of unconstitutional search and seizure procedures and other types of illegal invasions of privacy, police interrogations, internments, and self-incriminations.

Ira Glasser gave a good example of this point when he appeared on the *Oliver North* talk show. North began by criticizing the antiterrorism bill that was pending in Congress. The right wing had begun to understand the relation between this bill and what happened at Ruby Ridge when Randy Weaver's wife and child were shot to death. The right wing, which previously had no problem with the use of excessive police force when used against other groups, suddenly realized that they had become victims of that tactic. North noted the potential surprise of his audience that he was giving a forum to the head of the ACLU. He stated, "I just want to say I've never publicly thanked Mr. Glasser for the ACLU's filing of a Fifth Amendment brief in my case."

Glasser replied that Ollie had never privately thanked him either and elucidated that North had never been a big fan of the Fifth Amendment until he needed it to keep himself out of jail. He further indicated that if the ACLU hadn't been able to successfully use the Fifth Amendment protection against self-incrimination to defend accused Communists in the 1950s and alleged Mafiosi in the 1950s and 1960s, it would not have been there to keep North out of jail.

If schools really teach that authorities are not allowed to use force or excessive interrogation to make people incriminate themselves, citizens will not support such actions by authorities even when most citizens believe that the targets are guilty or reprehensible. Schools need to teach that the Fifth Amendment does not provide an escape hatch for the guilty; it offers a right that deters authorities from using torture to gain confessions. This is an important cornerstone of democracy that separates us from many other societies where torture and confinement are routinely used to extract confessions from both guilty and innocent people.

The Bill of Rights was rooted in self-interest because it was rooted in experience. The values underlying the Bill of Rights can not be learned only from classroom texts. Early Americans demanded the Fourth Amendment protections from search and seizure because they knew what it was like to have British soldiers burst into their homes without warrants. Teaching about the Bill of Rights today must also be connected to the real experiences of children.

Role-playing can be used to enlighten students about the Fourth Amendment. Students can enact scenes, both historical and contemporary, in which individuals are searched. Scenarios can include examples in which probable and reasonable cause are used correctly. Other scenarios can illustrate how authorities can justify unconstitutional searches that are based on neither probable nor reasonable grounds. Teachers can also use audiovisual media and other creative techniques to help students understand the implications of Fourth Amendment violations. These techniques can be used to expand on other themes such as warrantless invasions of privacy.

The Bill of Rights is a strategic document, not just a high-minded statement of principle. It is a mutual insurance policy and a statement of self-preservation. Many Americans do not understand the difficult concept that the only way to protect your own rights is to protect everyone else's rights. If we really want to live in a society in which it is safe to be different, we must have laws that protect all differences.

When teachers inequitably discipline and demean children of specific gender, race, or minority, they undo the Bill of Rights. This is a hard nut to crack since children learn by modeling. For instance, conservatives have attacked legislation intended to protect the rights of homosexuals. Homosexuals are seeking to legitimatize their sexual orientation, end promiscuity by engaging in stable relationships through the institution of marriage, and ensure equality of treatment in schools, the workplace, and society. Yet conservatives have attempted, too often successfully, to censor open discussion of these issues in schools. Both successful and failed attempts in this area undermine students' understanding of the necessity of protecting everyone's rights.

We realize that well-financed and highly organized groups believe that they are morally impelled to ban student discussion, consideration, and appreciation of many of the rights of others. These are not easy issues for school authorities, who in many cases view the Bill of Rights as an obstacle to the maintenance of order, discipline, and their version of morality.

Local, State, and National Policy Initiatives

Since most of the maltreatment discussed in this book is done in the name of discipline, it is important to eliminate or severely restrict these toxic and dangerous practices that undermine democracy. This may only be accomplished if you are willing to lobby for effective, positive methods of discipline and the prevention of misbehavior. If you wish to become involved, you can be an activist at the local, state, and national levels. Although not definitive, here are some suggestions to give you a place to start.

Making an Impact on Your School District

In the annual Gallup polls of the public's attitude toward schools, discipline invariably comes out as a top concern. Yet despite the importance of discipline, a national survey done in 1993 indicated that only about one-half of all accredited teachers colleges offered an undergraduate course in school discipline and only half of those required that all students take the course. This is ironic, given that all student teachers must succeed in classroom management in order to pass the basic requirements for graduation and entry into the profession. Further, once hired, teachers must demonstrate ability to control and motivate their students before they can receive tenure or renewed contracts.

When we give our discipline workshops to teachers, most who were trained before this decade indicate that they have not had any undergraduate or graduate courses in discipline. Few teachers are familiar with the research and literature on corporal punishment or psychological maltreatment. Many have had at least one in-service workshop on discipline, but these have generally been only a few hours each and the teachers often have only a vague idea about what they learned. Too often they seem to have the best recall about punishment techniques rather than prevention or positive methods. This is probably because punishment offers a quick and effective fix in the short run.

Considering the educational situation and the incidents you have read of in this book, you can lobby for extensive teacher training to improve school discipline and decrease abuses. Educators and school boards need to be sensitized to the issues discussed in this book. At the local level, school psychologists, mental health professionals, and child abuse experts can present workshops. At the regional level, there are probably college professors and others in your area with the needed expertise. Preferably, workshops should be part of an ongoing program of training and consultation to help teachers deal with more difficult behavior problems. Ideally, this approach would be integrated into a climate assessment and remediation project based on the principles we have already discussed.

If you live in one of the twenty-three states that allow corporal punishment, you can lobby to eliminate it in your school district. This book and the references we provide should give you plenty of ammunition to respond when educators use personal anecdotes to defend a practice that invariably leads to abuse. Local school districts should recognize psychological maltreatment in the classroom and write regulations forbidding it. These should be included in the district's statement of philosophy, goals, and objectives and should be included in discipline handbooks.

Fear of drugs has resulted in the introduction of police tactics and a pedagogical penchant for punishment, interdiction, and a police orientation to substance abuse education. We will never win the war on drugs with police-oriented education programs, such as DARE, which use scare tactics. Despite millions of dollars spent on these popular programs, research shows that most are either ineffective or counterproductive.

Change of national drug policy is difficult and considerations of this issue are beyond the scope of this book. This is because addiction, which science shows to be a medical problem, is treated as a moral issue. In other words, drugs such as nicotine, cocaine, and alcohol become addictive for physiological reasons that are better understood at the biological level. While it is true that everyone has a choice to try or not try addictive substances, morality does not shape or control the physiology of anyone's brain.

Drug prevention education in the schools can teach about addiction from a medical perspective rather than focusing on criminal issues. At a local level, schools and communities can decide how to design these programs. Student drug education programs should focus entirely on the social, medical, and psychological problems of substance abuse. They should be conducted primarily by psychologists, nurses, physicians, and others with similar expertise on brain and behavior. Programs should be developmentally sensitive and therefore targeted to the language, cognitive understanding, and emotional readiness of each age group.

For instance, kindergarten and primary grade children can easily be frightened and develop unrealistic fears about drug use by themselves and their family. Many adolescents go through a period of rebellion against authorities. Attempts to scare them with information they know or believe to be false may only encourage them to experiment with drugs or to test the limits of how far they can go to defy authorities.

Lobbying at the State Level

If your state allows corporal punishment in the schools you need to organize or join groups willing to lobby against this practice. Your allies can be drawn from child abuse agencies, domestic violence workers, former victims of maltreatment, and state professional organizations representing the various mental health professions. Also, you will find that most national organizations devoted to child welfare, such as the American Psychological Association, the National Association of School Psychologists, the National Education Association, the National Parent Teacher Association, and the American Academy of Pediatrics, have position papers or statements against corporal punishment in the schools.

You should urge your state representative to consider legislation that will enable your state to join the twenty-seven others and almost all the other Western democracies that are able to educate schoolchildren without paddling. You will of course need to connect with experienced lobbyists, whose addresses may be made available to you through state organizations interested in the issue. It will be a tough struggle, as we have discovered in Pennsylvania. After repeated attempts through Michael Veon, a state legislator, and cooperation by many professional and parent groups, we have still been unable to introduce a bill banning corporal punishment in Pennsylvania. The response we have encountered reflects the conservative, rural mind-set of a legislature wedded to pain and punishment in pedagogy. Our research shows that two-thirds of Pennsylvania schools report that they do not use corporal punishment, but the legislature continues to protect the ability of the remaining third to paddle students at will.

No state that we know of, except Connecticut, addresses psychological maltreatment in classrooms. However, many state departments of education have regulations that allude to prohibitions against emotionally damaging children. You should determine if and where these regulations exist and lobby for improvement in the wording and specification of penalties.

We have documented the realities of psychological maltreatment in classrooms, one of the most common types of abuse of students. Because it is widespread but little understood by so many educators, we believe legislators need to address this issue. We recommend that they mandate education on psychological maltreatment in the classroom for teacher training programs and for school staff. This can be accomplished without significant cost increases to colleges or school budgets. At the college level, training can be included in the curricula. Since most public schools require regular in-service training each year, this topic can be added to workshop schedules.

The more subtle maltreatment, which we described under the category of performance pressure, requires attention by both educators and parents. Schools have the responsibility to educate parents, especially those of vulnerable, hurried children whose lives are overscheduled. Teachers need to be informed about the stress symptoms that are often related to performance pressures. They should contact parents as soon as these symptoms are noticed.

Parents should be sensitive to their children's reactions regarding overscheduling and overdemanding academic requirements. For example, setting high expectations for bright children should not translate into excessive amounts of homework. A general rule of thumb is that the average child should not be required to do more than ten minutes of homework multiplied by their grade level. For instance, a seventh grader should generally spend no more than seventy minutes doing daily homework (10 minutes × 7th grade = 70 minutes).

Bright, highly motivated students enrolled in advanced courses may be expected to handle more homework than others. But some teachers of advanced courses mistakenly believe that the amount of homework is a measure of its value. They often assign lots of busy work that has no intrinsic value in terms of adding to the students' knowledge base or their ability to think critically. Students enrolled in multiple advanced courses may be victimized by too many teachers who subscribe to this belief. The solution is for parents to request a meeting with all of their child's teachers so that a team of staff, parents, and the student can develop a realistic limit to homework.

We believe that the violation of children's constitutional rights can be ameliorated at the state level. We propose that states establish a system of constitutional ombudsmen. We envision a system in which attorneys would provide pro bono (free) services to school districts. They would act as neutral ombudsmen when students, teachers, or parents feel that their constitutional rights have been violated. The ombudsman's task would be to educate individuals and groups within the school system about the constitutional issues involved in any particular situation.

Unlike attorneys who represent the school district or injured parties, constitutional ombudsmen would remain neutral and focus on educating people to make a decision about whether they believe they were denied their constitutional rights. For example, if a principal arbitrarily censored an article in the school newspaper, the writer could seek advice about case law involving similar situations. It would then be up to the student to decide what to do. The ombudsman's consultation could be directed to the writer, the newspaper staff, or the entire student body. The purpose would be to make the Constitution a living document and to frequently remind students and staff of the importance of the Bill of Rights in their daily lives.

Altering National Policy

You probably feel that you have little chance of directly influencing national policy. However, there are many legislators who support the premises discussed in this book—and they need people who are concerned and willing to work. I have testified in congressional hearings of bills to restrict the use of corporal punishment in the schools and to deter national policies of punitiveness. These efforts have always been blocked by conservative legislators, and admittedly this is an uphill struggle at this time. But we believe the country will eventually swing back to moderation and lobbying groups should be positioned to present meaningful legislation to make schools safer for children. You can get more information about national issues by contacting some of the resource groups listed at the back of the book.

. . .

When we began to work on this book the focus was on pedagogical and clinical aspects of dangerous and toxic schools. The point was to describe the issues of physical and psychological maltreatment by educators and the context within which you must function if you want to litigate against abusive educators or change punitive policies. But we had to expand our discussion as we dealt with the fact that schools reflect a society that is becoming increasingly punitive and toxic for many children and youth. This makes it more difficult to bring about change as we seem to be sliding deeper and deeper into a morass of punishment.

As the book developed, it was apparent that we were becoming increasingly enmeshed in constitutional issues. We realized that toxicity toward democracy in schools is intertwined with toxicity toward every individual's rights, including ours—and yours. We hope that you understand this truth and are willing to join the struggle to change our schools. While you may think that our portrayal is of doom and gloom, we obviously have hope. Otherwise, why write this book and continue to work with schools and parents? We continue the fight because we believe, given the facts rather than propaganda, that the majority of Americans will opt for reforms. Where do you stand?

Resources
and References

Resources

National Center for the Study of Corporal Punishment and Alternatives

The National Center for the Study of Corporal Punishment and Alternatives (NCSCPA) conducts research and consults about physical and emotional maltreatment of students, and about school discipline and school violence. Staff provide clinical and psycho-educational evaluations of victimized students, offer expert testimony, and conduct advocacy activities and workshops for educators, parents, and mental health professionals. Publications list available.

National Center for the Study of
Corporal Punishment and Alternatives (NCSCPA)
254 RHA
Temple University
Philadelphia PA 19122
Phone: (215)204-6091
Fax: (215)204-6013
Web site: http://www.temple.edu/education/pse/NCSCPA.html
E-mail: ncscpa@blue.vm.temple.edu

Constitutional Rights Foundation

The Constitutional Rights Foundation (CRF) is a nonprofit, non-partisan educational foundation. Its mission is to instill in our nation's youth a deeper understanding of citizenship through the values expressed in our Constitution and its Bill of Rights. The goal is to help schools educate students to become active and responsible participants in our society. CRF provides programs, curricula, and materials that focus on institutions, processes, roles, and issues relating to law and government, civic participation, and business.

Constitutional Rights Foundation
601 South Kingsley Drive
Los Angeles CA 90005-4128
Phone: (213)487-5590
Fax: (213)386-0459
Web site: http://www.crf-usa.org
E-mail: crf@crf-usa.org

American Civil Liberties Union

The American Civil Liberties Union (ACLU) represents parents and students when it appears that their constitutional rights have been violated. If you believe that your child's or other students' civil liberties have been violated, you may contact the national ACLU's Public Education Office, which will direct you to a local affiliate.

American Civil Liberties Union
125 Broad Street
New York NY 10004
Phone: (212)549-2565
Fax: (212)549-2646
Web site: http://www.aclu.org
E-mail: LSeigal@aclu.org

Family Research Laboratory

The Family Research Laboratory (FRL) conducts research in all areas of family violence, much of which is relevant to children's behavior in schools. Expertise includes homicides, missing and abandoned children, and physical, sexual, and spousal abuse. Staff activity is limited to research and consultation about research. FRL offers many publications that may be ordered through their Web site or by mail.

The Family Research Laboratory
University of New Hampshire
Durham NH 03824
Phone: (603)862-2594
Fax: (603)862-1122
Web site: http://unh.edu/frl/index.html
E-mail: MAS2@CHRISTA.UNH.EDU

End Physical Punishment of Children (EPOCH-USA)

End Physical Punishment of Children (EPOCH-USA) is the American chapter of the international EPOCH organization, which has its headquarters in England. EPOCH is dedicated to the elimination of corporal punishment in homes and schools. It provides literature, coordinates public awareness and education campaigns, and works to educate the public on the need for legislative reform.

EPOCH-USA
155 W. Main Street #100–B
Columbus OH 43215
Phone: (614)221-8829
Fax: (614)228-5058
Web site: http://www.stophitting.com
E-mail: nblock@infinet.com

National Committee for the Prevention of Child Abuse

The National Committee for the Prevention of Child Abuse is dedicated to eliminating physical, psychological, and sexual abuse and neglect of children. It conducts research on annual rates of abuse, publishes numerous pamphlets and articles, and participates in national conventions. Most states have affiliate chapters.

National Committee for the Prevention of Child Abuse
200 South Michigan Avenue
Seventeenth Floor
Chicago IL 60604-4357
Phone: (312)663-3520
Fax: (312)939-8962
Web site: http://www.childabuse.org
E-mail: ncpca@childabuse.org

Parents and Teachers Against Violence in Education (PTAVE)

Parents and Teachers Against Violence in Education (PTAVE) provides materials for parents, educators, and policymakers regarding the dangers of corporal punishment.

Parents and Teachers Against Violence in Education
P.O. Box 1033
Alamo CA 94507-7033
Phone: (925)831-1661
Fax: (925)838-8914
Web site: http://silcon.com/~ptave
E-mail: ptave@silcon.com

Additional Reading

Unless otherwise indicated, all the opinions and facts stated in this book are based on social science research and the opinions of scholars, legal experts, and clinicians. If you wish to read more, we have provided some references to get you started. For a central source of references and sources of information that will help you become an expert on school discipline, see this textbook:

Hyman, I., Dahbany, A., Blum, M., Brooks-Klein, V., Weiler, E., & Pokalo, M. (1997). *School discipline and school violence: The teacher variance approach*. Needham Heights, MA: Allyn & Bacon.

Other Publications by the Authors

Brassard, M., Hyman, I., & Dimmitt, C. (1991). What can children expect? Protecting and nurturing children in a school and community context. *School Psychology Review, 20*(3), 369–381.

Czumbil, M., & Hyman, I. (1997). What happens when corporal punishment is legal? An analysis of corporal punishment cases reported in newspapers from 1975 to 1992. *Journal of Interpersonal Violence, 12*(2), 309–315.

Hyman, I. (1990). *Reading, writing and the hickory stick: The appalling story of physical and psychological abuse in American schools*. Lexington, MA: Lexington Books.

Hyman, I. (1991). Institutionalized violence directed towards children. In R. Baenninger (Ed.), *Targets of violence and aggression* (pp. 159–210). Netherlands: North-Holland.

Hyman, I. (1995). Corporal punishment, psychological maltreatment, violence and punitiveness in America: Research, advocacy and public policy. *Applied and Preventive Psychology, 4,* 113–130.

Hyman, I. (1996). Using research to change public policy: Reflections on 20 years of effort to eliminate corporal punishment in schools. *Pediatrics-Supplement, 98*(4 [part 2 of 2]), 818–820.

Hyman, I. (1997). *The case against spanking: How to discipline your child without hitting.* San Francisco: Jossey-Bass.

Hyman, I., Cavallo, M., Erbacher, T., Spangler, J., & Stafford, J. (Fall 1997). Corporal punishment in America: Cultural wars in politics, religion and science. *Children's Legal Rights Journal, 17*(4), 36–46.

Hyman, I., Clarke, J., & Erdlen, R. (1987). An analysis of physical abuse in American schools. *Aggressive Behavior, 13*(1), 1–7.

Hyman, I., & Perone, D. (1998). The other side of school violence: Educator policies and practices which may contribute to student misbehavior. *Journal of School Psychology, 36*(1), 7–28.

Hyman, I., Snook, P., Berna, J., & Kohr, M. (1999). *My Worst Experience Scales.* Los Angeles: Western Psychological Services.

Hyman, I., Weiler, E., Perone, D., Romano, L., Britton, G., & Shanock, A. (1997). Victims and victimizers: The two faces of school violence. In A. Goldstein and J. Conoly (Eds.), *The school violence intervention handbook* (pp. 426–459). New York: Guilford Press.

Other References

Altemeyer, B. (1988). *Enemies of freedom: Understanding right-wing authoritarianism.* San Francisco: Jossey-Bass.

American Psychological Association. (1993). *Violence and youth: Psychology's response. Vol. 1: Summary report of the American Psychological Association Commission on Violence and Youth.* Washington, DC: Author.

Brassard, M., Hart, S., & Germain, B. (1987). *Psychological maltreatment of children and youth.* Elmsford, NY: Pergamon Press.

Bybee, R., & Gee, E. (1982). *Violence, values and justice in schools.* Boston: Allyn & Bacon.

Delafattore, J. (1992). *What Johnny shouldn't read: Textbook censorship in America.* New Haven, CT: Yale University Press.

Dewey, J. (1961). *Philosophy of education.* Paterson, NJ: Littlefield, Adams.

Froyen, L. (1993). *Classroom management* (2nd ed.). New York: Macmillan.

Fuentes, A. (1998). The crackdown on kids. *The Nation,* June 15–22, pp. 20–22.

Garbarino, J., Guttman, E., & Seeley, J. (1986). *The psychologically battered child.* San Francisco: Jossey-Bass.

Greven, P. (1980). *The Protestant temperament.* New York: Knopf.

Greven, P. (1991). *Spare the child: The religious roots of punishment and the psychological impact of physical abuse.* New York: Knopf.

Helfer, R., & Kempe, C. (1968). *The battered child.* Chicago: University of Chicago Press.

Helfer, R., & Kempe, C. (1987). *The battered child* (4th ed.). Chicago: University of Chicago Press.

Straus, M. A. (1994). *Beating the devil out of them: Corporal punishment in American families.* San Francisco: Jossey-Bass.

Wolfgang, C. H., & Glickman, C. D. (1986). *Solving discipline problems: Strategies for classroom teachers* (2nd ed.). Boston: Allyn & Bacon.

About the Authors

IRWIN A. HYMAN, EdD, is professor of school psychology at Temple University and is internationally recognized for his research and scholarship about student victimization. He is widely quoted in the media and has made numerous appearances on shows such as *Oprah, Sally Jessy Raphael, Ricki Lake, Today,* and *Good Morning America.*

PAMELA A. SNOOK, RN, MSN, is a psychiatric nurse and clinical specialist and coauthor of the *My Worst School Experience Scale.* She is a doctoral student in school psychology at Temple University, and has worked with a wide variety of victimized children.

Index